ON THE BORDER

ON THE BORDER

SOCIETY AND CULTURE BETWEEN THE UNITED STATES AND MEXICO

Edited by
Andrew Grant Wood

SR BOOKS
Lanham • Boulder • New York • Toronto • Oxford

Published by SR Books
An imprint of Rowman & Littlefield Publishers, Inc.
A wholly owned subsidiary of The Rowman & Littlefield Publishing Group, Inc.
4501 Forbes Boulevard, Suite 200
Lanham, MD 20706

PO Box 317, Oxford OX2 9RU, UK

Copyright © 2001 Arizona Board of Regents
First published 2001 as *Journal of the Southwest* 43, no. 4
(Winter 2001): 461–764
Published by SR Books 2004

British Library Cataloguing in Publication Information Available

Library of Congress Cataloging-in-Publication Data

   On the border : society and culture between the United States and
Mexico / edited by Andrew Grant Wood.
        p.   cm. — (Latin American silhouettes)
   Includes index.
      ISBN 0-8420-5172-4 (cloth : alk. paper) — ISBN 0-8420-5173-2
(pbk. : alk. paper)
      1. Mexican-American Border Region—Civilization.   2. Mexican-
American Border Region—History.   I. Wood, Andrew Grant, 1958–
II. Series.
   F787.05   2004
   972'.1—dc22
                                                           2003023426

Printed in the United States of America

♾ The paper used in this publication meets the minimum requirements of
American National Standard for Information Sciences—Permanence of Paper
for Printed Library Materials, ANSI/NISO Z39.48-1992.

Contents

Introduction

ANDREW GRANT WOOD

Whether one hears about the "New America" at the kitchen table, on the streets, in the classroom, on the Internet, at the movie theater, or on the news, addressing complex issues related to the environment, the economy, citizenship, social welfare, and culture is clearly on the minds of many people. Assuming for a moment that the present trend toward neoliberal economic integration combined with current levels of migration to the United States will only continue to "Hispanicize" the dominant culture of North America, it is worth considering the history of the borderlands as a way to envision larger social and cultural changes taking shape.

Indeed, as Mexicans live, work, and contribute in various ways to local communities not only in the Southwest but also throughout the country, one can appreciate the expression "the border is everywhere." As an attempt to reflect on the relationship between national cultures, this rather eclectic collection of essays offers a number of perspectives on the history and cultures of the U.S.-Mexican borderlands.

Lawrence Taylor's piece on mining during the second half of the nineteenth century tells of a lesser known "gold rush": one in the Baja California peninsula. He describes the early development of San Diego as a crossroads for prospectors, cattle, and assorted commodities, many on their way to northern California. When the frenzy had largely played itself out by the early 1850s, word of gold being discovered in Las Gallinas (east of present-day Ensenada) attracted a new wave of prospectors to the region. Thus began a new period of exploration and development that would stimulate growth in southern California and eventually give rise to the border town of Tijuana.

Urban growth and the problems associated with popular housing along the border is the subject of my essay on turn-of-the-century El Paso and Ciudad Juárez. In El Paso, hundreds of recently arrived Mexican migrants crowded into the southside Chihuahuita barrio, which soon became the target of urban reformers. Comparable conditions existed across the river in Juárez, where residents briefly organized a tenant association to protest high rents and substandard conditions in the spring of 1922. Subsequent attempts by city officials and visiting moral crusaders to rid the town of vice during the 1920s largely failed to improve popular housing.

Further work on twin cities is presented by Daniel Arreola, who takes us on a historic tour of the border towns of Nogales, Arizona, and Nogales, Sonora (together known as Ambos Nogales), to illustrate change in a single borderland-built environment over time. Assembling a fascinating sampling from his picture postcard archive, Arreola uses images of the city's border crossings (*garitas*) as a dramatic way to portray the evolution of the urban landscape during the twentieth century.

Exploring new themes in borderlands cultural geography, Victor Manuel Macías-González offers some preliminary ideas on the history of gay men in Northern Mexico. He contends that modern gay culture surfaced in Mexico—just as it did in the United States and Europe—with the development of capitalism and many social and cultural "revolutions" (that is, the rise of free labor, the expansion of commodity production, rapid urbanization, and changes in family relations). Combining a careful reading of memoirs by gay men, including the celebrated writer Salvador Novo, with descriptions of late-nineteenth-century recreational sites, including gymnasiums, bathhouses, and dormitories, in places such as Chihuahua City, Macías González suggests several future possibilities for scholars of Queer history in Mexico and the U.S. Southwest.

Eric Schantz's essay on Mexicali provides a stunning glimpse of border-town nightlife. He explains how the city's bustling vice commerce attracted scores of tourists while also alarming many residents. At the center of Mexicali's red-light district was the infamous Owl Café and Theater, a casino, vaudeville stage, and brothel owned by three businessmen (collectively known as the ABW Syndicate) who had left California in 1913. With new regulatory policies of Governor Esteban Cantú forcing many of Mexicali's sleaziest operations out of business, Schantz tells how the Owl's illicit entertainments were made somewhat "safe" for U.S. consumers. Relocating to the Chinatown section of the city, business boomed as gaming, alcohol, and prostitution revenues produced hefty profits for the café's ABW Syndicate owners and the governor himself. In carefully documenting the history of the Owl and related commercial operations elsewhere in Baja California, Schantz reconstructs an important slice of transnational social history.

Then, what first appears to be a forgotten, seemingly innocent trip to Tijuana taken by an American family turns out to be a scandalous "lost weekend" in which heavy drinking, kidnapping, sexual assault, and "shameful" death caused an international furor. In a real film-noir-style page-turner, Vincent and Juan Cabeza de Baca narrate the wild history of the Peteet family's last days before evaluating a flurry of cross-cultural misperceptions and anti-Mexican attitudes exhibited in the southern California press at the time. Without revealing all of the scintillating details of this torrid tale, it is safe to note that in the wake of the Peteet misadventure, pressure from the United States soon convinced Baja California governor Abelardo Rodríguez and Mexican president Plutarco Elías Calles to coordinate a "vice sweep" of Tijuana in mid-February 1926. In the process, Mexican authorities deported several hundred "bar girls," closed down some fifty-two saloons, and even tried to change the city's name to Zaragoza in order to avoid the negative associations that "Tia Juana" held in (largely American) minds. When murder charges brought against suspects in the Peteet family case did not stick, U.S. officials in Washington reacted by ordering the border closed after 6:00 P.M. Yet enforcement of the curfew would prove difficult in the coming years as thousands of American tourists made their way to Mexico (some through large holes illegally cut in the eight-mile fence erected during the Hoover administration) in pursuit of adult pleasures despite the self-righteous outrage whipped up by the Peteet affair.

Turning (this time in earnest) to film, María Arbeláez examines two *narco-ficheras* in the larger context of twentieth-century Mexican cinema. She contends that these budget films, largely dismissed by scholars for their lowbrow aesthetics, predictable plots, and stereotypic portrayals, are worthy of study because of their enormous popular appeal—especially among migrants and people living in the U.S.-Mexican borderlands (*fronterizos*). Deriving, in part, from Golden Age dance hall and rural comedy scripts, *narco-ficheras* produced in the 1990s melodramatically combined the well-worn themes of drugs, corruption, prostitution, and violence. Arbeláez suggests that these films, while relying heavily on stock characters and sensationalism, tell us something about the overt racism, classism, and sexism that the people who watch them face every day.

Next, Jeffrey Pilcher serves up a savory discussion of the four main regional cooking styles that constitute borderlands cuisine. He considers the influence, from pre-Hispanic times to the present, of available ingredients and the centuries-long process of culinary encounter. Taking seriously the adage "you are what you eat," Pilcher examines how Mexican Americans in the U.S. Southwest have constantly negotiated their cultural identity through food production and consumption. At the same time, he describes the often contentious way in which Anglo entrepreneurs have appropriated and subsequently "tamed" aspects of

Greater Mexico's culinary tradition for huge profits. At a time when salsa has surpassed catsup as the most popular condiment in the United States, Pilcher's tangy critique uncovers a host of complex flavors in telling us much about ourselves as related to a larger, transnational history of identity politics and the political economy of food.

Our final chapters offer different ethnographic approaches to the borderlands. Josiah Heyman considers Arizona and California port towns along the U.S.-Mexican border. Looking at local realities that have largely been ignored by scholars, Heyman discusses the different nature of these ports and their daily operations. He points out how each has its own character as shaped by history and the type and volume of traffic. Working to stop the flow of contraband, Heyman reveals how border personnel become attuned to the peculiarities of each locale in applying federal policies. Studying the articulation of state power at the local level, Heyman complicates our understanding of how immigration and trade policy is enforced. Moreover, he suggests that the application of federal legislation creates a highly charged "local state" environment with significant effects—not only on those who live and work in port-of-entry communities but for citizens of both countries.

Drawing upon previous views of unauthorized settlement or "squatting," Travis DuBry, together with Dominique Rissolo's striking photographs, documents life among residents of Imperial County, California's Slab City. Describing the history of the area as it became incorporated in 1848 as Section 36 land, a military camp in 1942, and, more recently, Bureau of Land Management property, he explains the various reasons why people have come to Slab City. Profiling three residents, including the internationally famous artist Leonard Knight, DuBry sees several common themes (among them, individualism, freedom, self-government, and democracy) that connect present-day California squatters with their nineteenth-century predecessors.

Paul Vanderwood's work on the Juan Soldado shrine in Tijuana, Mexico, gives us important insights into an often underappreciated subject for scholars: popular religion. Following the 1938 rape and murder of eight-year-old Olga Camacho, a soldier named Juan Castillo Morales was arrested. After he allegedly confessed to the crime and was executed, bizarre events—including the realization of certain "miracles"—soon began to take place at his gravesite. People then venerated the dead soldier, proclaiming him a saint. Since then, petitioners have made pilgrimages to the site where today a chapel stands. Conducting ethnographic work with his team of researchers, Vanderwood provides us with keen observations of this interesting scene in combination with some fascinating testimony from Juan Soldado devotees.

Devra Weber's photostory on Oaxacans in Los Angeles documents the high profile of recent Mexican migrants. Many provide essential services as workers in restaurants or on construction sites, and as gardeners or janitors. She observes how Oaxacans have retained their cultural integrity while at the same time remitting considerable sums to families and friends back in Mexico. Whether Mixtecs, Zapotecs, Mixes, Triques, or Chontales, ethnic groups have formed their own enclaves in and around the city. Evidence of this can be seen in their many community services, organizations, and cultural activities, including the famed *guelaguetza* celebrations.

Finally, my review of *The Mexican* and *Traffic* considers the power of popular media in shaping cross-border perceptions. In looking at these two recent films I argue that Hollywood has too often conjured up sloppy stereotypes of Mexico and Mexicans in the quest for the almighty entertainment dollar. Surprisingly, the Brad Pitt-Julia Roberts romantic comedy, *The Mexican*, positively pokes fun at past stereotypes. In contrast, I suggest that the socially conscious Steven Soderbergh film, *Traffic*, unnecessarily exoticizes Mexico in order to make its important point about drug consumption in the United States.

Because this volume got its start as a special issue of the *Journal of the Southwest* (Winter 2001), I would like to thank journal editors Joe Wilder and Jeff Banister. Subsequently, Richard Hopper at Scholarly Resources and Bill Beezley helped to make this edition (along with certain revisions) possible. While certainly not meant as a definitive take on borderland cities and cultures, this collection will, I hope, stimulate discussion, fresh research, and future cross-cultural understanding.

The Mining Boom in Baja California from 1850 to 1890 and the Emergence of Tijuana as a Border Community

LAWRENCE D. TAYLOR

In the period following the Mexican War of 1846–1848, many of the hordes of prospectors who participated in the California gold rush also became interested in mining possibilities in the Mexican northwest. During the 1850s, a series of gold and silver strikes in the northern part of the Baja California, or Lower California, peninsula resulted in a rush of U.S. and other foreign miners to the region. It was during this period that San Diegans and other Californians first became aware of the economic potential of the peninsular region and its relevance for their own growth and development. The great majority of the gold seekers left the territory once the mineral deposits had played out. Discoveries of precious metals in the area continued to occur throughout the following decades, with the exception of the 1860s, when the only notable strikes were those which took place in the southern and central portions of the peninsula.

It was also during this period that Tijuana began to emerge as a town on the border, owing to the strategic location of the Tijuana River valley on the route to the goldfields and other locations in the peninsula, as well as the influence of the southern California land development boom of the mid-1880s. A small community soon grew up around the customhouse and military post that had been established there as a governmental response to the increase in cross-border traffic and trade caused by the mining boom in the interior. In this way was formed the nucleus of what would eventually become the second largest metropolis in the Mexican northern border region.

PRELUDE TO THE BAJA CALIFORNIA MINING BOOM

Although precious metals had been mined in Baja California since the early part of the eighteenth century, mining activities had not in general developed to the same degree as they had in Sonora and other

1

regions of Mexico.[1] By the early decades of the nineteenth century, many gold and silver mines had been abandoned. The only significant mining site was the silver-producing region of San Antonio, located in the southeastern tip of the peninsula near Bahía Ventana.[2]

During the early national period in Mexico, the Mexican government removed obstacles to the establishment of mining ventures by foreigners. It also offered rewards for the discovery of ores and mercury deposits for the refinement of metal ores.[3] Although the mining of precious metals in Baja California increased somewhat during the 1840s, the Mexican War interrupted such activities.[4] In the course of the conflict, several Americans proposed that Baja California be included in the territorial cession to be imposed upon Mexico as part of the peace agreement. The Mexican government, considering the peninsula vital for the country's defense and believing that it contained valuable resources that had not yet been exploited, refused to consider this proposal. As a result, Baja California was not included among the Mexican territories ceded to the United States by the Treaty of Guadalupe Hidalgo signed on February 2, 1848.[5]

James W. Marshall's discovery of gold along the American River in the northern sierra region of California during the last week of January 1848 set in motion a great migration of miners from many countries to the area. Many miners made their way to the goldfields by traveling overland through Baja California. Mexicans and Chileans, who were among the first groups of miners to reach California and were accustomed to desert travel, particularly favored this route. Miners from northern Sonora made their way to the Gila River in southern Arizona, which at that time still belonged to Mexico, then headed westward to Los Angeles. Mexicans coming from regions farther south would depart by ship from ports on the Pacific such as Mazatlán, San Blas, or Guaymas; cross the Gulf of California to La Paz, the principal port and territorial capital of Baja California; then journey overland up the length of the peninsula.

Some of these miners remained for a time at certain camping spots in order to prospect for precious metals. The mines that were begun by Mexican and Chilean prospectors in the northern sierra districts or the central desert region further south continued to be worked by various owners long after the rush had ended. In fact, some would continue to produce ore up until the early decades of this century.[6]

Some of the Anglo-American miners who penetrated Baja California during this period were men who, while traveling by ship from Panama to San Francisco, had been shipwrecked along the southern coast of the peninsula and forced to make the remainder of the trip overland up the peninsula. Others, weary of the long ocean voyage, voluntarily went ashore in the belief that the overland trek to California would be less time-consuming and hazardous than continuing the trip by sea. Both types of travelers promptly found out that the overland journey up the peninsula was neither rapid nor always comfortable. In the course of these trips, none of the Anglo prospectors apparently detected the presence of gold or other precious metals in the region.[7]

Urban San Diego in 1848 consisted of what was referred to as Pueblo Viejo, or Old Town. Old Town contained a cluster of wooden and adobe structures around a dirt plaza that had grown up on the flat below the hill on which stood the former Mexican *presidio*, or garrison. Merchants, landowners, and cattlemen formed the bulk of the town's governing elite. The majority of the 300 to 400 inhabitants were Mexican, with a numerous Indian population in the outlying areas.[8]

At this time no gold had been found in the San Diego region, and several of its inhabitants had departed for the northern California gold-fields. Since California had only recently come under U.S. rule, many of these persons were of Mexican origin. Despite the migration of citizens to the northern goldfields, the town's population grew steadily. The stream of northern-bound miners from Mexico passing through the town stimulated business. During the early years of the rush, from 1849 to 1851, San Diegan entrepreneurs opened several new hotels, retail stores, and saloons to meet the prospectors' needs.[9]

Cattle from the surrounding region were also exported in considerable numbers to the northern California goldfields. Much of the cattle came from Baja California. The export from Mexico of cattle, together with other agricultural products, would come to form a principal part of cross-border commerce in the region over the ensuing decades.[10]

Andrew B. Gray, a surveyor with the U.S. commission charged with the task of demarcating the new international boundary, believed that a better site for the town lay on the shores of San Diego Bay, at a site near what is now the foot of Market Street. Anglo and Californio[11] speculators, believing that the land around the harbor area would become valuable once the community began to grow, bought up lots in that zone. The prosperity resulting from the flow of miners northward sparked a construction boom in both the Old Town area and the new area favored by Davis. By 1850, the population of San Diego had grown to 650.[12]

In that year, Gray met William Heath Davis, a San Franciscan merchant and coast trader, who had married into the wealthy Estudillo family of San Diego. Gray was able to interest Davis and several other prominent citizens in the New Town project. In March 1850, the partners bought up a 160-acre tract of land bounded by what is now Front Street, Broadway, and the waterfront. A grid of 56 blocks was laid out, wells were excavated, a warehouse constructed, and a wharf built. Fourteen prefabricated houses, shipped around the Horn from New England, were disembarked in the port and assembled in the new area. The U.S. Army also established a supply depot in the zone, further enhancing its prospects for development.[13]

Despite the growth in business and construction projects, San Diego still had very much the appearance of a rough-and-tumble frontier community. The streets were filled with garbage and cattle roamed them freely. The surrounding rural areas were dotted with Indian huts. The town possessed a transient element armed with pistols and bowie knives. The wild and woolly nature of San Diego during this period was captured by the artist H. M. T. Powell in his account of a two-month stay there while en route to the northern goldfields:

> Gamblers and gambling rife here, Sunday or no Sunday. . . .
> Everybody gets drunk. . . .The gambling and drinking of the officers . . . and their exceedingly supercilious manners to the Emigrants is very reprehensible. . . . A party came in from City of Mexico today. . . . They set up a Monte Bank in the evening; piles of doubloons; large lumps of gold. . . . Owens (Dragoon) died for cutting and maiming another Dragoon. . . . A Mexican soldier of Carrasco's Command murdered another right here in town last night. So little notice was taken of it that I did not hear of it until this evening.[14]

The Gold Strikes of the 1850s
in the Peninsula

In northern California, the period in which gold could be easily recovered from surface deposits had almost ended by 1850. Mining became increasingly competitive and dependent on the hiring of labor to work subsurface seams. Many miners began to consider the possibility of striking it rich in other areas that hitherto had not been exploited.

Given that gold was so abundant in the California sierra, to many of the gold seekers it seemed logical to suppose that it should also be plentiful in the mountain and desert regions of northwestern Mexico. They hoped that gold deposits equal or superior to those of California might be found and exploited in Baja California and Sonora.[15] It was rumored that Jesuit missionaries had discovered rich mines in the hinterland, the exact locations of which had been lost over time or maintained in secret. Rumors soon began to circulate among the California miners that great gold deposits could be found in these regions.[16] Some Americans asserted that the Spanish, and the Mexicans who later replaced them as the territory's rulers, had failed to develop these resources out of lethargy and indifference. "If a race like the Americans shall ever get the country under their command," a correspondent to the *Daily Alta California* boosted, "I am satisfied that fortunes will be made and riches brought to light of which but few of the present occupants of the territory ever dreamed."[17]

Some U.S. citizens had already journeyed to Baja California with that aim in mind. Several of them were veterans of the campaigns waged by U.S. forces against groups of Mexican patriots in the southern part of the peninsula during the recent conflict. Not all of these immigrants were prospectors; some were men who, having made some money in California, intended to settle in northern Baja California as farmers, ranchers, and traders.[18]

The interest of those who sought gold in Baja California was heightened by news of a number of discoveries of that metal in different localities in the northern portion of the territory (see map). Early in 1851, placer gold was discovered at a place called Las Gallinas, near San Antonio. The discovery prompted hundreds of persons from San Diego and other southern California communities to migrate to the vicinity in hopes of striking it rich. The strike evidently did not last long, as no further news was heard of it. It did, however, stimulate interest among San Diegans and Californians in general concerning mining possibilities in the peninsula.[19]

Some months later, in June 1851, other gold deposits were discovered in the vicinity of Santo Tomás, about three hundred miles south of San Diego. This strike proved somewhat longer lasting than the previous one at San Antonio. Although the gold was quite coarse, some miners were able to extract at least five dollars' worth a day from the diggings. Shortly thereafter, other deposits were discovered near the bay

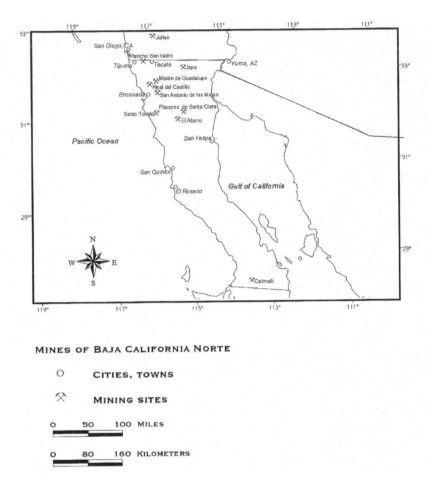

MINES OF BAJA CALIFORNIA NORTE

O   CITIES, TOWNS

⚒   MINING SITES

O   50   100 MILES

O   80   160 KILOMETERS

Cartography by Colegio de la Frontera Norte-Sistema de Información Geográfi-ca y Estadística sobre la Frontera, Tijuana, Baja California, México, based on an idea and design by Lawrence Taylor.

of Todos Santos. This bay, around which the port of Ensenada and its outlying settlements would emerge in the 1880s and 1890s, offered an easy entrance and good anchorage for ships en route along the coast.[20]

A much richer strike occurred on June 23, 1851, in Rancho San Isidro (also known as Aja-jolojol or Jesús María), approximately forty miles from San Diego in the vicinity of the international boundary. This property belonged to José López, a disabled ex-soldier to whom the parcel of land had been given as a pension by the government. Additional gold finds, as well as deposits of silver, were soon made in the same area or in regions farther south. The mines at these sites were developed by Mexican business partners José Matías Moreno and Guillermo Norlin. Norlin provided the capital for carrying out mining operations, while Matías Moreno obtained the necessary permit from the Mexican federal government. Together the two men organized the La Margarita mining corporation and sent shipments of silver to San Francisco via the Wells Fargo Express Company.[21]

Matías Moreno owned property on both sides of the border. He had investments not only in mining, but also in a variety of other activities including lumbering, land speculation, and cattle ranching. Reputed to have more influence with the regional Mexican government at La Paz than any other man, he was sought after as an agent by U.S. businessmen who wished to invest in Baja California. On one occasion, for example, he was paid two thousand pesos by Grisar-Brynes and Company of San Francisco for obtaining for this firm the rights to mine for salt in the San Quintín area.[22]

Further gold discoveries were made in the mid-1850s. In September 1854, a vein of gold-bearing quartz was discovered on the lands of the former Misión de Guadalupe, located about eighty miles southeast of San Diego.[23] In 1845, Pío Pico, the last Mexican governor of California, had given Juan Bandini, a Peruvian of Italian descent whose father had immigrated to California in 1820, a grant of land which included the mission property. Bandini improved the land and planted an orchard. Bandini's principal interests were in raising cattle and horses, and by 1852, his herds consisted of some three thousand of these animals. In 1853, the land reverted to government ownership when President Antonio López de Santa Anna declared void the land grants issued by Pío Pico.[24] Ten years later, in 1863, it was acquired by Matías Moreno. By then, the gold production had evidently ceased, since Matías Moreno makes no mention of it in an 1861 report to Teodoro Riveroll, the governor of Baja California, shortly after his appointment as *jefe político de la frontera* (political representative of the border zone).[25]

The majority of the gold discoveries of this period occurred south of the international boundary. Although two Indians reportedly found traces of gold pyrites in a gulch between Old Town and the Misión de Alcalá in the San Diego region in May 1852, gold was not discovered in significant quantities in the county until the large strike that began along Banner Canyon in the Cuyamaca sierra during the winter of 1869–1870.[26] The Banner Canyon strike spawned a series of mining towns east of San Diego in the early 1870s, among them Julian, Banner, and Cuyamaca City.[27]

For a time, the gold discoveries in Baja California caused San Diego's economy to stagnate. Each new gold strike attracted a flow of citizens to work the claims. In addition, as time went on, the flow of prospectors heading north to the goldfields of northern California gradually diminished, which also hurt business.[28]

Davis's New Town project had also floundered. One of the project's partners, Miguel Pedrorena, died of apoplexy shortly after the construction work commenced. Several of the older San Diego elites preferred to remain in the Old Town area. The U.S. federal government canceled its plan to construct a customhouse and post office in the New Town site. Davis had also suffered personal financial losses, chiefly as a result of a San Francisco fire that resulted in $700,000 in property and merchandise damages. The tragedy left him without money to invest in the New Town venture. The site was gradually abandoned as its inhabitants moved elsewhere and the buildings deteriorated.[29]

In time, however, the town's outlook brightened considerably. As the most important ocean port near the line of demarcation between the United States and Mexico, San Diego grew into an important departure point and supply depot for prospecting expeditions setting off into the mountainous interior of Baja California. Several local businessmen, such as Matías Moreno and Norlin, were themselves mine owners or had shares in some of the larger mines.[30]

San Diego's relative proximity to the Baja California goldfields and to Mexico created problems of security for the town, as well as difficulties with the Mexican government. As in the case of the northern California gold rush, there were numerous instances of crime and violence in the peninsular gold region. Two men, identified only by their surnames, Vanness and McDonald, attempted for several weeks in San Diego to organize an expedition with the intention of leading an attack against the mining encampments in Mexico and looting them, much as the desperado gang led by John Glanton and other parties had done to villages in northern Sonora, such as Cieneguilla. Unsuccessful in this endeavor, Vanness and McDonald crossed into Baja California and were subsequently slain during an encounter with either Mexican federal troops or miner-vigilantes.[31]

As time went by, robberies and crime in Baja California increased. Several persons convicted as bandits by the Mexican authorities were executed by firing squad over a five-year period from 1856 to 1861.

Many foreigners were expelled from the territory as part of a general governmental policy aimed at getting rid of such troublemakers.[32]

One incident involving violence in the goldfields almost led to a regional conflict between the two Californias. In 1858, William Cole and two other San Diegans, who had been mining in the vicinity of Santo Tomás, killed an American named Bill Elkins and a Mexican in the belief that they were guilty of horse theft. Cole and his companions were jailed by the local authorities. Thomas R. Darnall of San Diego, who journeyed to Santo Tomás to try to gain the men's release, was also imprisoned. San Diego citizens threatened to lead an expedition of volunteers from the town and Los Angeles to the peninsula in order to free the four men. Fortunately, the jailed men were freed by the Mexican authorities before the proposed expedition could be launched.[33]

In the following year, 1859, rumors abounded concerning possible raids on San Diego by armed bands of outlaws from Baja California. At a public meeting attended by several of the town's citizens, it was decided to appoint a special guard of twelve volunteers to maintain vigilance at certain designated spots around the town each night in order to warn the populace in case of an attack.[34]

Cattle thefts also became very common in San Diego during the gold-rush period. In most cases, crimes of this type were blamed on the Indians. Prior to this period, whipping had been the punishment commonly meted out to Indians caught stealing from members of the white population. Many Indians accused of stealing, however, were hung or shot. Those who killed Indians in this manner knew that in the event of a trial, they would not be convicted of homicide.

In 1850, the county of San Diego, in need of tax money, had sent Sheriff Charles Haraszthy among the Diegueño, Luiseño, and Cupeño tribes to collect taxes on cattle and other property. The Indians had numerous grievances against the whites, and the tax appeared to them to be the last straw. The missions that formerly had protected them had disappeared as a result of the secularization process from 1834 to 1845. The Indians were also much annoyed that the whites had despoiled them of their best lands and that increasing numbers of white settlers were entering the region. In 1851, the Indians refused to pay the tax and began a revolt. It was feared that a general native uprising would result, involving not only the tribes in the region, but also those of Baja California. Due to dissension among the Indians, the feared uprising did not materialize. The revolt petered out when the rebel leader, Antonio Garra, was captured and executed on January 10, 1852.[35]

The suppression of the Garra revolt put an end to any potential Indian threat to the white settlements. It did not, however, put an end to cattle rustling in the region, which increased in the years following the native revolt. Hanging eventually replaced whipping as the official punishment for all cattle rustlers, whether white or Indian.[36]

The Mexican government, concerned over the influx of Americans and other foreigners into Baja California, adopted measures to reinforce its control over the region. In July 1849, President José Joaquín Herrera issued a decree for the establishment of a number of military colonies along the Mexican side of the border. It was contemplated that these colonies, made up of soldier-civilians, would, like the colonial presidios or garrisons, serve as core areas around which civilian towns would develop and be governed by elected councils. The decree excluded foreigners—a provision aimed principally at U.S. citizens—from being eligible "either as military colonists or as civilians unless it be done personally and at the responsibility of the inspector, in order that there be no questionable motives behind their joining."[37]

The Herrera colonization project, together with subsequent plans elaborated by Congressman Mariano Paredes in 1850 and Senator Juan Nepomuceno Almonte in 1852, were weakened by a shortage of government funds, a failure to induce Mexicans to migrate and settle in the border areas, and a lack of initiative on the part of the authorities in promoting such projects.[38] The single *colonia militar* established in Baja California, which had to be moved from El Rosario on the coast to a more suitable location at Santo Tomás, experienced internal dissension from the beginning. The lack of water and lands for farming caused discontent among the soldiery, who, in the words of the distinguished California historian Hubert Howe Bancroft, "wandered about in quest of sustenance or deserted to the glittering placers of the gold region."[39] Mismanagement and personal rivalries among the officers of the region initiated a period of disorder among local factions struggling to assert their power over the northern half of the peninsula.[40]

In 1850, the expulsion from La Paz of two U.S. citizens suspected of attempting to promote the peninsula's annexation to the United States caused the Mexican federal government to issue a circular prohibiting the various state and territorial authorities from granting permits to U.S. citizens wishing to travel to Baja California.[41] Aware that prospectors and settlers were entering the territory in steadily increasing numbers, it instructed local commanders to turn back all foreigners at the border. Nevertheless, due to the unsettled conditions in the peninsula as well as a lack of soldiers to patrol the line, little could be done to stop the flow of immigrants.[42]

Although the Mexican government tried to send reinforcements to northern Baja California to preserve order and establish effective control, the ongoing power struggles in the area perpetuated the danger for miners and settlers. In 1852 a revolt led by local *caudillos* Antonio María Meléndrez and Santiago Alvarez against federal forces led by Juan Mendoza resulted in the sacking of Santo Tomás, the principal community. The attack provoked demands by U.S. property owners that the Mexican government provide them with protection. Some U.S. citizens who were suspected of collaborating with the rebels—including Isaac Van Ness of San Diego and an associate—were executed by government forces.[43]

On occasion, these peninsular political struggles also constituted a threat to San Diego's security. During the late 1850s, Mendoza, who had by then had been forced out of power, had established a base in the San Diego vicinity. With the aid of some U.S. citizens, he conducted a series of cross-border raids into Baja California. Several skirmishes were fought between Mendoza's men and Mexican troops along the dry bed of the Tijuana River. The proximity of the conflict to the San Diego region led some of her citizens to demand that the U.S. government strengthen its defenses against possible assaults on the town from Mexican territory.[44]

Filibuster attacks against Baja California posed an additional problem of security for the Mexican government during this period. A group of adventurers led by William Walker set out from San Francisco in mid-October 1853 with the goal of conquering Sonora. Due to the confiscation of the filibusters' brig, *The Arrow,* by U.S. Army authorities, the group was obliged to alter its plans. After plundering La Paz, the expedition made its way back up the Pacific coast of the peninsula to Ensenada, where it awaited reinforcements. Although Walker's associate in the enterprise, Henry Watkins, arrived at the end of December aboard the brig *Anita* with some two hundred volunteers, the expedition still lacked food and other urgently needed supplies. As a result, many of the new arrivals returned to California. In March 1854, Walker finally determined to march on Sonora. Shortly after crossing over into that state, he was obliged, due to desertions, to return to Baja California. In the meantime, the small garrison that Walker had left at San Vicente had been wiped out by a guerrilla group led by Antonio Meléndrez. Fighting constant rearguard actions against Meléndrez and his men, Walker and the remnants of his expedition eventually succeeded in reaching California and safety in early May 1854.[45]

In comparison with the mining strikes of later decades in the peninsula, the discoveries of the early 1850s were fairly modest in scale and did not result in the riches hoped for by prospectors and investors. Despite the small nature of the deposits, Californian promoters and speculators remained optimistic about the possibility of future and greater discoveries in the peninsula.[46]

For U.S. and other foreign miners in Baja California, water was a key determinant. Settlements could flourish and mining be conducted only in areas where a continuous supply of water could be found. Due to the fact that the peninsular watershed is very narrow, water from torrential cloudbursts occurring most commonly in winter is rapidly carried off to the Pacific Ocean or the Gulf of California. Periods of drought are also fairly frequent. The shortage of water greatly hindered the development of mining in the region, especially with regard to placer deposits.[47]

The lack of water was not as great an obstacle to Mexican miners, who had developed a technique called "dry-washing" to cope with the scarcity of water in arid regions. Miners who used this technique would deposit a quantity of ore into a *batea*, or conical wooden bowl. They would then toss a certain amount at a time into the air, allowing the wind to separate the lighter materials from the heavier metal ore, which collected in the bottom of the receptacle. Although simple, this placer method was not very efficient, since only the nuggets and larger flakes of gold could be recovered in such a manner. The gold dust simply blew away.[48]

Despite the limited nature of the Baja California gold deposits and the lack of water, a decree issued by the government of President Antonio López de Santa Anna at the end of June 1855 permitting the exportation of mineral ore from the country without the payment of taxes gave foreign prospectors and investors an incentive to develop their claims. The new law also permitted the importation, without charge, of equipment and other supplies needed to work the mines. In 1857 this special concession was renewed for an additional five years.[49]

The stepped-up flow of miners into the territory spurred by the liberalization of Mexican mining legislation only added to the security concerns of the regional authorities. In 1862, Teodoro Riveroll, the governor of Baja California, recommended to the minister of development and colonization in Mexico City that foreign miners be barred from the goldfields in La Frontera on the grounds that they provoked

violence and disorder. He also argued that the region lacked an adequate police force to contend with such disturbances. The central government, however, preoccupied with the even greater threat to national
security caused by the French intervention, decided that it could ill
afford to spare troops to send to the peninsula.[50]

THE RESURGENCE OF MINING
AND THE BIRTH OF TIJUANA

In the early 1860s, U.S. interest in mining development in Baja California shifted for a time to San Antonio on the southeastern coast,
where new silver deposits were discovered in the latter part of 1862.
During this period, several silver mines were also developed in the
Mulegé district in the central portion of the peninsula (see map).[51]

In the early 1870s, a number of new gold discoveries in the northern region served to reawaken U.S. interest in that area. By then, the
mines of Lower California had produced approximately half a million
dollars in gold. Miners and speculators were confident that a new El
Dorado would soon be discovered in the region.[52]

On January 1, 1870, San Diego once again was infected with gold
fever when a Mexican deposited some one hundred pounds of gold and
silver amalgam at the McDonald and Gale Lumber and Building Supply Company. The Mexican claimed that he had dug up the ore at an
unspecified location about sixty miles south of the international border.
Hundreds of persons were soon en route to the peninsula in hopes of
striking it rich. By February, however, the excitement had died down
as no additional discoveries had been reported. In any case, in the same
month, news of a much more significant strike in the Cuyamaca mountains east of the city more than made up for whatever deception San
Diegans felt concerning the earlier reported find.[53]

In 1870 and 1871 rich veins of gold and silver were discovered on
a ranch southeast of Ensenada belonging to Ambrosio del Castillo. In
this period, Emiliano Ibarra, a California prospector, made another significant find at Calmallí in the central desert region. In 1873, there were
further gold discoveries at Japa (also called Tres Pinos) and Juárez, some
110 miles from San Diego on the Mexican side of the border.[54]

The new strikes once again set in motion a southward migration of
prospectors and merchants from San Diego and other California towns.
In 1872, Real del Castillo, the town that grew up around the Rancho

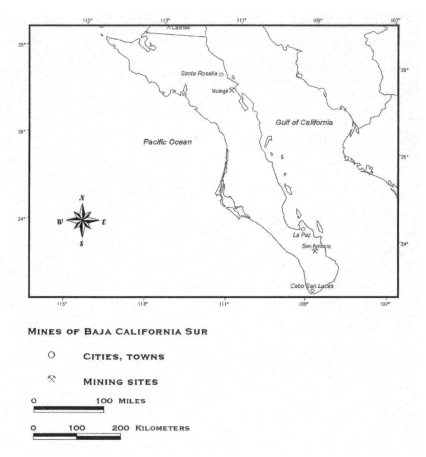

MINES OF BAJA CALIFORNIA SUR

○ CITIES, TOWNS

⚒ MINING SITES

0 ━━━━━ 100 MILES

0 ━━ 100 ━━ 200 KILOMETERS

*Cartography by Colegio de la Frontera Norte-Sistema de Información Geográfi-
ca y Estadística sobre la Frontera, Tijuana, Baja California, México, based on an
idea and design by Lawrence Taylor.*

Castillo mines, replaced Santo Tomás as the *cabecera*, or principal town,
of the Partido Norte, or northern portion of the peninsula. The Real
del Castillo mining boom lasted until the early 1880s, when production
declined. The Calmallí mines continued to produce gold until the end
of the century, finally being abandoned in 1912.[55]

It was during this period that the incipient town of Tijuana began
to take shape. In the 1860s, settlers had begun to farm in the Tijuana
River valley on both sides of the international line. The valley also constituted an important transit route to the gold-mining centers at Real del
Castillo and elsewhere in the peninsula. In mid-November 1869, Marre

and Company initiated regular stagecoach service from San Diego to Santo Tomás.[56] The cross-border traffic by way of the Tijuana Valley multiplied to such an extent that the Mexican federal government considered it expedient to establish an *aduana,* or customhouse, there in 1874 so as not to lose this important source of customs revenue. The customhouse employees resided in San Diego, from where they also dispatched its business. A small detachment of troops was also designated to guard the new port of entry.[57]

Miners crossing the border into Mexico found that the customs duties levied by the Mexican authorities often exceeded the cost of the equipment and goods taxed. Tijuana itself benefited little from this source of revenue, since the money resulting from customs fees was sent to Mexico City. The residents of the valley and nearby areas on the Mexican side of the border earned much more money from the export of produce and livestock.[58]

San Diego's economy, in the meantime, had entered a period of stagnation due to the uncertain conditions brought on by the panic of 1873 and the end of the gold mining boom in the Cuyamacas. Efforts by entrepreneur Alonzo E. Horton to revive the New Town project also faltered for lack of investor confidence. Hopes for injecting new life into the economy hinged on the construction of a rail line linking the city with Los Angeles, San Francisco, and the rest of the country. The completion of the line on November 9, 1885, inaugurated a regional boom in land speculation and construction. The boom, which was part of a nationwide upsurge of prosperity in the 1880s, was fueled by the promotional campaigns of the railway companies, which had millions of acres of land to sell.[59]

The San Diego boom was touched off when the Santa Fe Railroad withdrew from the Transcontinental Traffic Association, which its rival in the region, the Southern Pacific, interpreted as a declaration of war. The dispute led to a passenger rate war between the two companies, which allowed San Diego to tap a portion of the wave of immigrants arriving in California. New subdivisions were created within the city proper, while about twenty new towns were founded in the county as a whole. Public works undertaken during the boom period included the paving of streets and avenues, the construction of interurban rail and cable car lines, dams and flumes to provide the city with water, schools, a public library, and an opera house.[60]

The flurry of speculation that swept through San Diego in these years also had its gaudy or seamy side, a reminder that the city still retained some of the rougher edges of its frontier heritage. As Walter Gifford Smith, editor of the *San Diego Sun,* commented,

> A population drawn together from the adventurous classes of the world, imbued as it was with excitement and far from convention-al trammels, contained and developed a store of profligacy and vice, much of which found its way into official, business, and social life. Gambling was open and flagrant; games of chance were carried on at the curbstones; painted women paraded the town in carriages and sent out engraved cards summoning men to their receptions and "high teas." The desecration of Sunday was com-plete, with all drinking and gambling houses open, and with pic-nics, excursions, fiestas and bullfights. . . . Society retired to cover before the invasion of questionable people, and what came to be known as "society" in the newspapers, was, with honorable excep-tions here and there, a spectacle of vulgar display and the arro-gant parade of reputations which, in Eastern states, had secured for their owners the opportunity and the need of "going West."[61]

The greatest expansion of the city during this period was southward around the bay. The National City and Otay Railway Company, owned by the Land and Town Company (a subsidiary of the Santa Fe Railroad), constructed a line south from the National City terminal to Otay Mesa, with branches to the community of Tia Juana, on the U.S. side of the line, and to Oneonta, in Imperial Beach. A number of suburbs were planned in the areas served by these two branch lines: Tia Juana Heights, Fruitland, Tia Juana Junction, Tia Juana City, and Oneonta. Land values and sales in these areas rose sharply, owing to their proxim-ity to the border and the possibilities they offered for the expansion of agriculture.[62]

The effects of the land boom extended south of the border. The International Company of Mexico, a U.S.-Mexican firm that had been organized in March 1885 to take advantage of the liberal terms of the Mexican Colonization Act of 1883, hoped to sell the almost fifteen million acres it held in concession in the peninsula to colonists willing to settle in the region.[63] When the company failed in this task, its hold-ings were acquired in May 1889 by an English corporation, the Mexican Land and Colonization Company. A subsidiary, the Lower California Development Company, was formed in 1890 in order to develop the San Quintín Valley, located about 150 miles south of the border, into a major grain-growing region. The latter firm established the Peninsular Railway and Telegraph Company to construct a railway from San Quintín to San Diego, with a branch line to Yuma. Drought and the economic recession of the early nineties made investors leery, however, and the Mexican government eventually canceled both companies' concessions in April 1917.[64]

The Tijuana region was not initially affected by the development boom owing to a legal dispute over the lands of the ranch formerly belonging to Santiago E. Argüello, which comprised a substantial portion of the area, between his widow Pilar Ortega and other members of the ranch man's family.[65] Despite this litigation, a small settlement had begun to form in the area. In addition to the customhouse and the cattle ranch belonging to the Argüello family, there were also a number of wood and adobe huts, some stores (the largest of which belonged to William Lane), a butcher shop belonging to James Argüello, a school, and a church. A hotel and restaurant had also been erected some years previously at hot springs located a short distance south of town, where persons having rheumatism and skin diseases could be treated.[66]

The beginnings of what was eventually to become a flourishing tourist trade also linked the border communities with San Diego. An important attraction for tourists visiting San Diego, especially following the inauguration of the Hotel Coronado in 1888, was the Mexican town of Tijuana. The National City and Otay Railroad ran three daily excursion trains to Oneonta. From there, tourists could board horse drawn carriages to take them to the international boundary marker on the coast, where they could look into Mexico. Other excursion trains ran to Tia Juana, where tourists could board coaches that took them to the hot springs at Agua Caliente.[67]

On arriving in Tijuana, the tourists found a variety of interesting attractions and features to choose from. There were horse races, which were advertised daily in San Diego newspapers and often drew up to one thousand spectators. The races were organized by a group of merchants and ranchers in both Tia Juana and Tijuana, including Joseph Messenger, Alejandro Savín, and Felipe Crosthwaite. There were also bullfights, cockfights, and native dances. Certain Mexican festive holidays, such as Cinco de Mayo and 16 de Septiembre (National Independence Day), also attracted many visitors. All of the attractions were popular with San Diegans and other foreign visitors to Tijuana because they helped them feel that they were in a foreign country.[68]

At certain times, normally on Sundays, there were special shows and spectacles to delight the crowds. On one occasion, for example, a

Mexican circus visited Tijuana on a tour stop.[69] On another occasion there was a boxing match, refereed by the celebrated former lawman and gunfighter Wyatt Earp. Earp, having been indicted for murder in Arizona for shooting the men who had killed his brother Morgan, had been drawn to San Diego by news of the boom. Earp opened three casinos in the business district and invested money in land and other commercial ventures in the region.[70]

The development of this border tourist trade in 1888 and 1889, together with the presence of new settlers on the lands of the Argüello ranch, induced the Argüello family to reach a settlement concerning the property litigation. They were also motivated by the fact that several members of the family—as well as some of their relatives from the Olvera family of Tijuana property owners—resided in California and could see the advantages of opening the ranch property to town lot development. The agreement ending the litigation, which was approved on July 12, 1889, set aside a portion of the ranch to form the town site of Zaragoza de Tijuana. A plan for the new site was completed by engineer Ricardo Orozco, who was hired to carry out the task of surveying the town property.[71]

During the boom period, San Diego constituted the center of activities for the communities contiguous to the border. The inhabitants of these areas not only sold their products in San Diego, but also purchased a portion of their food, clothing, and implements in its shops and stores. They also attended social and religious meetings in San Diego. Even the Tijuana tourist trade was dependent on San Diego. The latter possessed the necessary infrastructure for business, while Tijuana provided the attractions for the visitor.[72]

By the late spring of 1888, the boom in San Diego had ended. Although the city's population dropped from 35,000 to 16,000 over the next half year, it was still approximately three times as large as it had been before the boom.[73] The population loss was not as severe in the rest of the county and in rural areas, since immigrants had arrived there principally to farm or conduct businesses unrelated to real estate speculation. Following the boom, the county population stood at about 35,000, or four times what it had been in 1880.[74] Although many persons lost money in the collapse of the real estate market, and construction work halted, the boom also resulted in many civic improvements that would facilitate future growth and development. With the expansion of the urban areas toward the border, San Diego had also become linked in a physical, economic, and social sense with the emerging town of Tijuana.[75]

Cross-border traffic between San Diego and Tijuana increased even further following the discovery in late February 1889 of a rich placer gold deposit in the Santa Clara district about sixty miles southeast of Ensenada.[76] The rumors that circulated in connection with this gold discovery compared it with the California strike of 1849.[77] People were predisposed to believe such rumors, given the end of the development boom. In the course of the new strike, an average of three hundred miners a day passed through San Diego en route to the Santa Clara gold-fields. Of these, some one hundred went by steamer to Ensenada and from there in wagons to the mining district. The rest made their way to the goldfields by the overland route via Tijuana. Those choosing the overland route went by carriage, wagon, burro, horse, or on foot. The peak of the rush was reached on March 5, when some six hundred prospectors departed from San Diego.[78]

The regions nearest the mines were depopulated almost immediately after the announcement of the gold strike. Almost all of the adult male population of Ensenada left for the gold region, and most of the town's stores, saloons, and barber shops were obliged to close for lack of personnel to manage them. In San Diego, the labor shortage caused by the rush was also acute. More than one hundred tracklayers on the San Diego, Cuyamaca, and Eastern Railroad walked off the job and headed for the mines, followed by engineers, brakemen, conductors, switchmen, and dispatchers. Restaurants also lacked kitchen help and waiters. The Hotel Coronado, for example, had to advertise for workers as far away as San Francisco.[79]

The Santa Clara strike lasted for a period of only about five weeks. Even so, it was the largest in the history of the peninsula, with as many as five thousand men participating in the rush. Some twenty thousand dollars worth of gold was ultimately extracted from the placers. The results appear somewhat diminutive considering that the miners expended almost a quarter of a million dollars getting to the diggings and working their claims. Each prospector not only had to spend an initial sum of about fifty dollars for equipment and food, but also an additional five or six dollars a day for living expenses while at the mines. Often miners did not have enough money for living expenses and had to use—in the case of the more fortunate ones—the gold they found at the site. As pointed out, customs duties charged at the Tijuana border crossing were often higher than the actual value of the goods brought into Mexico. Although burros and mares were admitted duty-free, other horses were taxed at forty dollars a head. In addition to the tax on equipment and livestock, the aduana also charged six dollars just for passage through the customhouse. Once the strike ended, most of the miners, who were mainly unemployed or low-income wage earners, returned to their places of origin.[80]

For San Diego, the rush offered a temporary respite from the slump caused by the end of the real estate boom. Since the city constituted the principal stopover point for supplies and transportation to the mines, merchants and businessmen were able to make enormous profits off those persons headed for the goldfields. Be that as it may, by 1890, Los Angeles, with its larger growth and more prosperous surrounding communities—such as Riverside, San Bernardino, and Redlands—had diverted much of the trade with the coastal interior away from San Diego. During the boom period, it eclipsed San Diego and became the hub of commerce on the West Coast that the latter had aspired to be.[81]

In 1896, with the outbreak of the independence struggle in Cuba, San Diego's economy began to experience another change that would define its character throughout much of the twentieth century. In that year, Congress decided on measures to greatly strengthen the port's fortifications and to establish a major naval and military base in the area.[82] San Diego's hopes for a direct rail connection to eastern U.S. markets were eventually fulfilled in 1919 with the completion of the San Diego and Arizona Railway, which linked the city with Yuma, Arizona.[83] By the end of the century, Tijuana was also well on its way to becoming a major metropolis in the region. Its tourist industry, although still dependent on San Diego, continued to grow during the 1890s. Several curio stores selling postcards and other souvenirs were opened, as well as eating establishments featuring Mexican food.[84] By 1900, the town's population stood at 242 inhabitants, with a further 108 inhabitants living in the outlying areas of the *sección municipal*, or municipal district.[85] So accelerated had been its growth during the first decade of its existence that in September 1901 it was raised to the category of *subprefectura* (subprefecture).[86] In 1925, a generation later, it became a full-fledged municipality largely as a result of Prohibition in the United States, which fostered the growth of cantinas, cabarets, and other forms of entertainment in the communities along the Mexican side of the border. The tourist and service sectors would constitute the mainstays of its economy until the advent of the maquiladora industry in the 1960s.[87]

CONCLUSION

The Baja California mining boom of 1850–1890 coincided with the gradual transformation of San Diego from a rough pioneer settlement into a small but burgeoning city with several modern attributes. Although the mineral strikes in northern California and the Baja California peninsula initially hurt the town's economy by draining off needed manpower, in time San Diego developed into an important departure point and supply center for mining operations in the latter region.

The Baja California gold strikes helped to buoy up San Diego's economy as the traffic to the northern California goldfields diminished. Additional strikes continued to do so periodically, such as during the period of economic depression during the early 1870s and in the late 1880s, when the southern California land boom ended.

By the end of the 1880s, Tijuana had begun to emerge as a border community in the ranching area adjacent to the international border. The substantial increase in cross-border traffic due to the discovery of significant deposits of precious metals in Real del Castillo and other locations in northern Baja California led to the establishment of an aduana and military post in the Mexican portion of the Tijuana River valley, around which a small settlement soon developed. The land boom of the mid-1880s, with the development of communities in areas contiguous to the international border and tourist excursions to the Mexican side, greatly increased economic and social ties between San Diego and Tijuana.

The mining boom from 1850 to 1890 in Baja California thus played an important role in the growth and development of San Diego and Tijuana, particularly the latter. In drawing the two communities more closely together, it also constituted in many ways the cornerstone of the building of a symbiotic relationship between the cities' inhabitants that has endured to this day. ✤

NOTES

1. Acknowledgement by the conde de Aranda of the report of an expedition to Sonora and the Californias, noting the discovery of new gold placer deposits in these regions. Archivo General de la Nación, México (hereafter cited as AGNM), Fondo: Historia, caja 2, exp. 16; in the Instituto de Investigaciones Históricas, Universidad Autónoma de Baja California (hereafter cited

as IIH/UABC), caja 2. exp. 16; correspondence relating to the discovery of a gold bar by an Indian belonging to the Mission of San Borja, January 29, 1774–July 8, 1775, in AGNM, Fondo: Provincias Internas, vol. 211, exp. 1, hs. 1–9; in IIH/UABC, caja 8, exp. 5; Miguel Del Barco, *Historia natural y crónica de la Antigua California,* ed. Miguel León-Portilla (México: Universidad Nacional Autónoma de México, 1988), pp. 153–55; Johann Jacob Baegert, *Noticias de la península americana de California* (México: Antigua Librería Robredo, 1942), pp. 60–63; Francisco Javier Clavijero, *Historia de la Antigua o Baja California* (México: Editorial Porrúa, 1982), p. 15.

2. Alexander Forbes, *California: A History of Upper and Lower California from Their First Discovery to the Present Time* (1839; reprint, New York: Arno Press, 1973), p. 63.

3. For the legislative act permitting foreign investment in Mexican mining, see Manuel Dublán and José María Lozano, eds., *Legislación mexicana, o colección completa de las disposiciones legislativas expedidas desde la independencia de la república,* 34 vols. (México: Dublán y Lozano, 1876–1904), 1:681.

4. Henry W. Halleck, "Report on Baja California," in Henry W. Halleck, *The Mexican War in Baja California: The Memorandum of Captain Henry W. Halleck Concerning His Expeditions in Lower California, 1846–1848,* ed. Doyce B. Nunis, Jr. (Los Angeles: Dawson's Book Shop, 1977), p. 203; Robert R. Alvarez, Jr., *Family: Migration and Adaptation in Baja and Alta California, 1800–1975* (Berkeley: University of California Press, 1987), p. 26.

5. United States Senate, *Senate Executive Document 52,* 30th Congress, 1st. Sess. (1847), Serial No. 509, p. 337; President Polk's Instructions to U.S. peace negotiator Nicholas Trist, April 15, 1847, in William R. Manning, ed., *Diplomatic Correspondence of the United States: Inter-American Affairs, 1831–1860,* 12 vols. (Washington, D.C.: Carnegie Endowment for International Peace, 1932–1939), 8:205–6.

6. Carl O. Sauer and Peveril Meiggs, "Lower California Studies I. Site and Culture at San Fernando Velicaté," *University of California Publications in Geography* 2, no. 9 (September 30, 1927), p. 294.

7. For accounts of such journeys, see "Our Golden Correspondence," *New York Herald,* October 15, 1849; James D. Hawks, "Journal of the Expedition of Mr. J. D. Hawks and Party, through the Interior of the Peninsula of Lower California, from San Domingo to San Diego," in J. Ross Browne, *Resources of the Pacific Slope* (New York: D. Appleton and Co., 1869), pp. 132–42; Patricia A. Etter, "Ho! for California on the Mexican Gold Trail," *Overland Journal* 11, no. 3 (Autumn 1993), pp. 2–12.

8. William E. Smythe, *History of San Diego, 1542–1908: An Account of the Rise and Progress of the Pioneer Settlement on the Pacific Coast of the United States* (San Diego: The History Co., 1908), pp. 238–49, 254–55.

9. Antonio Franco Coronel, *Tales of Early California (Cosas de California),* ed. Doyce B. Nunis, Jr. (Santa Barbara, Calif.: Bellerophon Books, 1994), pp. 54–55; Cave Johnson Couts, *Hepah, California! The Journal of Cave Johnson Couts,* ed. Henry F. Dobyns (Tucson: University of Arizona Press, 1961), pp. 82–88.

10. Horace Bell, *Reminiscences of a Ranger; or Early Times in Southern California* (1851; reprint, Santa Barbara, Calif.: Wallace Hebberd, 1927), pp. 10–11; A. B. Clarke, *Travels in Mexico and California,* ed. Anne M. Perry (1852; reprint, College Station, Tex.: Texas A&M University Press, 1988), pp. 93–94; Robert Glass Cleland, *The Cattle on a Thousand Hills: Southern California, 1850–1880,* 2nd. ed. (San Marino, Calif.: Huntington Library, 1951), pp. 102–16.

11. *Californio* has commonly been used to refer to a person born in California of Spanish-speaking parents. Some writers have used the term to refer exclusively to a member of the landowning class—*hacendados* and *rancheros*—that existed in California in the period before the war of 1846–1848 and for some decades afterward. It is in the latter sense that the term is used here. For explanations of the term in its historical context, see in particular Leonard Pitt, *The Decline of the Californios: A Social History of the Spanish-Speaking Californians, 1846–1890* (Berkeley: University of California Press, 1966), p. 309.

12. *Daily Alta California,* January 22, 1850; *San Diego Herald,* September 25, October 6, 1851; Smythe, *History of San Diego,* pp. 255, 275, 316–17; Richard F. Pourade, *The History of San Diego: The Silver Dons* (San Diego: Union-Tribune Publishing Co., 1963), pp. 157–64.

13. *San Diego Herald,* July 31, 1851; Smythe, *History of San Diego,* pp. 317–19.

14. H. M. T. Powell, *Santa Fe Trail to California, 1849–1852,* ed. Douglas S. Watson (San Francisco: Book Club of California, 1931), pp. 190–99.

15. "Lower California, No. 1," *Daily Alta California,* February 8, 1851; M. Paredes, "Sonora: placeres de oro y plata," article from the Mexico City newspaper *Siglo XIX,* June 9 [1850?], reproduced in José Francisco Velasco, *Noticias estadísticas del estado de Sonora* (México: Imprenta de Ignacio Cumplido, 1850), pp. 343–44 (see also pp. 296, 346–48); William Redmond Ryan, *Personal Adventures in Upper and Lower California,* 2 vols. (1850; reprint, New York: Arno Press, 1973), 2:331–38; William Perkins, *Three Years in California: William Perkins' Journal of Life at Sonora, 1849–1852,* ed. Dale L. Morgan and James R. Scobie (Berkeley: University of California Press, 1964), pp. 312, 351.

16. *Daily Alta California,* September 26, 1851, August 16, 1852; Hubert Howe Bancroft, *History of California,* 7 vols. (San Francisco: History Co., 1884–1890), 6:583; Ernest De Massey, *A Frenchman in the Gold Rush: The Journal of Ernest De Massey, Argonaut of 1849,* ed. Marguerite Eyer Wilbur (San Francisco: California Historical Society, 1927), p. 153.

17. "Lower California, No. 2," *Daily Alta California,* February 21, 1851. See also the first part of this news report in the edition of February 8, 1851, as well as the article entitled "The Mines of Lower California" in the August 11, 1851, edition.

18. *Daily Alta California,* March 16, 1851; Alexander S. Taylor, "Historical Summary of Baja California from Its Discovery in 1532 to 1867," in J. Ross Browne, *Resources of the Pacific Slope* (New York: D. Appleton and Co., 1869), p. 55; Hubert Howe Bancroft, *History of the Northwestern States and Mexico,* 2 vols. (San Francisco: History Co., 1889), 2:727.

19. "Lower California, No. 2," *Daily Alta California*, February 21, 1851; James Smith, Jr., correspondent for the *Daily Alta California*, to the newspaper's editor, February 17, 1851, *Daily Alta California*, February 27, 1851.

20. *San Diego Herald*, July 17, 1851; "The Mines of Lower California," *Daily Alta California*, August 11, 1851.

21. José Matías Moreno, "Descripción del partido norte de la Baja California, 1861," in David Piñera Ramírez and Jorge Martínez Zepeda, ed., *Fuentes documentales para la historia de Baja California*, vol. 1, pt. 2 (December 1984), p. 27; *San Diego Union*, February 17, 1870; Robert W. Long, "The Life and Times of José Matías Moreno" (Ph.D. diss., Western University, 1972), pp. 241–42; Robert W. Long, "José Matías Moreno, Secretary to Pío Pico, the Last Mexican Governor of California," in George M. Ellis, ed., *Brand Book Number Three* (San Diego: San Diego Corral of the Westerners, 1973), pp. 183–84.

22. Letters from José Matías Romero to Rafael Espinosa, governor of Baja California, November 29, 1851, in Amado Aguirre, *Documentos para la historia de Baja California* (Tijuana: Instituto de Investigaciones Históricas UNAM/Centro de Investigaciones Históricas UNAM-UABC, 1977), pp. 64–66; Matías Moreno, "Descripción," p. 31; Ulises Urbano Lassepas, *Historia de la colonización de la Baja California y decreto del 10 de marzo de 1857* (1859; reprint, México: Universidad Autónoma de Baja California/Secretaría de Educación Pública, 1995), pp. 131–32.

23. *San Diego Herald*, September 16, 1854.

24. Bandini, like Matías Moreno, possessed properties in both Upper California and Lower California. In the early 1850s he moved his business operations to the peninsula, where he focused on developing copper mining. For the Mexican government, Bandini's claim to Rancho Guadalupe was further weakened by the fact that he had supported the United States during the war of 1846–1848 and had become a U.S. citizen residing in San Diego. Lassepas, *Historia de la colonización*, p. 283; Smythe, *History of San Diego*, pp. 164–66.

25. Robert W. Long, "Annals of the Rancho Ex-Misión de Guadalupe," in Abraham P. Nasatir, ed., *Brand Book Number Four* (San Diego: San Diego Corral of the Westerners, 1976), pp. 129–33.

26. *San Diego Herald*, May 15, 1852. There was also news of a later discovery in 1855. See *Daily Alta California*, March 19, 1855. The earliest report of indications of gold in the San Diego area was that of Father Antonio de la Ascensión, a member of the expedition led by Sebastián Vizcaíno. Father Antonio was a member of a shore party that examined the San Diego bay region on November 10, 1602. Gold was also reportedly mined to a limited extent in the region of Escondido and Black Mountain, east of Peñasquitos. Antonio de la Ascensión, "A Brief Report of the Discovery of the South Sea," in Herbert Eugene Bolton, ed., *Spanish Exploration in the Southwest* (1908; reprint, New York: Barnes and Noble, 1963), p. 117; Richard F. Pourade, *The History of San Diego: The Glory Years* (San Diego: Union-Tribune Publishing Co., 1964), pp. 34, 50.

27. For a history of the discoveries in the Cuyamaca range, see Horace F. Wilcox, "How the Julian Mines Were Discovered," typescript manuscript, San

Diego Public Library, California Room; and Gale W. Sheldon, "Julian Gold Mining Days" (master's thesis, San Diego State College, 1959).

28. *Daily Alta California,* February 27, 1851; Pitt, *Decline of the Californios,* p. 111.

29. The abandonment was completed in 1866, when the military barracks were vacated by the army. Elizabeth C. MacPhail, *The Story of New San Diego and of Its Founder Alonzo E. Horton* (San Diego: San Diego Historical Society, 1979), pp. 17–18.

30. Long, "José Matías Moreno," pp. 241–42; María de Jesús Ruiz, "José Matías Moreno (1848–1870): economía y política en la frontera de Baja California" (Unpublished paper, Universidad Autónoma de Baja California, Tijuana, 1998), n.p.

31. Pourade, *Glory Years,* p. 187.

32. Taylor, "Historical Summary," p. 67; Pourade, *Silver Dons,* pp. 209–10; Pitt, *Decline of the Californios,* p. 259; Dean T. Conklin, "Tijuana: génesis y primeras noticias," in Miguel Mathes, ed., *Baja California: textos de su historia,* 2 vols. (México: Instituto de Investigaciones Dr. José María Luis Mora, SEP/Programa Cultural de las Fronteras/Gobierno del Estado de Baja California, 1988), 1:426.

33. Pourade, *Silver Dons,* pp. 212–13.

34. Ibid., p. 213.

35. For accounts of the Garra revolt, see Arthur Woodward, "The Garra Revolt of 1851," in *The Westerners Brand Book: 1947* (Los Angeles: Los Angeles Corral of the Westerners, 1947), pp. 111–17; Noel M. Loomis, "The Garra Uprising of 1851," in *Brand Book Number Two,* pp. 4–23; Leonard B. Waitman, "Chief Antonio Garra's Insurrection and the Confederation Myth of 1851," in Ellis, *Brand Book Number Three,* pp. 98–101.

36. Pourade, *Silver Dons,* p. 213.

37. "El plan de México para establecer las colonias militares," taken from AGNM, Ramo: Secretaría de Gobernación, archivos viejos, 1833–1854, Indios bárbaros, exp. 35, reproduced in Rufus Kay Wyllys, *Los franceses en Sonora, 1850–1854: historia de los aventureros franceses que pasaron de California a México* (México: Editorial Porrúa, 1971), p. 184; Joseph Allen Stout, Jr., *The Liberators: Filibustering Expeditions into Mexico, 1848–1862, and the Last Thrust of Manifest Destiny* (Los Angeles: Westernlore Press, 1973), pp. 27–30.

38. Mariano Arista, "Military Colonies: A Project for Their Establishment on the Eastern and Western Frontiers of the Republic" (translation of: *Colonias militares, proyecto para su establecimiento en las fronteras de oriente y occidente de la república*), July 20, 1848, in Odie B. Faulk, ed., "Projected Mexican Military Colonies for the Borderlands, 1848," *Journal of Arizona History* 9, no. 1 (Spring 1968), pp. 40–45; Patricia R. Herring, "A Plan for the Colonization of Sonora's Northern Frontier: The Paredes *Proyectos* of 1850," *Journal of Arizona History* 10, no. 2 (Summer 1969), pp. 104–11; Juan Nepomuceno Almonte, "Proposals for Colonization Laws" (translation of "Proyectos de leyes sobre colonización," January 26, 1852), in Odie B. Faulk, ed., "Projected Mexican Colonies in the Borderlands, 1852," *Journal of Arizona History* 10, no. 2 (Summer 1969), pp. 119–28; Stout, *The Liberators,* pp.

28–35.

39. Bancroft, *History of the Northwestern States,* 2:720.

40. Adrián Valadés, *Historia de la Baja California, 1850–1870* (México: Universidad Nacional Autónoma de México, 1974), pp. 21–25; Angel Rivera Granados, "La colonia militar en Baja California, 1849–1853," *Calafia* 4, no. 6 (April 1982), pp. 20–23; Angela Moyano Pahissa, "Instrucciones para el cuidado de la frontera de Baja California en 1848," *Secuencia* 5 (May–August 1986), pp. 81–86; Bancroft, *History of the Northwestern States,* 2:720–21. For correspondence and other documents dealing with problems related to border security and the establishment of the military colony in Baja California during this period, see Aguirre, *Documentos,* pp. 98–101.

41. Luis G. Zorrilla, *Historia de las relaciones entre México y los Estados Unidos de América,* 2 vols. (México: Editorial Porrúa, 1977), 1:304.

42. Acknowledgement from Robles, of the Ministerio de Gobernación, of receipt of communication from the Ministerio de Relaciones Exteriores in regard to the report from the *jefe político* of Baja California, July 4, 1851. AGN, Fondo: Gobernación, leg. 2111, caja 2599, exp. 2; in IIH/UABC, caja 16, exp. 22.

43. *San Diego Herald,* May 15 and 22, 1852, June 28, 1852; Valadés, *Historia,* p. 25; Adalberto Walther Meade, *Antonio María Meléndrez: caudillo y patriota de Baja California* (Mexicali: Universidad Autónoma de Baja California, 1988), pp. 19–22.

44. Benjamin Hayes, *Pioneer Notes from the Diaries of Judge Benjamin Hayes, 1849–1875* (Los Angeles: McBride Printing Co., 1929), pp. 235–41; Pourade, *Silver Dons,* p. 209; Conklin, "Tijuana," p. 426.

45. Manuel Diez de Bonilla, ministro de relaciones exteriores, to James Gadsden, U.S. minister to Mexico, August 20, November 15, and November 30, 1853; Gadsden to Diez de Bonilla, November 18, November 29, and December 2, 1853; Gadsden to Secretary of State William L. Marcy, November 18–20, 1853, December 4, 1853, July 3, 1854; Juan M. Almonte, Mexican minister to the United States, to Marcy, December 21, 1853, and January 20, May 16, and May 31, 1854; John S. Cripps, U.S. chargé d'affaires ad interim at Mexico City, to Bonilla, February 1, 1854; all in William R. Manning, ed., *Diplomatic Correspondence of the United States: Inter-American Affairs, 1831–1860,* 12 vols. (Washington, D.C.: Carnegie Endowment for International Peace, 1932–1939), 9:601–2, 663–78, 685–86, 696–97, 699–700, 706–7, 710–12, 719–21; *Daily Alta California,* December 1, 1853, January 3, 1854, and January 10, 1854; *San Diego Herald,* December 3, 1853 and May 13, 1854; "California Filibusters," *Daily Alta California,* June 15, 1854; Arthur Woodward, ed., *The Republic of Lower California, 1853–1854, in the Words of Its State Papers, Eyewitnesses, and Contemporary Reporters* (Los Angeles: Dawson's Book Shop, 1966), pp. 39–42; William Walker, *The War in Nicaragua* (Tucson: University of Arizona Press, 1985), pp. 18–24.

46. Charles Nordhoff, *California for Health, Pleasure, and Residence: A Book for Travellers and Settlers* (1873; reprint, Berkeley, Calif.: Ten Speed Press, 1974), pp. 12, 21.

47. A particularly serious drought, which occurred in 1863–1864 throughout the Californias and on a global scale, affected mining operations in the sub-

sequent decade. In the state of California, this period of drought followed one of heavy rains in 1861–1862. J. Ross Browne, *Explorations in Lower California* (1868; reprint, Studio City, Calif.: Spencer Murray, 1966), p. 27; Taylor, "Historical Summary," pp. 67–68; Bancroft, *History of the Northwestern States,* 2:726; Ruth Elizabeth Kearney, "American Colonization Ventures in Lower California, 1862–1917" (Ph.D. diss., University of California, 1944), pp. 1–2.

48. For an excellent description of this technique, see William Redmond Ryan, *Personal Adventures in Upper and Lower California,* 2 vols. (1850; reprint, New York: Arno Press, 1973), 2:13–15; see also Otis E. Young, "The Spanish Tradition in Gold and Silver Mining," *Arizona and the West* 5 (Winter 1965), pp. 306–7, 313–14.

49. Permission for the export of mineral ore mined in the territory of Baja California; in AGNM, Fondo: Gobernación, vol. 2 (1855); in IIH/UABC, caja 9, exp. 18; AGN, Fondo: Fomento, Serie: Decretos, circulares y leyes, vol. 3, exp. 5 s/2; in IIH/UABC, caja 1, exp. 36; Dublán and Lozano, *Legislación mexicana,* 7:472; extension of the decree regulating the export of mineral ore from Baja California for a period of five years, 1857; in AGN, Fondo: Gobernación, vol. 458, sección s/s, exp. 7; in IIH/UABC, caja 9, exp. 43; AGN, Fondo: Fomento, Serie: Decretos, circulares y leyes, vol. 5, exp. 4 s/s; in IIH/UABC, caja 1, exp. 38; Dublán and Lozano, *Legislación mexicana,* 8:382–83.

50. Teodoro Riveroll to the ministro de fomento y colonización, April 2, 1862, in AGNM, Fondo: Justicia, vol. 659, leg. 217, ff. 242–43; in IIH/UABC, caja 9, exp. 53.

51. *Mining and Scientific Press,* October 1, 1864, and January 21, 1865; Browne, *Explorations,* pp. 23–27; Browne, *Resources,* pp. 119–21; Taylor, "Historical Summary," pp. 55, 59; Manuel Rivera Cambas, *México pintoresco, artístico y monumental,* 3 vols. (México: Imprenta de la Reforma, 1880–1883), 3:616–33.

52. *San Diego Union,* December 11, 1873.

53. *San Diego Union,* January 27 and February 10, 1870.

54. *San Diego Union,* December 11, 1873; Donald Chaput, William M. Mason, and David Zárate Loperena, *Modest Fortunes: Mining in Northern Baja California* (Los Angeles: Natural History Museum of Los Angeles County, 1992), pp. 53–55, 102–12.

55. David Goldbaum, *Towns of Baja California: A 1918 Report,* ed. William O. Hendricks (Glendale, Calif.: La Siesta Press, 1971), pp. 27–31, 51–52; Robert R. Alvarez, *Familia: Migration and Adaptation in Baja and Alta California, 1800–1975* (Berkeley: University of California Press, 1987), pp. 42–43, 51–53; Don Meadows, "A Forgotten Capital of Baja California," in *Westerners Brand Book Number Five* (Los Angeles: Los Angeles Westerners, 1953), pp. 103–8.

56. Conklin, "Tijuana," p. 426; Celso Aguirre Bernal, *Tijuana: su historia, sus hombres* (Mexicali: n.p., 1975), pp. 91–92; David Piñera Ramírez and Jesús Ortiz Figueroa, "Inicios de Tijuana como asentamiento urbano," in David Piñera Ramírez and Jesús Ortiz Figueroa, eds., *Historia de Tijuana,* 2d. ed., 2 vols. (Tijuana: Universidad Autónoma de Baja California, Centro de Investi-

gaciones UNAM-UABC/Gobierno del Estado de Baja California/XII Ayuntamiento de Tijuana, 1989), 1:60.

57. "Decreto para el establecimiento de una aduana fronteriza en el punto denominado Tijuana: 1874," AGNM, Fondo: Gobernación, leg. 1183(2), caja 1434, exp. 3; en IIH/UABC, 1874.11; Jesús Ortiz Figueroa, "La Comisión de Terrenos Baldíos y el primer proyecto de la fundación del pueblo de Tijuana," in Piñera Ramírez and Ortiz Figueroa, *Historia de Tijuana,* 1:23–24; Piñera Ramírez and Ortiz Figueroa, "Inicios de Tijuana," p. 62.

58. Richard E. Lingenfelter, *The Rush of '89: The Baja California Gold Fever & Captain James Edward Friend's Letters from the Santa Clara Mines* (San Diego: Dawson's Book Shop, 1967), p. 36; Bascom C. Stephens, *The Gold Fields of Lower California, Being a Complete Guide Book with Official Maps, Revenue and Mining Laws, etc., etc., for Miners and Settlers* (Los Angeles: Southern California Publishing Co., 1889), pp. 24–27; T. D. Proffitt III, *Tijuana: The History of a Mexican Metropolis* (San Diego: San Diego State University Press, 1994), pp. 217–18.

59. Glenn S. Dumke, *The Boom of the Eighties in Southern California* (San Marino, Calif.: Huntington Library, 1944), pp. 17–27; MacPhail, *Story of New San Diego,* pp. 26–52.

60. Smythe, *History of San Diego,* pp. 413–52; Dumke, *Boom of the Eighties,* pp. 136–42.

61. Walter Gifford Smith, *The Story of San Diego* (San Diego: City Publishing Co., 1892), pp. 153–54.

62. *San Diego Union,* October 1, 1887; Dumke, *Boom of the Eighties,* pp. 154–56. In 1908, William E. Smythe established a colony of U.S. farmers in Tia Juana called "Little Landers," meaning people who possessed small land lots. The settlement motto, "A Little Land and a Living," expressed the working principle of the colony: that a family could gain a livelihood from cultivating an acre of land. The colonists later changed the name of their community to San Ysidro, the patron saint of Madrid and of agriculture. John L. Cowan, "The Hope of the 'Little Landers,' " *The World's Work* 23, no. 1 (November 1911), pp. 96–100; Robert V. Hine, *California's Utopian Colonies* (New Haven, Conn.: Yale University Press, 1953), pp. 144–48; Laurence B. Lee, "The Little Landers Colony of San Ysidro," *Journal of San Diego History* 21, no. 1 (Winter 1975), pp. 26–48. Oneonta, named after a town in New York state, was never developed. It remained as a name on the promotional maps of the time to indicate an area lying south of the present-day community of Imperial Beach and north of the Tijuana River.

63. *San Diego Bee,* December 23, 1888 (supplement); Angela Moyano de Guevara, "La Compañía Internacional en Ensenada," in Angela Moyano de Guevara and Jorge Martínez Zepeda, coords., *Visión histórica de Ensenada* (Ensenada, B.C.: Centro de Investigaciones Históricas, Universidad Autónoma de Baja California, 1982), pp. 125–35.

64. Interview with Elena Martínez Davidson conducted by Marguerite Reeves, June 4, 1981, in the Oral History Collection, San Diego Historical

Society, San Diego, Calif., Document No. SDHS/CH, p. 5; James Knapp Reeve, "The Peninsula of Lower California," *Lippincott's Monthly Magazine* 53 (January–June 1894), p. 77; decree of President Venustiano Carranza canceling the concession of the Mexican Land and Development Co. and the Lower California Development Co., April 17, 1917; in Pablo L. Martínez, *Historia de Baja California* (La Paz, B.C.S.: Patronato del Estudiante Sudcaliforniano, A.C./Consejo Editorial del Gobierno de B.C.S., 1991), pp. 473–75; Moyano de Guevara, "La Compañía Inglesa," in Moyano de Guevara and Martínez Zepeda, *Visión histórica*, pp. 143–45, 152–53.

65. Jesús Ortiz Figueroa, "Evolución de la propiedad en el Rancho de Tijuana, 1829–1900," in Piñera Ramírez and Ortiz Figueroa, *Historia de Tijuana*, 2:84–85.

66. *San Diego Union*, April 15, 1881; *Daily San Diegan*, August 22, 1885.

67. *San Diego Union*, August 1, 1888; *Otay Press*, June 13, 1889.

68. *San Diego Daily Bee*, September 6 and 18, 1887; *San Diego Sun*, August 3, 1888; *San Diego Union*, August 6, 1888.

69. *San Diego Sun*, August 3, 1884; *San Diego Daily Bee*, September 6, 1887; *San Diego Union*, August 6 and September 5, 1888.

70. Interview with Adalaska Pearson, law enforcement officer for the area between National City and the Mexican border, 1928, in Kenneth R. Cilch and Kenneth R. Cilch, Jr., *Wyatt Earp, the Missing Years: San Diego in the 1880s* (San Diego: Gaslamp Books/Museum, 1998), pp. 34–35; Jerry McMullen, "Wyatt Earp and the Best 100-Round Boxing Match," *San Diego Union*, July 23, 1961; Stuart N. Lake, *Wyatt Earp: Frontier Marshal* (1931; reprint, New York: Pocket Books, 1994), p. 370.

71. *Otay Press*, May 2, 1889; Transacción que dio al litigio promovido en el intestado de doña Pilar Ortega viuda de Argüello, July 12, 1889, in Ortiz Figueroa, "Evolución," pp. 86–87; Medición y evalúo del predio de Tijuana por el ingeniero Ricardo Orozco, 1889, AGNM, Fondo: Dirección General del Gobierno, 2,382(30)24554, tomo II, caja 70, exp. 20/1; en IIH/UABC, caja 27, exp. 35; Federico Barrientes de la Torre, "El trazo original de Tijuana," *Calafia* 4, no. 8 (June 1983), pp. 31–33.

72. Ileana Gil Durán, "Tijuana y Tia Juana, dos pueblos fronterizos," in Piñera Ramírez and Ortiz Figueroa, *Historia de Tijuana*, 2:61; Ileana Gil Durán, "La influencia del turismo en el nacimiento y desarrollo inicial de Tijuana, 1888–1900," *Review of Latin American Studies* 2, nos. 1–2 (1989), p. 36.

73. Don M. Stewart, *Frontier Port: A Chapter in San Diego's History* (Los Angeles: Ward Ritchie Press, 1965), pp. 4–5; Robert Mayer, *San Diego: Chronological and Documentary History* (Dobbs Ferry, N.Y.: Oceana Publications, 1978), pp. 40, 45.

74. Pourade, *Glory Years*, p. 216.

75. Dumke, *Boom of the Eighties*, pp. 260–71; Gil Durán, "Tijuana y Tia Juana," pp. 65–66.

76. In reality, gold had been discovered by Basilio Padilla, a Mexican, in December 1888. Nevertheless, it was not until February 1889 that a U.S.

prospector named Luman H. Gaskill learned of Padilla's find and publicized it. *San Diego Union,* February 27 and March 15, 1889.

77. *Los Angeles Times,* March 7, 1889.

78. *San Diego Union,* March 3, 1889; *Los Angeles Times,* March 7, 8, and 13, 1889; Stephens, *Gold Fields of Lower California,* p. 49. See also various reports from the *San Diego Sun* and the *Lower Californian,* an English-language newspaper published in Ensenada, in Nordhoff, *Peninsular California: Some Account of the Climate, Soil Productions, and Present Condition Chiefly of the Northern Half of Lower California* (New York: Harper, 1888), pp. 124–26.

79. *San Diego Union,* March 6, 1889.

80. *Los Angeles Times,* March 8, 1889; *Mining and Scientific Press* 68, no. 11 (March 16, 1889), p. 181; Lingenfelter, *Rush of '89,* p. 58. Quartz mining in the mines at El Alamo and other nearly sites continued to produce ore on and off for many years. Goldbaum, *Towns,* pp. 52–53; Chaput, Mason, and Zárate Loperena, *Modest Fortunes,* pp. 137–51.

81. *Los Angeles Times,* March 8, 1889; Dumke, *Boom of the Eighties,* pp. 46, 49.

82. Smythe, *History of San Diego,* pp. 503–5, 507–8.

83. The SD&AR project had been initiated thirteen years earlier, in 1906, by city magnate John D. Spreckels. Through traffic on the line began suffering interruptions from 1976 on and ceased entirely in the early 1980s. Smythe, *History of San Diego,* pp. 529–34; Robert M. Hanft, *San Diego & Arizona: The Impossible Railroad* (Glendale, Calif.: Trans-Anglo Books, 1984), pp. 9–78.

84. *San Diego Union,* May 3 and 6, 1896, and September 17, 1898.

85. Piñera Ramírez and Ortiz Figueroa, *Historia de Tijuana,* 2:334.

86. Adalberto Walther Meade, "La subprefectura política de Tijuana," *Calafia* 4, no. 7 (December 1982), p. 9; Adalberto Walther Meade, *El distrito norte de Baja California* (Tijuana: Universidad Autónoma de Baja California, 1986), pp. 133, 143–48.

87. Decrees of October 15 and November 20, 1925, regarding the establishment of the municipality of Tijuana, *Periódico Oficial del Distrito Norte de Baja California,* November 10, 20, 1925; Arturo Ranfla González, Guillermo Alvarez de la Torre, and Guadalupe Ortega Villa, "Expansión física y desarrollo urbano de Tijuana, 1900–1984," in Piñera Ramírez and Ortiz Figueroa, *Historia de Tijuana,* 2:327–29.

Anticipating the Colonias: *Popular Housing in El Paso and Ciudad Juárez, 1890–1923*

ANDREW GRANT WOOD

The visitor who arrives in El Paso with the idea that it is a barren waste, desert-like, where, of course, nothing green, like flowers and trees, grow, is subjected to an immediate disillusionment.

—*El Paso Times,* May 25, 1922

Today along the U.S.-Mexican border, popular settlements known as *colonias* are growing at a rate of approximately 10 percent per year.[1] Located at the periphery of large cities, these settlements host an array of improvised shelters fashioned out of plywood, tarpaper, old bricks, discarded garage doors, and found scraps of tin. Water and electricity are often scarce, and many areas have little or no access to urban services of any kind.[2] Yet while life in the colonias may be shocking to observers today, a look at the history of popular housing along the border during the first decades of the twentieth century shows that the task of securing adequate shelter along the border has long been a difficult one for many. In what follows, I briefly describe the housing situation in El Paso and Ciudad Juárez during the early decades of the twentieth century, as well as some early attempts at urban reform.

BORDER BOOM TOWNS

Beginning in the 1880s a mining boom in northern Mexico helped spark a period of dynamic growth in transportation, agriculture, and commerce between Mexico and the United States. At that time, border towns grew as the prospect of jobs and a better life attracted migrants from both the interior of Mexico and the eastern United States. Subsequently, revolution in Mexico (1910–1917) and Prohibition in the United States (1918–1933) accelerated rates of exchange and settlement.

Between 1900 and 1930, the population of cities on both sides of the border increased sharply (see table 1). Not surprisingly, rapid rates

31

of urbanization during the first three decades of the century posed certain problems. One of the most troubling was the housing situation in El Paso and Ciudad Juárez.

Table 1. Border City Populations, 1900–1930

City and State	1900	1910	1920	1930
Matamoros, Tamps.	8,347	7,390	9,215	9,733
Brownsville, Tex.	6,305	10,517	11,791	22,021
Reynosa, Tamps.	1,915	1,475	2,107	4,840
McAllen, Tex.	—	—	5,331	9,074
Nuevo Laredo, Tamps.	6,548	8,143	14,998	21,636
Laredo, Tex.	13,429	14,855	22,710	32,618
Piedras Negras, Coah.	7,888	8,518	6,941	15,878
Eagle Pass, Tex.	—	3,536	5,059	6,459
Ciudad Juárez, Chih.	8,218	10,621	19,457	19,669
El Paso, Tex	15,906	39,279	77,560	102,421
Nogales, Son.	2,738	3,117	13,445	14,061
Nogales, Ariz.	—	3,514	5,199	6,006
Mexicali, B.C.	—	462	6,782	14,842
Calexico, Calif.	—	797	6,223	6,299
Tijuana, B.C.	242	733	1,028	8,384
San Diego, Calif.	17,700	39,978	74,683	147,897

Source: David Lorey (ed.), *United States–Mexico Border Statistics since 1900* (Los Angeles: UCLA Latin American Center Publications, 1990), p. 33.

Figure 1. House in El Paso, Texas, circa 1910. (Courtesy of University of Texas at El Paso Library, Special Collections Department)

During the summer of 1910 a reporter for the *El Paso Times* antic-ipated difficulties in the local rental housing market, writing that the city "was filling up rapidly and soon there will be a shortage of hous-es." Similarly, a spokesperson for the real estate firm of J. H. Smith esti-mated that "if the demand kept up . . . there would not be a vacant house in the city by the first of September." Citing a flow of migrants from Mexico and elsewhere in the United States as the cause of the increase, another resident declared that "there are fewer desirable homes in El Paso now than there have [ever] been." Anticipating that all available homes would soon be rented out, some imagined that late-comers to the city "would have to build their own residences or live in tents this winter if they wished to be enrolled among the residents of El Paso."[3]

Figure 2. Popular housing in winter, El Paso, Texas, circa 1910. (Courtesy of University of Texas at El Paso Library, Special Collections Department)

These and other observations suggest that the supply of affordable housing in the city had become scarce. As a result, many crowded into a south-side neighborhood known as Chihuahuita. As a rapidly grow-ing district of El Paso around the turn of the century, Chihuahuita quickly became the area where the majority of Mexican immigrants set-tled after crossing the Río Grande.[4] Not surprisingly, many Anglos viewed the neighborhood with suspicion, considering the neighborhood a dangerous place where disease and social pathologies lurked. Soon, reformers took action in an effort to "clean up" Chihuahuita and comparable working-class areas across the border in Ciudad Juárez.

On June 16, 1910, members of the El Paso City Council heard Dr. J. A. Samaniego complain that heaps of trash had collected in several Chihuahuita streets and alleys. Interestingly, he told public officials that city engineers rather than local residents were to blame for the accumulation. "These people may be poor, but they are human beings, entitled to humane treatment," Samaniego argued. In response, Mayor Robinson and Alderman Clayton initially claimed that they had no information on patterns of city trash disposal. Later, however, the two municipal officials indicated that they would look into the matter and conceded that "now is the time to inaugurate a cleaning crusade in the south side."[5]

A month later the El Paso City Council again discussed the southside neighborhood. This time officials made plans to pave several streets and expand water service in the area. According to reports, however, difficulties between the water company and the city soon resulted in delays. Meantime, inspection teams sent by the El Paso Health Department counted more than five hundred dwellings in the city that were "crowded and in extremely poor condition." Relaying this information to municipal officials, a local health official proclaimed, "what a deplorable condition exists when almost one-half of these houses are marked uninhabitable." To this he added, "taking into consideration that there are five persons to each house and usually more, you have over two thousand persons living in houses not fit for animals." To remedy the situation, it was recommended that the city sewer system be extended south "as far and as soon as possible" and that property owners rather than tenants be held accountable for housing conditions. By mid-September 1910, Health Department officials had determined that 1,500 houses on the south side should be torn down. Shortly thereafter, city officials asked police for help in relocating renters.[6]

With the housing stock for residents diminished, a story published later that fall documented a growing housing crisis in El Paso and elsewhere along the U.S.-Mexico border. In a November 19, 1910, article titled "Passage to Texas" published in the *Survey*, Francis H. McLean, field secretary for the Charity Department of the Russell Sage Foundation, commented on the condition of popular housing in several Texas cities: "From El Paso, with its miserably damp and dark Mexican adobes

Figure 3. Women in a yard, El Paso, Texas. (Courtesy of University of Texas at El Paso Library, Special Collections Department)

fringing the international boundary along the historic Río Grande, to the opium shacks in the bottoms of Dallas, there is in every one of the five cities a need for some rudimentary housing regulation." Yet McLean continued by describing how El Pasoans had prepared for a visit by U.S. and Mexican Presidents William Howard Taft and Porfirio Díaz earlier that year by simply building a fence to hide the various dilapidated shacks from the politicians' view:

> There is an amusing yet sardonic tale of the time when the presidents of the United States and Mexico were to meet at the Río Grande. It was discovered that a most irreverent, unreasonable and utterly miserable group of so-called houses border[ing] the line of progress refused to hide itself. What easier than to hide it with a huge fence! That is the logic which El Paso used.[7]

While simply hiding the unattractive housing of the urban poor from visiting elites may have been a temporary solution, McLean's account leaves little doubt that urban reform measures were needed. Attempting another quick fix a few years later, General "Black Jack" Pershing sent troops from nearby Fort Bliss to Chihuahuita in 1914.

Still, the city's housing problems—at least in the Mexican neighborhood—had not been resolved. A local report produced in 1915 suggested, "Probably in no place in the United States could such crude, beastly, primitive conditions be found as exist in Chihuahuita." The following year, El Paso leaders decided to deal with the matter by simply tearing down much of the popular housing in the area. Many of those Mexicans displaced by the action were forced to make their way back across the Río Grande to Juárez.[8]

Housing in El Paso continued to be in much demand. Commenting on the situation in early 1922, Real Estate Board President W. K. Ramsey noted the city's lack of surplus rental housing. Talking with a staff member from the *El Paso Times*, Ramsey said that "cottages and close-in stuff" as well as "bungalows of the 'far-out' sections" of town had all been rented out.[9]

U.S. and Mexican labor representatives who gathered in El Paso in mid-April sent a petition to the Texas State Federation of Labor demanding that the issue of rental housing be addressed immediately. On Saturday, April 22, 1922, the *El Paso Times* announced that a resolution declaring affordable housing a matter of "public utility" had been passed unanimously. Over the next few months, however, no follow-up to the labor-backed proposal appears to have taken place. Instead, city officials took to publishing delinquent tax rolls in the *Times* during the hot summer months.

TENANT ACTION AND EARLY REFORM CAMPAIGNS

Meantime, in the spring of 1922, collective action by tenants in several central Mexican cities (e.g., Veracruz, Mexico City, Guadalajara) inspired house renters in the northern state of Coahuila to issue demands for improved housing conditions and reduction of rents to 1910 levels. Similarly, tenants in the city of Torreón announced that they had formed a syndicate of renters and were busy negotiating with local landlords—many of whom had formed their own association (see figure 4).[10]

Then on May 4, 1922, renters in Ciudad Juárez announced that they were also in the process of forming a tenant organization. According to the San Antonio newspaper *La Prensa*, socialist Cástulo Herrera had called for a public meeting on Sunday, May 7, in the Plaza de Gallos, with the purpose of officially founding the Sindicato Fronterizo de Inquilinos (Border Syndicate of Tenants). In his communication, Herrera indicated that the Juárez syndicate "would be similar to those created in Veracruz and Mexico City." The Sunday gathering attracted

Figure 4. Mexican tenant handbill, ca. 1922. (Courtesy of Archivo General de la Nación, Mexico City)

nearly five hundred Juárez renters who, maintaining a peaceful and nonmilitant tone, elected a governing board for the new renters' syndicate. New members were organized by neighborhood and paid a small fee to help fund the association. A week later, local landlords requested that syndicate leaders communicate their demands in writing. Following the example set by groups in central Mexico, renters requested the lowering of rents to 1910 levels or by 75 percent for more recent construction, improved housing conditions, legal protections against eviction, and recognition of tenant syndicates.[11]

Little is known regarding the outcome of renter lobbying in Juárez and other towns such as Piedras Negras, Coahuila. However, the nearly four thousand tenants in Monterrey who had come together under the banner of the Tenants Union of Nuevo León, as an important component of the Monterrey labor movement, managed a significant presence in that city. They claimed that housing costs ate up nearly half a typical worker's salary, and in one of their direct actions, renters invaded the state congress. Subsequently, their organizing efforts helped influence legislation that offered a tax break to property owners who cut their rates.[12]

Yet despite various grassroots organizing efforts, urban elites continued to view popular neighborhoods as "low life" areas that hosted criminal and other "dangerous" elements. In conjunction with various renewal projects intended to beautify border cities, local boosters stepped up campaigns to eliminate "unsightly areas" altogether during the 1920s. One such campaign came after the reorganization of the El Paso City Health Department in the fall of 1922. Headed by R. E. Tarbett, sanitation officials initiated a new inspection campaign of tenements, apartment houses, hotels, and residences. For his part, Tarbett

ordered that close attention be paid to a variety of critical issues including water supply, waste removal, and animal control. In a short article
in late September, the *El Paso Times* reported, "Inspection of residences and tenements began yesterday under the direction of the city
health department. Three inspectors began work south of the tracks.
They have orders to inspect every house in which people are living. . . .
The work is expected to take six months. The condition of every residence, rooming house and tenement . . . will be recorded in the office
of the city health department." The article noted how inspectors would
detail important information, including ownership, management, type
of house, condition, number of rooms and inhabitants, water supply,
availability and condition of toilets, provisions for garbage, and "number of horses, mules, cows, goats, rabbits or fowl on the premises."[13]

During the inspection, El Paso Mayor Charles Davis, various councilmen, and members of the planning commission toured sections of the
city. Despite describing various plans for modifying streets, drainage
facilities, and other public utilities to *El Paso Times* reporters, Davis
nevertheless acknowledged that full realization of El Paso's beautifica-
tion program would take several years.[14] Curiously, the newspaper
reported nothing about official plans to address problems in poorer
districts of the city.

Across the River in Juárez

Meantime, the advent of Prohibition in 1920 had sparked a significant increase in tourism across the U.S.-Mexican border to Ciudad
Juárez. Concerned about what the trade meant for U.S. citizens, evan-
gelist Bob Jones visited the northern Mexican town in September 1922
to heighten public awareness of the situation. In a series of public
addresses reported on at length in local newspapers, Jones complained
about the condition of Juárez and declared the city a vice-stricken "hell
hole." Shortly thereafter, Chihuahua governor Ignacio Enriquez told
those attending a Chamber of Commerce banquet in El Paso of his
plans to "clean up" the city. "Frankly," he confessed to the audience,
"we are ashamed of Juárez."

At the top of the governor's list were some seventy-five saloons he
intended to close by the end of November 1922. In addition, Enriquez
indicated that cabarets would be regulated and the city's vice district
brought under state supervision and moved to a western section of the

city. Known gringo drug addicts were to be deported, while any Mexicans engaged in criminal activities would be rounded up and shipped
off to Chihuahua City for trial. Those saloons allowed to remain open
would not be allowed to tolerate "women of questionable character" loi-
tering on or near their premises. Explaining the longer-term goals of
the effort, Enriquez declared, "I want Juárez to be such a city that citizens of the United States and Mexico will not be afraid to go to with
their family and friends." Hoping to promote cooperative relations
between the twin cities, Enriquez claimed, "El Paso is important to
Juárez" because "it is the gateway to Mexico." Working to build support for the campaign, the governor encouraged Juárez residents to
appreciate the long-term effects of his initiative and not to give in to
commercial interests who opposed his efforts to "moralize" the city.[15]

While the campaign proved difficult to sustain over time, immediate
reports suggest that the governor's plan helped reduce crime, with one
account stating, "In contrast to before the measure, four days have
now passed without any assaults, robberies or violent crime being
reported in Juárez." According to other reports, neighborhoods in
Juárez had taken on a renewed tranquility after government agents had
expelled "pernicious foreigners" and "any persons not engaged in making a respectable and honest living." Still, the central streets of Juárez
were filled—as they had been for several years—with tourists from
neighboring El Paso who had come to "pass the day in the Juárez

*Figure 5. International Bridge, El Paso, Texas. (Courtesy of University of Texas
at El Paso Library, Special Collections Department)*

saloons and central vice district." Noting the continued problem of vice tourism, the Chihuahua state legislature passed legislation containing elaborate plans for a new, regulated red-light district to be built outside of town. This, lawmakers hoped, would provide the necessary resources for the "moralization" of the city. In the following months, however, mismanagement of municipal and state funds significantly hurt reform efforts.[16]

CONCLUSION

With the acceleration of commercial activity along the U.S.-Mexican border around the turn of the century, towns such as Ciudad Juárez and El Paso grew significantly. Not surprisingly, rapid urbanization led to housing shortages, problems related to public health, and other social ills. In their responses to the situation, elites in both cities showed little sympathy for the urban poor. Instead of developing measures designed to remedy housing shortages, officials choose either to ignore the problem or to blame residents for the often dilapidated state of popular neighborhoods.

Anticipating efforts by colonia dwellers today, residents in Ciudad Juárez organized a tenant union in the spring of 1922. Protesting high rents and substandard conditions, they lobbied municipal officials and local landlords for changes. Soon, renters in a few other northern Mexican cities did the same. While little is known about the outcome of their protests, it is important to note that collective action dedicated to improving the living conditions of the urban poor in cities along the U.S.-Mexican border has a long and still largely unknown history. ✤

NOTES

1. *Borderlines 42*, vol. 6, no. 1 (February 1998). Available on the World Wide Web at http://www.us-mex.org/borderlines/bkissues.html.

2. For an interesting article on the use of recycled garage doors in Tijuana colonias, see "In Castoff Doors, the Making of Castles," *Los Angeles Times,* May 30, 2000. On the lack of urban services see *Borderlines 65*, vol. 8, no. 3 (March 2000); Mike Davis, *Magical Urbanism: Latinos Reinvent the U.S. City* (New York and London: Verso Press, 2000), pp. 31–32. On problems and temporary solutions relating to water supply in the colonias see "Long Wait for Water Ending on Texas Border," *New York Times,* October 27, 1997. Other

recent contributions to the study of urbanism along the border include David Lorey, *The U.S.-Mexican Border in the Twentieth Century: A History of Economic and Social Transformation* (Wilmington, Del.: SR Books, 1999); Peter Ward, *Colonias and Public Policy in Texas: Urbanization by Stealth* (Austin: University of Texas Press, 1999); Daniel Arreola and James Curtis, *The Mexican Border Cities: Landscape Anatomy and Place Personality* (Tucson: University of Arizona Press, 1993); and Lawrence Herzog, *Where North Meets South: Cities, Space, and Politics on the U.S.-Mexican Border* (Austin: Center for Mexican American Studies, 1990). For discussion of related issues see "Contested Terrain: The U.S.-Mexico Borderlands," *NACLA Report on the Americas* 33, no. 3 (November–December 1999), pp. 13–47.

3. *El Paso Morning Times,* August 7, 1910; Oscar Martínez, *Border Boom Town: Ciudad Juárez since 1848* (Austin: University of Texas Press, 1975).

4. Because the land was prone to flooding, some soon made their way to higher ground north of downtown, establishing an adobe tenement village called Stormsville. Martínez, *Border Boom Town,* p. 34.

5. *El Paso Morning Times,* June 17, 1910.

6. Ibid., July 29, 1910; September 16, 1910. Having cleared the way for demolition of the south-side houses, councilmen then unanimously approved plans for the construction of a new meatpacking plant.

7. *Survey,* November 19, 1910, p. 291. Meanwhile, the *El Paso Morning Times* reported on November 20, 1910, that an anti-prostitution campaign had begun in the city.

8. Martínez, *Border Boom Town,* pp. 45–46. Attempting to deal with the situation, municipal leaders founded a Public Welfare Committee in 1918 and empowered members to find those individuals they deemed most destitute and provide them with shelter five days out of the week. Hoping to improve the overall sanitation of other residents, the Juárez Water Department also established public baths in several of the city's poorer neighborhoods. The Spanish flu epidemic that year did much to reverse these efforts, however, as hundreds soon fell victim to the disease.

9. *El Paso Times,* February 22, 1922. From reports that spring, food prices also had risen considerably. *El Paso Times,* April 8, 1922.

10. On the history of the renters' movement see Andrew G. Wood, *Revolution in the Street: Women, Workers, and Urban Protest in Veracruz, 1870–1927* (Wilmington, Del.: SR Books, 2001). On the Torreón syndicate, see *La Prensa,* San Antonio, Tex., June 1, 1922. On February 16, 1922, *La Prensa* reported that landlords in Mexicali, B.C., had selected a new board of directors for the property owners' organization there. News of tenant action in Veracruz, Guadalajara, and Mexico City was reported in the same paper beginning in March and continuing throughout much of the spring, summer, and fall of 1922. Regarding Veracruz, see March 23 and 24; May 30; June 5 and 11; July 13, 17, 23, and 27; August 5, 7, and 24; September 23; November 2, 3, 7, and 9. Regarding Guadalajara, see March 27 and September 21. Regarding Orizaba, see April 4 and August 5. Regarding Mexico City, see April 11, 29, and 30; May 1, 2, and 9; and August 31. Regarding Tampico, see August 2 and 6 and September 1, 12, 13, and 19. Regarding Merida, see August 13.

11. *La Prensa,* May 8, 1922, May 13, 1922, May 14, 17, June 1, 1922.

12. Michael Snodgrass, "Deference and Defiance in Monterrey: Workers, Paternalism, and Revolution in Mexico, 1890–1942," Ph.D. diss., University of Texas–Austin, 1998. In November 1922 the state legislature of Sonora considered and rejected a proposal for a Law of Rents similar to what had been passed in early 1923 in the state of Veracruz. *La Prensa,* November 13, 1922.

13. *El Paso Times,* September 26, 1922.

14. Ibid., September 28, 1922.

15. Ibid., October 10, 1922. See also *La Prensa,* October 10, 1922, October 14, 1922.

16. Ibid., October 18, 1922.

The Fence and Gates of Ambos Nogales: A Postcard Landscape Exploration

DANIEL D. ARREOLA

Charting the cultural geography of Mexican border cities is an ongoing project. Early writings laid a foundation for understanding spatial patterns and place characteristics of these cities (Herzog 1990; Arreola and Curtis 1993; Méndez Sáinz 1993). Further topical explorations have expanded this vision (Curtis 1993, 1995; Arreola 1996, 1999; Herzog 1999). Missing from the literature, however, is any effort to assess landscape change through time at a single border locale. This essay explores that possibility through the use of postcard imagery, a special source of visual evidence.

Unlike conventional photographic imagery about place that one might excavate from an archive, postcards, as mass commercial products, combine accessibility with visual repetition. Whereas archival photography can reveal an image of a city that is like a window to a particular time and place, repeat inspection of the same view at another time is not typically possible (Hales 1984). A diachronic, or time-series, record is therefore difficult to reconstruct from archival imagery. This problem is remedied somewhat by the strategy and application of repeat photography and by the transcription and comparison of archival photographs for selected cities (Foote 1985). In the case of Mexican border cities, however, no single historical repository of photo images has been assembled, although a portfolio of 1964 Tijuana has recently been published (Ganster 2000). No known repeat photography project is in progress.

In contrast to archival photographs, postcard views of a townscape allow images to be evaluated serially because postcard photographers typically were attracted to similar view sites, which were documented repeatedly. Over several decades, postcard views of the same landscape can be used to create a diagnostic visual interpretation of place.

The history of postcards is more recent than that of photography (Newhall 1982), and picture postcards as view cards first evolved in Europe during the last quarter of the nineteenth century. Although many countries restricted early postcard circulation to domestic mail, Germany, Switzerland, and Austria encouraged international postcard circulation with *Gruss aus,* or "greetings from," cards. These postcards depicted local views and scenes in art nouveau style on the borders of the front, or message, side of the cards; the back was by law reserved for the mailing address only (Staff 1966). After 1902 in Europe and 1907 in the United States, divided-back postcards appeared, allowing for a message and the mailing address on the back of the card while the front was entirely devoted to a view.

During the early postcard era in the United States, two Chicago-based companies came to dominate commercial production, Detroit Publishing Company and Curt Teich. Detroit Publishing is known to have printed postcards from seventeen thousand different images between 1895 and 1935 (Stechschulte 1994). By the 1910s, Curt Teich was selling some 150 million postcards annually, mostly view cards of scenes in the United States. During the 1930s and 1940s, Curt Teich was the most prolific publisher of linen postcards, so-called because the front view simulates a linen texture (Miller and Miller 1976). In Mexico, early postcard printers included the Sonora News Service, founded and operated by American photographer C. B. Waite (Montellano 1994). Perhaps the largest single Mexican producer of postcards from the 1930s to the 1950s was México Fotográfico, a Mexico City company whose real photo cards recorded scenes in many border towns as well as across the country.

While corporate postcard publishers dominated national production, independent photographic postcard producers operated in towns and cities across the country and in Mexico (Fernández Tejedo 1994). Eastman Kodak Company, for example, marketed postcard-size photographic paper that could be used to print directly from a negative, and this innovation was quickly copied by other companies, enabling amateur photographers and independent printers to begin producing postcards (Morgan and Brown 1981). Brownsville, Texas, photographer Robert Runyon (1909–1968) is an example of an independent border-town postcard entrepreneur (Samponaro and Vanderwood 1992). A local professional photographer, Runyon produced his own postcards and also contracted companies to convert his photos to postcards. He then made arrangements with local drug and cigar stores and other small retailers to sell his cards. In addition, regional distributors such as Gulf Coast News and Hotel Company, which had curio stores in San Antonio and Houston, bought several thousand of Runyon's postcards, which included landmark scenes from Matamoros, Mexico, across from Brownsville, especially his always-popular bullfight views. Runyon and his brother-in-law, José Medrano Longoria, opened a curio store on the plaza in Matamoros in 1925, and this, too, became a strategic outlet for his postcards until they sold the business in 1939.

Postcards provided popular imagery about places before personal cameras and television became widely available. Ironically, postcard photographers sought the unique in the landscapes they documented, but typically they tended to capture the ordinary (Jakle 1982). Representations of the ordinary or vernacular landscape give postcard imagery great utility in historical geographic research. Their repetitive renderings of local scenes make them an excellent source of historic views about a place, especially if that place was popularly photographed over time and if the postcard images are compared serially by a researcher.

Mexican border-town landscapes have appeared in postcard images since the 1890s, yet there is great variability in the coverage of particular towns. If my private collection is any indication, almost half of all border-town postcards are scenes of Ciudad Juárez and Tijuana, the two largest and most famous border cities. Other popular border towns that have moderate postcard coverage include regional tourist destinations such as Nuevo Laredo, Matamoros, and Reynosa on the Texas border, and Mexicali on the California boundary, but the number of cards representative of these places is decidedly inferior to those picturing Ciudad Juárez and Tijuana. Small towns such as Tecate, Naco, and Ojinaga are poorly represented in postcards.[1]

AMBOS NOGALES

Nogales, Sonora, is across the border from Nogales, Arizona, and together the towns are known as Ambos Nogales. My postcard collection of Nogales, Sonora, includes 290 individual images. This makes the town the third most popularly rendered border location in postcards after Ciudad Juárez and Tijuana. This is curious given the apparent relationship between the size of a town and its tourist potential (and, therefore, potential postcard popularity). Based on its size, Nogales should not be such a popularly depicted border town. Before 1980, Nogales, Sonora, had fewer than 70,000 people and thus was considered a medium-sized border town (Arreola and Curtis 1993, table 2.2). Nogales, nevertheless, has long competed as a tourist destination because of its historic advantage on the Arizona boundary, its hinterland access to nearby Tucson and Phoenix, its tradition of promotional effort, and media exposure (Arreola and Madsen 1998; see figure 1). No less important has been the town's status as a curio mecca (Arreola 1999).

Nogales, Sonora, and Nogales, Arizona, were first settled in 1880. By 1882, a railroad linking Guaymas, Sonora, on the Gulf of California with Benson, Arizona, across the international boundary created Ambos Nogales. The earliest town plat suggests the peculiar asymmetrical morphology of the towns, which straddle the railroad corridor as well as the boundary (see figure 2). The irregular blocks to the east represent the nucleus of pre-railroad settlement in the narrow pass, whereas the blocks to the west show a rigid perpendicular alignment to the border. The boundary follows International Street (Calle Camou), yet Nogales, Arizona, hugs tight to the line east of the railroad—lending the city its early nickname of Line City—while Mexican Nogales is set back from the boundary. To the west, blocks on either side of the border are equally set back.

Table 1. Nogales Postcards by View Depicted

View	Number of Images
Gate crossings	38
Avenida Obregón	29
Panoramas	27
Public buildings and monuments	25
Fence line	24
Miscellaneous	21
La Caverna	20
Plazas	20
Calle Elías	20
Calle Campillo	15
Bullfights	12
Residential areas	11
Total	**262**

Source: Author's postcard archive.

Table 1 categorizes postcards of Nogales by the dominant location depicted in the view. The premier tourist street of the city, Avenida Obregón, is the second most popular depiction, and Calle Campillo, a secondary tourist street that leads to Obregón, has fifteen images. Calle Elías, ranking just above Calle Campillo, was the border town's first tourist street until the 1940s. The celebrated bar and eatery La Caverna was situated on Calle Elías, and, combined, these two locations rival gate crossings as the most popular Nogales postcard view. There are an unusually high number of panoramas, accounted for by the fact that Nogales is spread out along a narrow pass creating spectacular vistas. Since the 1940s, when the population began to swell through in-migration (Arreola and Curtis 1993, fig. 2.3), housing has pushed up and over these steep hills. Public buildings and monuments combine for a significant postcard category in part because Nogales has been from its founding a railroad gateway and official customshouse (*aduana*) location. The old aduana built in 1894 and razed in 1963 was a neo-classical architectural landmark of the border and the spotlight of many postcard views.

Garitas, or gate crossings, are, however, the most popular postcard views; combined with views of the famous border fence, they total almost one-quarter of all Nogales postcard depictions (see table 1). In the discussion that follows, I use only these postcard image categories to narrate landscape change along the boundary. The fence line, the Morley-Elías gate, and the main gate are the principal view sites assessed. Twenty-two postcards are arranged topically and mostly chronologi-cally, and a separate caption interprets each postcard image or set of images. Information other than landscape description presented in the figure captions is drawn from standard histories and writings about the towns (Rochlin and Rochlin 1976; Ready 1980; Flores García 1987; Sokota 1990–91; Tinker Salas 1997) and from Sanborn fire insurance maps for 1890, 1893, and 1917.

The first fence dividing a Mexican from an American border town was erected at Nogales. Gate crossings evolved as official ports of entry along a declared buffer zone between the Sonora and Arizona towns. These landscapes became photographed as postcard views when Ambos Nogales began being promoted as a tourist destination. The fence line and gate crossings were fixed features of border-town identity by the early twentieth century.

For almost a century, postcards have faithfully recorded changes in landscape features along the boundary separating Ambos Nogales. Table 2 illustrates the frequency of borderline views by era. The fence-line view of the two towns looking west from Chureas Hill is perhaps the dominant postcard fix for Ambos Nogales, a landscape consistent-ly rendered by postcard photographers of each generation. The Morley-Elías gate crossing was a popular depiction early in the century, especially during Prohibition (1919–1933), when Americans could easily cross the street to bars along Calle Elías. This gate survived as a postcard image until 1960, but from the 1940s on, this landscape lost photographic allure as tourists and curio seekers increasingly opted for the main gate crossing and its proximity to Calle Campillo and Avenida Obregón, the premier tourist districts in the postwar period. This is demonstrated quite dramatically by the large number of postcard views of the main gate crossing during the 1950–1969 era, as well by the substantial number of depictions of this landscape during the 1930s and 1940s.

Table 2. Frequency of Nogales Border Postcard Views by Era

View	1910–1929	1930–1949	1950–1969	1970–1995
Fence line	10	6	6	2
Morley-Elías Gate	3	3	2	0
Main gate	2	7	11	8
Other gates	2	0	0	0

Source: Author's postcard archive

Table 2 also suggests that postcards no longer dominate as a visual medium for recording Ambos Nogales. Only two images of the fence line and eight of the main gate are available for the quarter century from 1970 to 1995. This is remarkable because Nogales, Sonora, is today a more popular tourist destination than perhaps it has ever been, attracting some 700,000 visitors each year (*Arizona Daily Star* 1997; *Arizona Republic* 1998). Tourists, however, have changed their visiting habits, making chiefly day-tripping excursions rather than overnight visits. The combination of shorter, more frequent visits with a general decline in traditional forms of correspondence like postcards means that postcard views have less credibility for travelers than they did in the past. Besides, many of the excursionists to Ambos Nogales today bring their own cameras and snap away at a myriad of views to capture their own images.

Still, picture postcards remain an important form of visual evidence for understanding and reconstructing place. These images are especially valuable for our appreciation of the towns of the Mexican-American border because other photographic sources are generally lacking or inaccessible to the researcher. A postcard archive of Mexican border cities can prove a useful lens through which one might view these evolving communities. ✤

NOTE

1. My postcard archive consists of some 2,200 individual postcards of Mexican border towns. Approximately 600 postcards are of Ciudad Juárez and 400 are of Tijuana. There are about 160 postcards of Nuevo Laredo, 152 of Matamoros, 140 of Mexicali, and 120 of Reynosa. Other towns such as Agua Prieta, Ciudad Acuña, and Piedras Negras account for between 65 and 95 postcards. The archive contains less than 20 postcards for the following Mexican border towns: Tecate, San Luis Río Colorado, Sonoita, Naco, Palomas, Ojinaga, Miguel Alemán, and Camargo.

Figure 1. Between 1927 and 1929, Nogales was advertised regularly in U.S. national magazines as a tourist destination. Note the reluctance to use the word Mexican, which is substituted for by the ethnic referent Spanish. (Collier's, The National Weekly, *January 28, 1928, p. 42.)*

Stop off, where the Arizona-Mexico border line runs down the middle of a main street!

You'll like the gayety and entertainment of this Spanish-American city...the hunting, fishing and scenic attractions nearby. Invigorating sun-shine every day; nights cool; altitude 3869 feet.

Everybody has a good time in Nogales—a mighty good place to live!

Transfer at Tucson—two hours away.

NOGALES WONDERLAND CLUB, Inc., Nogales, Ariz.

Please send me free booklet (106)

Name _____

Address _____

Figure 2. Railroad engineers Bonillas and Herbert drafted this plat of Ambos Nogales in 1884. The railroad ran between the older, pre-railroad settlement aligned diagonal to the boundary at the bottom of the map and the grid of blocks arranged perpendicular to the border west of the tracks. The first rail-road depot actually straddled the border. (After reproduction in Silvia Raquel Flores García, Nogales: un siglo en la historia, *1987, p. 32.)*

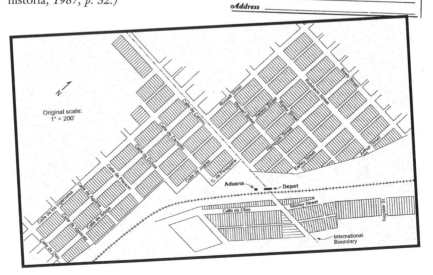

*Figure 3. Ambos Nogales buffer zone, circa 1916. In 1896 by presidential procla-
mation buildings previously built up to the boundary on the Nogales,
Arizona, side were razed and set back sixty feet. This created a 110-foot buffer
between the two halves of Nogales because Mexico had created a fifty-foot setback
in 1884. In this view looking west from Chureas Hill, a favorite vista point
for photographers, no fence exists, but the boundary line is foreshadowed by
the telephone poles immediately north of the Mexican kiosks. Several Model T auto-
mobiles with open carriages are discernible on the Mexico side near the
railroad track. Kiosks stand at the boundary where Calle Elías meets International Street and at Railroad Avenue. The two-story brick building southwest
of the kiosk is the Banco de Sonora. On the Arizona side, the triangular building
at the corner of International Street and Morley Avenue is the Ville de Paris store,
opened in 1901. The long roof of the new railroad depot built in 1905 to replace
the original structure, which burned, is visible just beyond. An arroyo that cuts
across the boundary near present Grand Avenue is discernible by
the Bonillas Bridge, a stone structure across this channel west of the railroad
corridor. This arroyo was filled and leveled in 1918. (All postcards are from the
author's personal collection and printed here courtesy of Daniel Arreola)*

International Street—Dividing

Es propiedad Sono

2700

Figure 4. *International Street looking south at Calle Elías, circa 1908. No fence is visible in this ground-level view of the buffer zone. A Mexican kiosk, telephone poles, and a single boundary marker define the border, which extends across the lower portion of the postcard view creating a triangular building, the Banco de Sonora, at right.*

een the United States and Mexico.

mpany, City of Mexico.

Figure 5. A fortified line, circa 1925. A simple wire fence was erected in 1918 by the U.S. government after hostilities erupted between U.S. and Mexican guards at Ambos Nogales, precipitating the so-called Battle of Nogales, a one-day clash on August 28. Officially, Mexico and the United States announced that the conflict was stirred by German spies. Unofficially, Mexicans insisted that the exchange erupted after months of resentment stemming from ill treatment of their countrymen by Americans. The American consul in Nogales, Arizona, refused to acknowledge that story, preferring to believe that Mexican border guards created the disturbance. Brigadier General D. C. Cabell, dispatched to Nogales from his post in Douglas, Arizona, recommended the construction of a fence, which was built entirely on the U.S. side of the boundary. As seen here, several sentry kiosks and the fence filled the buffer space between the towns. In time seven gatehouses were built, four near the Elias-Morley crossing, two others set back near the railroad crossing (hereafter referred to as the main gate), and one on the Mexican side near Calle Arispe (the present Avenida Obregón) beyond.

Figure 6. Calle Elías, gateway to wet Mexico, circa 1919. The wire fence is now visible and two kiosks are evident on the Mexican side. The former Banco de Sonora building has been converted to the Cosmopolitan Bar and Café, and the former single-story structure on the opposite corner is now the two-story Concordia Bar. Calle Elías became a street of wet palaces during Prohibition. Americans were enticed across the street for meals and entertainment served in the company of orchestras, surrounded by dance floors, and celebrated with legal disregard for the Volstead Act.

Figure 7. Two countries divided by a mere fence, a view circa 1935. In 1929 a new wire mesh fence replaced the simple strand-wire fence built in 1918. Masonry posts with lamps were added to the new fence at the Elías-Morley and main gate crossings, and electric light standards were erected along the border fence. The old kiosks were replaced with rectangular structures topped with tile roofs. An additional sentry house is now visible on the Mexican side at the base of Chureas Hill. The new U.S. Customs and Immigration Station, completed in 1934 in fashionable Spanish revival architectural style, is evident immediately west of the main gate crossing.

Figure 8. A second view of the fence, circa 1935. This view from slightly south
of the line reveals the new Mexican railroad depot across the street from the
town's principal public space, Plaza Trece de Julio. Like the U.S. Customs
building, it is built in Spanish-revival style. The clock tower and neoclassical
facade of the Mexican aduana (customshouse) are visible in this view south
of the railroad depot. The arroyo along the border on the Mexican side is now
a concrete channel beyond Calle Arispe.

Figure 9. Main gate crossing, circa 1930. This view looks north from the Mexican garita through the improved 1929 fence of wire mesh with lighted masonry pillars. The U.S. gatehouse is partially visible behind the left pillar, and the U.S. railroad depot is in the center background. The dome of the Santa Cruz County Courthouse is visible in the far background.

Figure 10. Morley gate, circa 1935, looking north along Morley Avenue into downtown Nogales, Arizona. Lighted masonry pillars like those found at the main gate (see figure 9) are also evident here. In the right foreground is the Mexican garita with seated guard in front, and in the midground is the over-hang of the U.S. gatehouse through which autos are lined up. Ville de Paris and Bracker's Department Store signs are partially visible on the right. Two fig-ures shake hands across the boundary at left, with one man shouldering a serape. Given the heavy coats with fur lining sported by the ladies on the right and the absence of leaves on the tree behind the gatehouse, this is probably a winter scene. Nogales, as some visitors perhaps failed to recognize, is situated at almost 4,000 feet elevation.

Figure 11. Main gate, 1939. This view looks south from outside the U.S. Customs and Immigration Station, out of view to the right. The U.S. gatehouse and Mexican garita are visible, as is the chain-link fence that replaced the single-strand wire fence. Railroad cars on the far left are crossing into the United States from Mexico. The tracks visible near the striding figure and motorbike in motion are those that cross to the Mexican side from the United States. The second story of the Mexican railroad depot appears over the top of the Mexican garita, and the clock tower and neoclassical facade of the Mexican aduana are visible in the right background.

Figure 12. Main gate crossing, circa 1935. This unusual view looks east along the border fence from the main crossing with the back of the Mexican garita in the right foreground and the U.S. gatehouse in the left midground. The chain-link fence is seen extending over Chureas Hill in the far background. The Mexican garita at the Elías-Morley crossing is visible in the center midground.

Figure 13. Main gate, circa 1945. This view is north from the Mexican railroad depot toward the main gate crossing. The Mexican garita is now a two-story structure, and the U.S. gatehouse is visible on the right just beyond. Curio stores and the leading edge of Plaza Trece de Julio are seen on the left. The tile roof of the U.S. Customs and Immigration Station is visible in the upper left. In 1940, Nogales, Arizona, had 5,135 residents, while Nogales, Sonora, totaled 13,866.

Figure 14. Main gate, circa 1952. The perspective is similar to that in figure 13, but the Mexican garita has been renovated into a single-story, flat-roofed, modern architectural style. A Safeway supermarket is now visible on the U.S. side. Many U.S. chain stores entered Nogales, Arizona, after World War II, and this Safeway store earned a reputation for high-volume sales because of the large number of Sonorans who would regularly shop across the border. On the Mexican side, the high art-deco facade facing Plaza Trece de Julio is the Teatro Obregón, featuring "Nuestras Vidas" on the marquee and "Gavilán Pollero" on the banner.

Figure 15. Los dos Nogales, circa 1950. By 1954, Ambos Nogales was a major automotive gateway to the west coast of Mexico, and a paved roadway extended from the border through Sinaloa to the national capital. Fence-line postcard views looking west from Chureas Hill now include the newly constructed million-dollar, high-rise Marcos de Niza Hotel. Auto traffic through Nogales nearly doubled in terms of passenger transit, from 38,000 in 1954 to 73,000 in 1959. This view shows that the Mexican garita at the main crossing is still a two-story structure in Spanish-revival style whereas the U.S. gatehouse has been renovated in a sleek, flat-roofed modern look.

Figure 16. Linea divisoria, circa 1955. This view, while similar to that in figure 15, was actually taken several years later, because the Mexican garita at the main gate is the same flat-roofed structure pictured in figure 14, and the new Safeway store is visible to the right of the U.S. Customs and Immigration Station. With the new emphasis on automobile tourism through Ambos Nogales, the curio district of Nogales, Sonora, shifted west from Calle Elías to Calle Campillo, and eventually, to Avenida Obregón. The Marcos de Niza Hotel on the corner of Calle Campillo and Avenida Obregón became a beacon drawing pedestrian and automotive tourists to a new district of the border town that only a decade earlier had been primarily a residential zone.

Figure 17. Morley gate crossing, circa 1960, looking north along Morley Avenue with the Mexican garita and U.S. gatehouse on the right. One of the 1929 masonry pillars has been removed (cf. figure 10), and a sign at the lower left as well as the sliding gate suggest that this crossing actually closes during certain hours. This implies that the Morley Avenue shopping scene was chiefly a daytime activity by the 1960s. The signature Eiffel Tower sign of Ville de Paris and signs for Valley National Bank, Kress, and the El Paso Store are visible along Morley.

Figure 18. Main gate crossing, circa 1960. An unusual view of the main gate crossing loc east with the Mexican garita on the right and the U.S. gatehouse on the left. Billboards decorating building rooftops and the hillside advertise not only local sites such as La Cave Cafe and Dance Club and La Azteca Silver Shop, but also air travel to the Mexican inte This is the first postcard in this survey that is a color photograph, or chrome card, as this st came to be called because of the suffix associated with Kodak color film, Kodachrome. The photographer was Stan Davis, and the postcard was published by Petley Studios in Phoenix

Figure 19. Birdseye view of Ambos Nogales, circa 1965. This oblique view looks north from just above the main gate crossing. The boundary is traceable as an east-west diagonal that cuts across the north-south-trending street and railroad corridors. In 1964, the Mexican national government through the Programa Nacional Fronterizo (PRONAF) completely modified the main gate crossing with a dramatic double-winged gateway and surrounding new buildings thematically connected to the garita by their white color and arched roofs. Gone is the old Plaza Trece de Julio, replaced with several traffic islands and associated ornamental landscaping. On the U.S. side, a new U.S. Immigration and Port of Entry in boxy, modern architectural style is positioned immediately north of the new PRONAF gate and aligned to the border. Each structure is massive in contrast to previous gatehouses, and multiple lanes accommodate increased automobile traffic. Roads that cross under these new gates have been expanded and realigned for single-direction passage. Both Mexican and U.S. railroad depots have been removed and relocated away from the gate, although a railroad crossing gate persists. On the U.S. side the 1934 U.S. Customs and Immigration Station remains standing. To the left of this facility on a nearby city block is an open lot with docking facilities used for inspection of trucks importing Mexican produce. Trucks lined up and crossed at the main gate every winter from 1950 until 1974, when the new Mariposa gate was opened several miles west of this view.

Figure 20. Fence line looking west, circa 1965. This view shows clearly how the new U.S. Immigration and Port of Entry squats directly in the old buffer zone and hard against the borderline, whereas the new Mexican garita is set well back from the line, a posture that respects the old transition space. The fence is still chain link with barbed wire along the top. Gone, however, are the trees that once fronted the Ville de Paris store along International Street on the Arizona side. Not visible in this chrome postcard view is Interstate 19, which would be completed in 1966. On the Mexican side an open lot at the intersection of Avenida López Mateos and Calle Campillo is the former site of the old aduana, which was razed in 1963.

Figure 21. Mexican garita, circa 1968. This ground-level view looks south into Mexico through the double-winged canopy built by PRONAF in 1964. Vehicles move into Mexico on the right and exit at the left. Traffic islands with ornamental vegetation and a flag standard display are visible in front of and behind the arched gateway. In 1969, the Nixon administration launched Operation Intercept, intended to combat drug trafficking at border crossings. The ensuing delays harmed border-area businesses and created traffic congestion at gate crossings.

Figure 22. U.S. Immigration and Port of Entry, circa 1968. This ground-level view looks south from immediately north of the main gate crossing on the U.S. side. The 1934 U.S. Customs and Immigration Station is out of view to the right. Unlike the double-winged gateway on the Mexican side, the American port of entry almost completely obscures any view of Nogales, Sonora, creating a defensive posture at the border. Compare this perspective with figure 11, photographed three decades earlier.

Figure 23. La linea divisoria, circa 1980. This view looks west along the borderline privileging more of Mexico than the United States. The fence is still chain link and is seen extending west beyond the built-up area of either town. The Elías-Morley gate is now permanently closed to automotive traffic and survives only as a pedestrian access across the line. Visible at the upper right as it cuts across a steep hill and winds down on the Arizona side is Interstate 19, completed in 1966. Curio shops now fill the space where the Mexican aduana once stood at Calle Campillo and Avenida López Mateos.

Figure 24. Ambos Nogales borderline, circa 1995. This look westward reveals the first postcard representation of the metal fence made of surplus military tarmac, creating a black line that now defines the border. The 1964 U.S. Immigration and Port of Entry is substantially renovated and extended in a postmodern disguise of battleship gray accented with a hot-pink color scheme; it is also renamed to honor former U.S. senator from Arizona Dennis DeConcini. An elevated tower positioned immediately east of the railroad corridor on the U.S. side monitors train crossings, which have increased greatly with the importation of vehicles from the Ford Motor plant in Hermosillo, Sonora. Faintly visible about one-half mile west of the main gate on the U.S. side is a closed-circuit television camera mounted on a tall standard; the camera scans the border to alert the U.S. Border Patrol to illegal crossings. On the Mexican side, three small tile-roofed pavilions are barely visible along the railroad track east of the double-winged gateway. These are part of a newly created public space called Garibaldi Plaza, where street musicians gather on weekend nights following the close of the bars and nightclubs on the Sonora side.

References

Arizona Daily Star. 1997. Nogales, Sonora: Foreign and familiar, 23 November.

Arizona Republic. 1998. Nogales to get face lift, 24 March.

Arreola, Daniel D. 1996. Border-city idée fixe. *Geographical Review* 86(3):356–69.

———. 1999. Across the street is Mexico: Invention and persistence of the border town curio landscape. *Yearbook, Association of Pacific Coast Geographers* 61:9–41.

Arreola, Daniel D., and James R. Curtis. 1993. *The Mexican border cities: Landscape anatomy and place personality.* Tucson: University of Arizona Press.

Arreola, Daniel D., and Kenneth Madsen. 1998. Variability of tourist attractions on an international boundary: Sonora, Mexico, border towns. *Visions in Leisure and Business* 17(4):1–10.

Curtis, James R. 1993. Central business districts of the two Laredos. *Geographical Review* 83(1):54–65.

———. 1995. Mexicali's Chinatown. *Geographical Review* 85(3):335–48.

Fernández Tejedo, Isabel. 1994. *Recuerdos de México: la tarjeta postal mexicana, 1882–1930.* México: Banco Obras Públicos.

Flores García, Silvia Raquel. 1987. *Nogales: un siglo en la historia.* Hermosillo: INAH-SEP Centro Regional del Noroeste.

Foote, Kenneth E. 1985. Velocities of change of a built-environment, 1880–1980: Evidence from the photoarchives of Austin, Texas. *Urban Geography* 6(3): 220–45.

Ganster, Paul, ed. 2000. *Tijuana 1964: A photographic and historic view.* San Diego: San Diego State University Press.

Hales, Peter Beacon. 1984. *Silver cities: The photography of American urbanization, 1839–1915.* Philadelphia: Temple University Press.

Herzog, Lawrence A. 1990. *Where north meets south: Cities, space, and politics on the U.S.-Mexico border.* Austin: Center for Mexican American Studies, University of Texas.

———. 1999. *From Aztec to high tech: Architecture and landscape across the Mexico–United States border.* Baltimore: Johns Hopkins University Press.

Jakle, John A. 1982. *The American small town: Twentieth-century place images.* Hamden, Conn.: Archon Books.

Méndez Sáinz, Eloy. 1993. De Tijuana a Matamoros: imágenes y forma urbana. *Revista de El Colegio de Sonora* 4(6):45–61.

Miller, George, and Dorothy Miller. 1976. *Picture postcards in the United States, 1893–1918.* New York: Clarkson N. Potter.

Montellano, Francisco. 1994. *C. B. Waite: una miranda diversa sobre el México de principios del siglo XX.* México: Editorial Grijalbo.

Morgan, Hal, and Andreas Brown. 1981. *Prairie fires and paper moons: The American photographic postcard, 1900–1920.* Boston: David R. Godine.

Newhall, Beaumont. 1982. *The history of photography from 1839 to the present.* Revised and enlarged edition. New York: Museum of Modern Art.

Ready, Alma, ed. 1980. *Nogales, Arizona, 1880–1980, Centennial Anniversary.* Nogales: Nogales Centennial Committee.

Rochlin, Fred, and Harriet Rochlin. 1976. The heart of Ambos Nogales: Boundary monument 122. *Journal of Arizona History* 17(2):161–80.

Samponaro, Frank N., and Paul J. Vanderwood. 1992. *War scare on the Rio Grande: Robert Runyon's photographs of the border conflict, 1913–1916.* Austin: Texas State Historical Association.

Sokota, R. Paul. 1990–91. Ambos Nogales, on the border: A chronology. Tucson: Udall Center, Studies in Public Policy, University of Arizona. Typescript.

Staff, Frank. 1966. *The picture postcard and its origins.* New York: Praeger.

Stechschulte, Nancy Stickels. 1994. *The Detroit Publishing Company postcards.* Big Rapids, Mich.: Nancy Stickels Stechschulte.

Tinker Salas, Miguel. 1997. *In the shadow of the eagles: Sonora and the transformation of the border during the Porfiriato.* Los Angeles: University of California Press.

A Note on Homosexuality in Porfirian and Postrevolutionary Northern Mexico

VÍCTOR MANUEL MACÍAS-GONZÁLEZ

Scholars of Queer history in Mexico have tended to focus on a series of scandalous events—most notably those documented in the Inquisition files or the quintessential modern gay scandal, the 41 affair in the Porfiriato—and in doing so have failed to apply to Mexican gay, lesbian, bisexual, and transgender studies the numerous approaches developed in the historiography of the urban gay experience in the United States and Western Europe.[1] Somehow, the lavender past (and present) south of the Río Grande must forever remain arcane, exceptional, or otherwise exoticized. Perhaps it is the fault of historians of Latin America, who have left historical studies on (homo)sexuality to other social scientists and well-meaning but misinformed scholars.[2] Given what we know about Mexico's social, political, economic, and cultural developments in the late nineteenth century,[3] however, the origins of today's modern gay community and identity must be explained along lines similar to those found elsewhere in the transatlantic world.

In the late nineteenth century, the urban areas of northern Mexico, like those of the densely populated center, offered the industrial capitalist conditions for homosexual identity to emerge. According to John D'Emilio, the existence of a free labor system and the expansion of commodity production made it possible for individuals to free themselves from dependency on the family in order to develop "an autonomous personal life . . . independent and disconnected from how one organized the production of goods necessary for survival."[4] The rise of wage labor thus allowed individuals to abandon their families and finally to begin exploring and acting upon their repressed homosexual desires. During the Porfiriato, employment opportunities in urban areas, particularly in northern Mexico (where wages were higher), attracted large numbers of single young people. There, countless mining camps, cattle ranches, and bustling commercial and manufacturing centers offered individuals new social spaces and a certain anonymity that allowed them to look outside the confines of heterosexuality.

A history of single *norteños* would go a long way toward opening the door on the Queer family past. While French scholars suggest that it was in the nineteenth century that the bachelor came to embody modernity as the ultimate example of individuation, he also became a social suspect.[5] Folklore warning people of the evils of "men alone" may well relate an awareness of the novel forms of being that the invisible, silent "hombres solos" experienced. *Hombre sin mujer no es de ver:* A man without a woman is not a sight to see.[6] How many anecdotal bachelor uncles—like the Tío Guillermo that Elías Nandino relates in his memoirs[7]—may in fact have been gay men, exiled from family life—and family histories—for the sin of being men without women? If the rejection they felt led them to explore other possibilities, how did they craft their new or alternative gendered identities? What role, for example, did geography and consumption play in this process?

The cities of Porfirian Mexico offered bachelors and other men social spaces rife with homoeroticism: sports clubs, gymnasiums, bathhouses, school dormitories, seminaries, military garrisons, and jails. The same spaces that other scholars have analyzed to explore the way in which Porfirian elites sought to instill novel practices such as time management, hygiene, the work ethic, and temperance upon the large, floating, working-class population should also be analyzed to understand how northern Mexicans experienced same-sex love between men.[8] Clubhouses, cafés, bars, spas, gyms, and sports teams merit increased attention because they were important sites of cultural bricolage. Within the safe confines of spas, for example, people of diverse social and ethnic backgrounds came together to learn novel modes of consumption and leisure while remaining productive and respectable.[9] These sites also allowed people to fashion new class and gender identities in tune with their evolving notions of the self; white-collar workers, for example, employed membership in the Young Men's Christian Association (YMCA) to separate themselves from workers while cultivating a moral manhood that would potentially cure modern society of prostitution, gambling, alcoholism, vagrancy, and idleness.[10]

The geography of leisure offered many options to the young men of northern Mexican cities. In Chihuahua even people of the middling sort found that with a peso or two per month they could gain access to the city's well-appointed clubhouses, cafés, bars, and sports clubs. The city boasted a local branch of the YMCA, the Foreign Club, the Chihuahua 1910 American Football team, the Bohemian Club, the Cosmopolitan Confectionery, the Seminary's Baseball Club, Delmonico's Restaurant, the Spanish Colony's Black and White Club, the Omega Baseball Club, the Atheneum, the Literary and Scientific Institute, and the Shooting Club. Great resources were dedicated to the construction and upkeep of these spaces. Plans to remodel the city's premier social club, the Casino de Chihuahua, included a bathhouse, library, billiards room, bar, restaurant, and barber shop at a cost of 100,000 pesos.[11]

The posh pleasure palaces of northern Mexico were on a par with similar establishments elsewhere in the country. Whether in Chihuahua, Guadalajara, or Mexico City, dapper young men treated themselves to the hedonistic pleasures of bathhouses, gymnasiums, and sports clubs. There they soaked, scrubbed, steamed, sweated, and swam before having a massage, manicure, and pedicure and having their hair coifed or their moustaches trimmed and waxed. The entire ritual of primping and preening before going out on the town took as long as three or four hours in bathhouses whose comfort and charm were more in keeping with Oriental harems. Advertisements touted "modern comfort and Oriental luxury with fluffy pillows, divans, magazines, newspapers, books, and a well-stocked buffet table."[12] These facilities did more than stimulate sweat glands and blood flow; some clients used the saunas for occasional sensual encounters, despite bath house regulations warning clients against scrubbing each other and prohibiting more than one person to share a bathtub. Elías Nandino, a poet and physician close to the Contemporáneos literary circle, had his earliest homosexual intercourse shortly after 1911 in Cocula, Jalisco, at "Los Baños del Pensil":

> I invited him and he accepted. We undressed, I saw his body and he saw mine. We were like rifles. We got into the water. We played and without meaning to, our bodies touched. I already knew how to kiss. I knew their impact, their meaning. We shared one. We got out of the tub, and in the place where we were supposed to scrub, we pleasured each other. I found his back. Thereafter, each week, he came looking for me.[13]

Such encounters are well documented in police archives as far back as the sixteenth century, but what proved novel for Porfirians was that these incidents seemed to occur in greater frequency, forcing society to take measures to combat them.

In the early twentieth century, authorities increased their surveillance of spaces where same-sex-attracted males were feared to congregate. Regulations for spas throughout Mexico urged bathers not to
dawdle any longer than they had to in the various departments of the
bathhouses, suggesting that some of the clientele cruised the baths for
sex.[14] Access to bathing facilities at schools and dormitories was subsequently limited. Beginning in 1905, for example, students at the
National Preparatory School could enter the showers only after having
exercised—and not prior.[15] Gradually, steps were taken to curb the
public expression of same-sex attraction. A new criminal code created
for the State of Chihuahua in 1905 included new measures that not
only penalized sexual harassment but also made veiled reference to
homosexuality. Article 769 punished "immodest acts against morality
performed in public" with arrest and fines of $5 to $500 pesos. Article 771
defined "crimes against morality" as "any offensive, shameless act that
is not copulation but is carried out on another person's body without
the individual's permission, regardless of the person's sex."[16]

Social reformers stressed the need for state authorities to police
sites of social danger. Countless conferences, legislative projects, and
prescriptive books reiterated the need to regulate the behavior of students, office workers, and soldiers in bathrooms, gymnasiums, dormitories and bathhouses. Porfirians dictated strict procedures and
specifications in order to contain all acts indicative of what they saw as
the primitive animal nature in the human being. These sites were
regarded as dangerous, unhealthy, and immoral since it was here that
the male genitalia were exposed, bringing with this exhibitionism a
thousand dangers, and here where evils of great transcendence must be
avoided at all costs with ample moral vigilance while still allowing for
the conduct of very necessary acts in an environment of the greatest
decency and decorum and in the most hygienic conditions possible.[17]

While the historical record speaks amply on the subject of homosexuality in bathhouses and restrooms, relatively little attention has
been given to dormitories (*internados*) and the homosocial culture that
they fostered. In the late 1870s and 1880s, shortly after Díaz came to
power, the dormitories of the National Preparatory School (as were
those of nearly all schools that depended on the National Treasury)
were closed. Northern schoolboys, newly arrived from Chihuahua and
elsewhere, where the use of dormitories apparently continued, were
dismayed to see the homosocial spaces thus disrupted.

In his later years, the successful northern businessman and bohemian Jesús E. Valenzuela—who relates in his all-too-frank memoirs of his meeting Oscar Wilde in New York City and Philadelphia and of having Manuel Gutiérrez Nájera plant kisses on his hands—looked back fondly on his internado years.[18] From 1873 to 1876, the period directly preceding the closing of the dormitories, Valenzuela lived raucous years, adding homoerotic-tinged tales to the usual stories of drunken student mayhem. One such incident became celebrated in the prep school's history as "the abduction of Malpica." According to Valenzuela, student gangs organized war parties and raided the dormitories of rival groups. During one raid, an upperclassman known as "El Soldado" carried off a younger student known as "Malpica" as his trophy. El Soldado was reportedly seen taking Malpica over his shoulders into the night and supposedly neither was heard from again. The object of such a raid is unclear from the testimony, but its presumably homoerotic overtones scandalized the school. Dr. Gabino Barreda, the prep school director, urged his protégé Valenzuela to find other lodgings.[19]

Secular leaders wanted to avoid for their presumably superior schools the behavior that was assumed to be commonplace in religious institutions. And while the Church endeavored to curtail same-gender eroticism in its schools, the testimony of Elías Nandino, who studied at various seminaries in Jalisco and Michoacán, suggests that homoeroticism was rife in Catholic institutions. At the Jacona Seminary, despite measures curtailing nudity and prohibiting students from socializing in groups of fewer than three, Nandino befriended youths who smilingly groped each other under the table while gazing into each other's eyes.[20] Later, at the short-lived Seminary of La Ascensión, which Nandino christened "La Sodoma Nueva," the priests frequently had their way with seminarians.[21]

If dormitories justifiably attracted the attention of authorities, they did not avert their surveillance from other homosocial spaces. School officials monitored lavatories in particular out of a sense that students and other social inferiors had traditionally used restrooms as a refuge from adult supervision. As such, these places became suspect since they were regarded as a site that encouraged the breakdown of individual discipline. Because the restroom represented "the only place where they could enjoy their liberty," officials recommended that vigilance with respect to lavatories be doubled, advocating, for example, that stall doors should not have locks on the inside and that they be made to allow for the head and legs to be visible from the outside.[22] Victoriano Salado Álvarez recounts in his memoirs how youths congregated in the "smelly latrines" of his school to smoke and talk about sex, sharing their readings of "dirty pseudoscientific books" while gawking at French pornographic images. "It was thus," don Victoriano noted, "that I came to learn of the full horror of the most terrible perversions."[23] In the school that Salvador Novo attended in Jiménez, Chihuahua, he and his classmates lived in fear of being sodomized—*cochados*—by older boys who prowled the lavatories for sex.[24] Two rubicund siblings, the Botello brothers, were the constant targets of their chums' affections. Older schoolboys enjoyed caressing and kissing them, "two or three times a day," relates Novo, who secretly hoped one day to be likewise ravished.[25]

Novo's memoirs are perhaps the best printed source for the study of homosexuality in urban areas of early-twentieth-century northern Mexico. They suggest that there were many homosocial spaces such as schools, baths, sports clubs, and hospitality establishments that catered to or fostered a nascent gay community. They also hint that dissident masculinities coexisted with that of the macho. Middle-class families, for example, thought nothing of having their pubescent schoolboys cross-dress in their daily games. Effeminate cooks and house servants were commonplace. And, most interesting, we learn that attractive young strangers, teachers, and coaches frequently approached the effete young Salvador for sex. His tutor in Jiménez, Chihuahua, was promptly dismissed after caressing his crotch and teaching him the word "penis."[26] In Torreón, Coahuila, he shared his first kiss with a classmate, Jorge González, who "melted his mouth into mine in a long wet kiss; he penetrated all my senses with his tongue, he dissolved the sweetness of his kiss throughout my body."[27]

Novo's and Nandino's youthful experiences confirm the existence of a gay subculture in urban areas of northern and western Mexico, lending credence to the proposition that Mexican Queer history bears many more similarities to the experience of homosexuals in North America and Western Europe than the present state of scholarship would have us believe. Rather than focus on Mexico and the rest of Latin America as an exotic aberrant from the development of homosexual subcultures in the Western world, we should focus on the shared experience, not merely in oppression but also related to urban geography and homosocial spaces. As more work is done on this topic— particularly in the urban, developed areas—scholars will find that research on Queer history south of the border need not be an arcane, needle-in-a-haystack experience. By focusing on identifying similarities and disparities based on what we already know about the evolution of homosexual identity and community life in other locales, we can perhaps better work to fill the great void in Mexico's Queer past.

Study also needs to be made of the presence of a Mexican gay community in the U.S. Southwest. This Queer Mexican diaspora, with origins in the nineteenth century, included a number of prominent literary and artistic figures who tired of the deceitful life of "bachelorhood" and escaped to the United States. There, a number found positions as language teachers, journalists, entertainers, and artists. Antonio Adalid arrived penniless in San Francisco in late 1901, disinherited from one of the largest fortunes of Porfirian Mexico for his participation in the "41 Scandal." Thanks to impeccable English acquired during his studies in Great Britain, he became a teacher of Spanish at St. Mary's School, surviving on this salary until, after his mother's death, he received her inheritance—and his father's forgiveness. Antonio returned to Mexico with his partner and lived to a ripe old age.[28] Many more men came with the Revolution, among them the pianist Ricardo Alessio Robles, the famed tenor José Mojica, and silent film actor Ramón Novarro, who spent significant time in the United States.[29] What was their relationship to the greater U.S. gay community and— most important—did they function as cultural brokers in the process of transplanting gay identity to Mexican same-sex-attracted males? How did their experiences in the United States subsequently influence the development of Mexico's gay community? The answers to these and other questions await. ❖

NOTES

Research and writing of portions of this paper was made possible thanks to a generous gift from the University of Wisconsin, La Crosse, International Faculty Development Fund. I wish to thank John Magerus for his commentary.

1. On scholarship in the colonial period, refer to Serge Gruzinski, "Las cenizas del deseo: homosexuales novohispanos a mediados del siglo XVII," in *De la santidad a la perversión: o de por qué no se cumplia la ley de Dios en la sociedad novohispana*, ed. Sergio Ortega (Mexico City: Editorial Grijalbo, 1986), 169–215; Clark L. Taylor, "Legends, Syncretism, and Continuing Echoes of Homosexuality from Pre-Columbian and Colonial Mexico," in *Latin American Male Homosexualities*, ed. Stephen O. Murray (Albuquerque:

University of New Mexico Press, 1995), 80–99; Enrique Dávalos López, "La sexualidad en los pueblos mesoamericanos prehispánicos. Un panorama general," in *Sexualidadcs en México: Algunas aproximaciones desde la perspectiva de las ciencias sociales* (Mexico City: El Colegio de Mexico, 1998), 71–106; Guilhelm Olivier, "Conquistadores y misioneros frente al pecado nefando," *Historias* 28 (1992): 47–64; and Ramón Gutiérrez, *When Jesus Came, the Corn Mothers Went Away* (Stanford: Stanford University Press, 1992), 76. Regarding the 41 scandal, refer to Rob Buffington, "Los Jotos: Contested Visions of Homosexuality in Modern Mexico," in *Sex and Sexuality in Latin America*, ed. Donna I. Guy and Daniel Balderston (New York: New York University Press, 1997), 118–32; Carlos Monsiváis, " 'Los que tenemos unas manos que no nos pertenecen' (A propósito de lo 'queer' y lo 'rarito')," *Debate Feminista* 16 (October 1997): 11–34; and Robert McKee Irwin, Edward J. McCaughan, and Michelle Rocío Nasser, eds., *The Famous 41: Sexuality and Social Control in Mexico, 1901* (New York and London: Palgrave MacMillan, 2003).

2. See Joseph Carrier, *De los Otros: Intimacy and Homosexuality among Mexican Men* (New York: Columbia University Press, 1995); and Annick Prieur, *Mema's House, Mexico City: On Transvestites, Queens, and Machos* (Chicago: University of Chicago Press, 1998). While pioneering in nature, the research of Carrier and other anthropologists like Prieur has received strong criticism from colleagues. See Matthew C. Gutmann, "Home and Habitus in Latin America," *GLQ* 6, no. 1 (2000): 125–28.

3. Refer to the scholarship of William French, "Prostitutes and Guardian Angels: Women, Work and the Family in Porfirian Mexico," *Hispanic American Historical Review* 72, no. 4 (1992): 529–52; William H. Beezley, *Judas at the Jockey Club and Other Episodes of Porfirian Mexico* (Lincoln: University of Nebraska Press, 1987); Mauricio Tenorio-Trillo, *Mexico at the World's Fairs: Grafting a Modern Nation* (Berkeley: University of California Press, 1996); Pablo Piccato, "*El Paso de Vénus por el Disco Sol*: Criminality and Alcoholism in the Late Porfiriato," *Mexican Studies/Estudios Mexicanos* 11, no. 2 (1995); as well as Steven B. Bunker's manuscript on consumerism in the Porfiriato.

4. John D'Emilio, "Capitalism and Gay Identity," in *The Lesbian and Gay Studies Reader*, ed. Henry Abelove, Michèle Aina Barale, and David M. Halperin (New York and London: Routledge, 1993), 467–76.

5. Jean Borie, *Le célibataire français*, rev. ed. (Paris: Grasset, 2002).

6. *Hombre sin mujer, no es de ver:* "A man without a woman is not a sight to see" could also be interpreted as "A man without a woman is a duty unmet *(deber).*"

7. Elías Nandino, *Juntando mis pasos* (Mexico City: Editorial Aldus, 2000), 2.

8. William E. French, *A Peaceful and Working People: Manners, Morals, and Class Formation in Northern Mexico* (Albuquerque: University of New Mexico Press, 1996).

9. Douglas Peter Mackaman, *Leisure Settings: Bourgeois Culture, Medicine, and the Spa in Modern France* (Chicago: University of Chicago Press, 1998).

10. Víctor M. Macías-González, "Sports and the Porfirian Gentleman," unpublished manuscript; Glenn Avent, "A Popular and Wholesome Resort:

Gender, Class, and the Y.M.C.A. in Porfirian Mexico" (M.A. thesis, University of British Columbia, 1996); and John Donald Gustav-Wrathall, *Take the Young Stranger by the Hand: Same Sex Relations and the YMCA* (Chicago and London: University of Chicago Press, 1998).

11. José María Ponce de León, Manuel Aguilar Sáenz, and Manuel Rocha y Chabre, eds., *Album del centenario. Chihuahua en 1910* (Chihuahua, Mexico: Imprenta del Gobierno, 1910), 15, 51.

12. *El Hamm Am. Baños turco-romanos en la gran Alberca Pane. Hidroterapia completa. Guía del bañador* (Mexico City: Tipografía Berrueco Hermanos, 1887), 6–7, 38.

13. Nandino, 39–40.

14. *Ligeros apuntes históricos sobre el baño en México y datos históricos y estadísticos del Gran Baño de San Felipe de Jesús en la capital de la República* (Mexico City: Tipografía Vázquez e Hijos, 1911).

15. Escuela Nacional Preparatoria, *Prescripciones disciplinarias aprobadas por la Secretaría de Educación Pública y Bellas Artes para que rijan en esta Escuela en sustitución de las que se expidieron el 16 de Noviembre de 1903* (Mexico City: Tipografía Económica, 1905).

16. Estado de Chihuahua, *Código penal del Estado Libre y Soberano de Chihuahua* (Chihuahua City: Imprenta del Gobierno, 1905), 178–79.

17. Consejo Superior de Salubridad, *Memorias del primer Congreso Higiénico-Pedagógico reunido en la ciudad de México el año de 1882* (Mexico City: Imprenta del Gobierno Dirigida por Sabas A. y Munguía, 1883), 37.

18. Jesús E. Valenzuela, *Mis recuerdos, Manojo de rimas* (Mexico City: Consejo Nacional para la Cultura y las Artes, 2001), 59–72. Valenzuela devoted his fortune to the patronage of the arts. He sponsored the works of many Porfirian literati but is primarily known for his relationship to the literary circle associated with the decadent, modernist journal *La Revista Moderna*. Some of these artists were gay, like Bernardo Couto Castillo. On Valenzuela's meeting with Wilde—to which he dedicated a poem—see p. 93 and pp. 202–3. On the kisses Valenzuela received from *la duquesa Job*, see p. 100.

19. Valenzuela, 62.

20. Nandino, 29–31.

21. Ibid., 47.

22. Consejo Superior de Salubridad, 54–56.

23. Victoriano Salado Álvarez, *Memorias*, vol. 1, *Tiempo Viejo* (Mexico City: EDIAPSA, 1946), 76. He claims that he read a French translation of Krafft Ebbing's *Psychopathia Sexualis* at age 14, in 1883. The book in question only appeared in German in 1886 and was not translated into French until 1890. It is likely he saw a precursor text, like Ambroise Tardieu's *Les attentats aux moeurs* (1857).

24. Salvador Novo, *La estatua de sal* (Mexico City: Fondo de Cultura Económica, 1998), 48–51.

25. Ibid., 51.

26. Ibid., 57–59, 50–51.

27. Ibid., 65.

28. Ibid., 108–10.

29. Good biographies of these individuals are lacking. Available accounts include highly censored memoirs, such as José Mojica, *Yo pecador, autobiografía* (Mexico City: Editorial Jus, 1956), or second-rate apologies, such as Allan R. Ellenberger, *Ramón Novarro: A Biography of the Silent Film Idol, 1899–1968; With a Filmography* (Jefferson, NC: McFarland and Company, 1999).

All Night at the Owl: The Social and Political Relations of Mexicali's Red-Light District, 1909–1925

Eric Michael Schantz

What is in the name Mexicali? Engineers and planners at the turn of the century crafted the place-name Mexicali and that of its border twin, Calexico, as monuments to the transborder irrigation project that integrated Baja California's Mexicali Valley and California's Imperial Valley into a single regional economic unit. Scholars of the U.S.–Mexico border point to the construction of this twin city and the transformation of the Colorado Desert into a modern zone of commercial agriculture as testimony to the triumph of international capitalism and symbiotic relations.[1]

In contrast, a popular and unthinking way of viewing Mexicali developed that was ultimately the cultural by-product of the border vice-tourism industry which emerged in the first third of the twentieth century. In 1920 the Mexican consul in Douglas, Alfonso Pesqueira, lamented to General Alvaro Obregón, "Our border cities began to look like red-light districts," echoing what many U.S. moral crusaders and Mexican nationalists, including Obregón's Constitutionalist faction, had long vehemently protested. Likewise, Obregón noted with horror to General Plutarco Elías Calles that American tourists had begun calling Nogales' principal street, Calle Elías, "Mexicali Street." The proliferation of Mexicali (as a place-name) in media productions, postcards, and music may be viewed as off-site markers referencing the border city's attractions and personalities. Whether self-referential or naming some other commodity, Mexicali came to evoke associations with red-light Chinatown ambience, saloon culture, and the hybridization of the U.S.–Mexico border. Interactively engaging print media and hearsay, sightseers to Mexicali sowed the seeds of this international topographic imagination as they digested and related their experiential consciousness. Ultimately, the media and consuming public participated in the unconscious interpretive act of integrating Mexicali into a larger sociocultural topography of the international border. Besides the transmission of print media and promotional literature, official records from both the U.S. and Mexican governments as well as popular protests helped cement the image of Mexicali as a border town specializing in red-light diversion.[2]

The negative publicity from whistle-blowing temperance reformers firmly established Mexicali's notoriety and further enticed those inclined to subvert conventional morality. Protests organized by temperance and civic groups bent on extending the moral imperative of Progressivism beyond international borders led to the U.S. Treasury Department decision to close international border ports as early as 6:00 P.M. between 1924 and 1929.[3]

Mexican *fronterizos* with nationalist credentials, such as General Abelardo L. Rodríguez, bemoaned the sensationalizing tendencies of these reform groups and warned of a second coming of the black legend. As governor of Baja California, Rodríguez loudly criticized the U.S. government and reform groups for injuring the tourism industry. Having capitalized his diversified economic empire largely from revenues generated by Tijuana and Mexicali's vice-tourism industry, General Rodríguez was predictably defensive. Ironically, Rodríguez supported the Sonoran faction of Constitutionalists, a faction which betrayed the influences of U.S. Progressivism, especially with regard to vice and leisure. This ideological disposition conditioned the diatribes that the Sonoran clique leveled at Governor Esteban Cantú (1915–1920) and his "reactionary" political economy nourished on gaming, inebriants, and prostitution revenue. Once in power, however, Governor Rodríguez's policies were not that different from Cantú's. Both shared a regulationist approach to vice tourism, one that would prevent "liberty from degenerating into *libertinage*."[4] The rhetorical tightrope that Constitutionalist governments were forced to walk exposed the paradoxical ideology of paternalistically fostering the growth of the working classes while aggressively negotiating, if not courting, foreign investment. This paradox was highlighted when Plutarco Elías Calles, the renowned prohibitionist governor of Sonora, became president and investment partner with Governor Rodríguez at Baja California's most extravagant tourist complex, the Agua Caliente Casino and Spa.

With the Progressive reforms and World War I engendering dry option and red-light abatement laws, vice concessionaires fled the United States seeking business opportunities in Cuba, Canada, and Mexico. As Oscar Martínez astutely notes, the vice-tourism industry expanded into Mexico well before the United States passed the Volstead Act in 1919.[5] Arriving by rail and increasingly by motor tour, tourists flocked to Mexicali's premier casino, brothel, and vaudeville theatre, the Owl, or El Tecolote as it was referred to in Spanish (see figure 1).

Perhaps more important than the often-mentioned prohibitionist push factors were the pull factors deriving from regional economic and social development. Unlike in Tijuana, vice tourism in Mexicali emerged from the structural changes transforming one of the world's harshest desert environs into a dynamic zone of commercial agriculture. This structural transformation of the periphery attracted workers from Mexico and the United States, especially indentured Asian laborers. It was no coincidence that the Owl clientele was similar in makeup to the consumers of Chinatown red-light attractions of the nineteenth century in that patrons varied along gender, class, ethnic, and racial lines. Too, the Owl resembled other segregated vice districts in the way that bourgeois tourists "slummed" with workers and rubbed elbows with an international cast of hustlers, pimps, and drug dealers. "Famous from the Yukon to Panama City, the history of the Northern District of Lower California has centered around the Owl to some extent since its construction." This irresistible promotional line from the *Los Angeles Times* exemplifies the public relations hype around the area.[6]

This article examines the history of the Owl Café and Theatre from 1909 to 1925 as a window through which the transcultural relations that characterize frontier and border societies may be viewed. This cross-cultural fertilization surfaces in the political and social relations of vice regulation as well as the urban geography of Mexicali's red-light district. While I acknowledge the asymmetrical relations of power and wealth between the two countries, in the research presented here, I illuminate many of the shared assumptions about race and ethnicity, gender, and economic class. At the same time, the incendiary history of the Owl—fires ravaged the establishment in 1920 and 1922—offers a unique vantage point from which to evaluate issues relevant to the study of the Mexican Revolution. For example, antagonistic center-periphery relations, historically a prickly issue for the Mexican state, come into acute focus from Baja California's new capital of Mexicali. Beyond the tainted social status of vice-tourism capital, the tight relationship forged by local government and high-profile foreign concessionaires such as the ABW Syndicate necessarily centered the Owl in the ideological machinations and power relations undergirding center-periphery conflict. The dialectical tension between central authority and Mexico's renegade border must be triangulated to accommodate the powerful external influences exercised from the north. Like other foreign

Figure 1. Photograph of the original Owl, 1914–15, on Avenida Porfirio Díaz. (Courtesy of Archivo Historico del Estado, Baja California Norte)

enclaves, Mexicali's Owl symbolized to Mexican nationalists and labor activists U.S. domination of labor and leisure markets.[7]

Disorganized and Unregulated Vice Commerce, 1909–1914

Fleeing California's red-light abatement initiative, Marvin Allen, Frank "Booze" Byers, and Carl Withington, who collectively became known as the ABW Syndicate, moved their operations to Mexicali, where they established the Owl on Avenida Porfirio Díaz, a de facto red-light boulevard. By the time the Owl landed in 1914, Mexicali already had a reputation as a border town specializing in dangerous diversions. One Mexican immigration inspector calculated that Mexicali's red-light attractions drew 2,500 tourists on a typical weekend day in 1913. Mexicali's vice trade provoked widespread indignation among the *gente decente,* whose protests began in 1909.[8] Cantinas, cabarets, and cafés constituted 75 percent of Mexicali's commerce, complained Enrique de la Sierra, the Mexican consul at Calexico, in 1909. He objected, as did his successors, to the fact that the vice business huddled almost exclusively along Ave. Porfirio Díaz. While neon signs from the Paris Café, Swiss-Italian Cantina, and Climax Cantina promised adventure and lustful diversion, Mexican officials bemoaned the public relations message they sent to Mexicali's twin city. Calexico stood directly across from Mexicali's main street, and the symbolically charged location of red-light business along Porfirio Díaz showed no other zoning logic than to capture the imagination of potential customers from across the border.

Mexican officials joined the gente decente of the Mexicali and Imperial Valleys in protesting the disorganized red-light geography that smothered Mexicali's port of entry. The daily immigration of prostitutes proved to be most disturbing. The free association and transit of *mujeres públicas* to and from Mexicali not only disquieted civic sensibilities and violated Mexican immigration law but jeopardized family tourism and cross-border curio shopping. Mexicali's crimson ambience undermined the sense of honor of women and children who were forced to cross through the gauntlet of iniquity that was the de facto red-light district huddled near Mexicali's entrance. In addition, mismanagement and unequal development forced Mexicali's schoolchildren to seek their schooling in Calexico, and the juxtaposition of students and migrating prostitutes raised the issue of social geography of the border to a symbolic high. The town's honorable families petitioned Porfirio Díaz to relocate the town's red-light services to a segregated district far from the gaze of the town's children. Mexicali's only school had been devastated by the 1907 Colorado River flood. Despite promises from Baja California's *jefe político* Col. Celso Vega, it had not been rebuilt. To local families this failure, or sin of omission, loomed even greater because Vega owned and collected rent from the cantina and prostitution services at the Hotel Emporio. In the eyes of upstanding Americans and Mexicans, Vega's sins of commission placed him in the camp of those jefes políticos, mayors, and law officers who used official power as a remunerative device, especially with regard to prostitution and gambling.[9]

Mexicali's unregulated red-light menu posed a threat to international relations. Pointing to the border's porous condition—it was demarcated only by a rather narrow canal—Consul Enrique de la Sierra expressed fears that the escalation of petty violence resulting from conflicts over "wine, women, and gambling" would spiral into a serious conflict between the two countries. A knifing involving two mulatto prostitutes alongside the New River symbolically defined Mexicali for the upstanding citizens as "wild and uncut wastes."[10] Mexicali's disorganized commerce threatened the honorable families with disease and shame. "Suffering to a very evident extent with an unmentionable disease," one syphilis-ridden saloon operator symbolized the ills of Mexicali's red-light sector. The people it attracted "were subversive to public morality and hurtful to the substantial progress not only of the said Town of Mexicali, but its twin sister, the City of Calexico and indeed the entire Imperial Valley." As the *Chronicle* quipped, Mexicali's prostitution services attracted those males whose class standing was sufficient that they could afford to send their family to the cooler environs of the Pacific littoral during the hot summer months of the Colorado Desert, though in some cases their sense of shame ensnared their honesty: "Some men are liars, and others say they are lonesome while their wife is at the coast on her vacation."[11]

To upstanding citizens of the region, crossing the border into Mexicali appeared to be an act of social and cultural degeneracy. In the nineteenth and early twentieth centuries, the "drunken Indian" was an iconographic symbol of a backward and unredeemable genetic and cultural group. Calexico's post office offered a postcard photograph of

Borrego, a centenarian Apache of local fame, and tourists "who were doing Mexicali last winter." The photograph documented the momentous commercial transaction whereby Borrego sold his scalp for a bottle of alcohol. An editorial from the same paper revealed the cultural and economic antagonisms that galvanized U.S. Progressive and Mexican Constitutionalist ideology: "Don't cross the line. Save a little money and buy a home for that little girl who will some day be your wife."[12] Concerns shared by U.S. and Mexican reformers over vice and excessive consumerism extended beyond morality and personal health to national political economic development and cultural well-being. Personal happiness and the future economic success of the region, as the following passage infers, hinged upon avoiding the earthly temptations that Mexicali offered and disciplining the savings habits of the wage-earning classes.

> In a few years some of these young men who are making good money and spending it all across the line will wake up to the fact that they could just as well have sidetracked ten dollars a month from their wages and bot [*sic*] a lot in Calexico. Real estate is going to take another jump one of these days and that day is not far distant. You can't imagine how easy it is to buy a lot until you get in and try. Call on a realty man and start in now. . . . When that official announcement is made that the San Diego and Arizona railroad will go thru Calexico to Yuma you will wonder why you did not take on a town lot when you could at half the figure they will then be.[13]

Ward Hull, an Episcopal minister from El Centro, betrayed the cultural tension and dismay that Mexicali's "wild and uncut" wastes provoked among the upstanding and decent citizenry on both sides of the border. In 1910, Ward "took some [clergy] friends over the border the other day on a little pleasure and sight seeing trip . . . quite the thing here, you know, show your friends the 'sights' across the line." They were "astonished to identify seemingly good moraled and virtuous men . . . down in Mexicali."[14] Not only did Hull's "pleasure and sight seeing trip" suggest that visiting Mexicali's "sights" had become a popular practice for the local population, but it evokes the notion of class cultural digression, or "slumming." Before Baja California's border vice attractions could truly appeal to the Babbitts, or weekend consumers of prohibited leisure services, Mexicali required certain internal reforms and boosterism to reassure anxious foreigners that they would be safe from the dangers and depredations of "barbarous Mexico." Such a shift in local politics as well as external perceptions of the border and Baja California came in 1915 with the ascendance to power of the military governorship of Col. Esteban Cantú.

THE SOCIAL AND ECONOMIC ANATOMY OF VICE TOURISM, 1915–1920

The key to Governor Cantú's success was his ability to project the illusion of order to Americans who had reservations about their personal security in Mexico. The *regiomontano* governor focused policy (both de facto and de jure) on three areas that directly applied to the Owl and Mexicali's vice-tourism economy: a fiscal policy of prohibitive taxation; a segregated vice district and tightly regulated prostitution; and a collaborative relationship with the United States. Aggressive taxation and vigilance of order were the economic and political cornerstones to Governor Cantú's effective administration of the border vice-tourism sector. He left his name on policies that helped imbue the border with a sense of order and progress without sanitizing its vice-based ingredients of sex, drugs, and gaming. The Owl fit nicely into the strategy because it housed the subversive commerce of prostitution, provided generous latitude for gaming, and accommodated the social anxieties of Euro-Americans by providing "white" space and special viewing booths for couples hoping to observe the dangerous diversions from a safe distance.

Fiscal Policy: Prohibitive Taxation and Vice Tourism

Though only in power a month, Cantú began to make his political power felt immediately following the New Year's celebrations of 1915, when he imposed a tax hike designed to moralize the tawdry attractions of Mexicali and Tijuana. "Mexicali Celebrated Only As Mexicali Can" read the *Los Angeles Times* headline covering the celebration. The Cantú government punctuated this tax hike with a bold power play amidst the climaxing New Year's fiesta. The *Times* reported that the "wildest night was cut short at midnight when the voices of the bouncers in the gambling rooms, dance halls, saloons, and opium joints made everybody clear out and the doors were bolted."[15]

Prohibitive taxation constituted the main ingredient in Cantú's fiscal policy. It was a policy lever designed to contain the disorder created by the vice trade while inducing "upwardly mobile tourism." The *Chronicle* predicted that this new fiscal policy would bring about Mexicali's "final regeneration" by eliminating the "disreputable saloons" and "cheap places." Resonant with the cultural hues and moralizing undertone that characterized discussions of working-class health in the nineteenth century, allusions to morality could not disguise the policy's rather transparent class trajectory. "The moral tone of Mexicali [would] be improved" by offering the "very best liquors obtainable" instead of the "vile alcohol disguised as whiskey being sold to the pauper class."[16] Besides calculating the costs of social opportunities to maximize "order," prohibitive taxation deftly exploited the inelastic demand upon which sex, drug, and gaming markets operate. While the juridic border ensured that Mexico's border economies wielded comparative advantages not obtained on the other side of the boundary, local governments could tax and extract revenue from a seemingly relentless demand for vice services. Cantú proved skillful, though hardly original, in threatening Mexicali's gaming and prostitution concessionaires with definitive closure. In actuality, his eradicative posture dissimulated a strategy to net greater revenues.[17]

The power of the U.S. dollar in the border zone combined with the inelastic demand for drugs and other dangerous diversions provided Cantú and the local government with unprecedented amounts of revenue. Federal officials like Cantú had long rehearsed the justification for extracting revenue from red-light services in terms of endemic shortfalls in budgetary assistance from the central government. Not only had the already meager federal budget outlay for the district government of Baja California disappeared, but the revolution and internecine conflict across the republic generated an outflow of workers who migrated to the Mexicali Valley only to find that land and labor markets were dominated by foreign immigrants. Cantú apprehended this logic, justifying licensed opium dens, casinos, and brothels by claiming that the destruction created by the Mexican Revolution necessitated emergency financing. Cantú's success owed to his ability to channel vice revenues to stabilize troops, foment infrastructure development and education in Baja California, and subject foreign investment and workers to regular, rather than forced, tax levies. While credited with executing a modest land distribution to peasants and soldiers, Cantú did not actively respond to the situation by implementing national employment as his successor, General Abelardo Rodríguez, did.

The economic resources that the "Kingdom of Cantú" commanded came largely from the vice-tourism economy, which by 1916 was dominated by the Owl.[18] Foreign and national observers unanimously concluded that vice-tourism revenues underwrote the political autonomy that allowed Governor Cantú to resist the advances of the Mexican state between 1915 and 1920.[19] *Los Angeles Times* journalist and regional booster Harry Carr sounded the widely held opinion that gaming provided the "the chief source of the Governor's revenue." Gaming taxes produced the lion's share of this revenue, although regulated opium commerce probably generated greater wealth than gaming commerce. Carr credited Cantú's fiscal discipline with having transformed Mexicali from a "stinking hole into an enterprising western town." Together, Cantú and his Austrian father-in-law, Paul Dato, oversaw the transformation of Mexicali from a "collection of bad smelling hovels" into a symbol of progress, modernity, and enterprise.[20] It was no secret, U.S. Consul Edward Simpich reminded the State Department in 1917, that vice-tourism revenue constituted 90 percent of Governor Cantú's income. Nor was it a secret that the U.S. dollar was the official currency of the Cantú administration and the de facto specie at the border. According to Simpich, the Owl casino drained the wages of "respectable people" from the surrounding communities, but Cantú's commitment to private property and order made his administration the lesser of evils encountered by Americans elsewhere in the tumultuous republic.[21]

Analysis of vice taxes paid by the Owl reveals the fiscal moorings of its primary attractions and the economic sources of political power in the border. The original Owl concession contract signed in 1916 by Governor Cantú and Carl Withington, the principal investor and the *W* in the ABW Syndicate, set gaming taxes for district government at $8,000 dollars monthly, totaling $96,000 for 1916. Gaming-tax obligations grew during the next four years, despite the slowdown in U.S. patronage of border attractions due to the wartime restrictions imposed by the State Department in 1918. Together, the Owl and the rest of the ABW holdings in Tijuana provided the Cantú government with steady income to finance the ambitious public works and education improvements during his administration.[22]

Revenues netted by Mexicali's municipal government from prostitution, gaming, and alcohol enable a limited time-series analysis of the fiscal significance of the border vice-tourism economy between 1915 and 1926. Indeed, the real (or at least official) story presented by the numbers illustrates that prostitution, followed by gaming and alcohol, were the real income producers for Mexicali's municipal government during the period. Tijuana paled by comparison. The change in regime ushered in by the Agua Prieta Revolt in 1920 did not substantially slow the red-light commerce in Mexicali. On the contrary, by 1922 all three sectors began recording income levels that surpassed the levels of the Cantú period. The impulse toward political centralization notwithstanding, allegations of corruption and scandal were so rife that Abelardo Rodríguez disbanded Mexicali's *ayuntamiento* in 1925, a year that witnessed record levels of income for all three sectors (see table 1).[23]

Table 1. Vice Tourism and Immigration Income for Mexicali's Municipal Government (in Percent of Revenues)

	1915	1916	1917	1918	1919	1920	1921	1922	1923	1924	1925	1926
Prostitution	26	10	10	9	5	4	3	5	5	8	13	14
Gaming	8	2	2	2	1	1	7	20	19	30	17	12
Alcohol	1	4	5	5	3	6	2	2	12	10	12	10
Immigration	30	29	21	30	28	19	n/a	n/a	n/a	n/a	n/a	n/a

Source: Figures extrapolated from municipal tax records of *cortes de caja,* in AHE, *Periódico Oficial,* Ayuntamiento de Mexicali, 1915–1926.

Conversely, the border revenue bonanza from vice and king cotton fired the central government's resolve to replace the recalcitrant caudillo. President Carranza sent Modesto Rolland to head a commission that investigated the political and economic conditions of Baja California in 1919. A devotee of Henry George's single tax, Rolland naturally despised Cantú's fiscal policy, which he characterized as an opaque tangle of internal taxes (*alcabalas*). Harry Carr addressed the importance of Cantú's fiscal policy for creating order and political stability in two articles penned in support of the governor. Carr's enthusiasm for Cantú and hostility toward First Chief Venustiano Carranza were not unrelated to issues of private property and taxable wealth, and certainly echoed the sentiment of most foreign interests operating in the "Kingdom of Cantú." Compared to bloody Mexico, the peace that reigned in the Kingdom of Cantú justified the steep tax bill in Baja California Norte. Carr's justifications for the tax burden (the cost of "peace comes high in Lower California") mirror Cantú's policy statement justifying a tax rise on opium laboratories or the Owl concession.[24] Carr criticized the Carranza administration for its blundering attempt to control the wealth and economy of the border zone:

> Very naturally, the big sums coming in from the taxes on the American ranchers, from the gambling houses of Mexicali, and from the horse races and prize fights at Tia Juana created a delicious odor of prosperity that titillated the olfactories of all the revolutionary chiefs who came and went in the City of Mexico. For a long time Carranza has been wild to get into this dough.[25]

Besides not sending Carranza tax revenue, Cantú declared his opposition to Villista and Constitutionalist tax raises on items that would directly impact agricultural producers in the Mexicali Valley. Opposition to constitutional Article 27 placed Cantú squarely in the camp of U.S. oil interests and made him a favorite caudillo spoiler to rally opposition against Carranza, and later Alvaro Obregón.[26] Walter Boyle, the U.S. consul dispatched to Mexicali in 1919, offered a qualitative insight into Cantú's political economy of vice tourism. Boyle acknowledged the extraordinary influence and allegiance Cantú commanded over many reputable U.S. citizens, including high-ranking military officials. He attributed this allegiance in part to the governor's debt-conversion policy, whereby gambling losses were quietly transferred into political credits. "Concessions, private understandings, special privileges, etc. . . . were handed out to Americans of supposed influence. The gambling institution of course was in this respect an agent of the Cantú Government. By many it is believed that the Cantú government even corrupted minor officials of the United States."[27] The political influence that Governor Cantú commanded over the ABW Syndicate as well as U.S. officials must not be underestimated, considering the support they gave Cantú's unsuccessful rebellion against President Alvaro Obregón in 1921. Calling the Constitution of 1917 a "tyrannical document," he characterized the movement as one of *"Mexicanos de sangre y corazón"* who rejected "seizures and despoilment as means to introduce reforms."[28] While the lucrative vice trade invited greater scrutiny from the central government after years of neglect, the money to be made in casinos, cabarets, and other sizzling nightspots drew increasing numbers of Mexican migrants who faced severe barriers of entry to a racially segregated labor market.[29]

Regulating Prostitution and Tempering Disorder

Governor Cantú understood that to maximize revenue and instill confidence in Mexico's uneasy neighbor to the north, his government must discipline and order Mexicali's booming sex and gaming trade. Beginning in 1911 as division commander of Mexicali's infantry, Cantú had personally witnessed the immigration of prostitutes and the scandals of competing political authorities vying for control over Mexicali's red-light strip on Ave. Porfirio Díaz. Cantú and Mexicali's new ayuntamiento government announced that Mexicali's red-light commerce would relocate from Porfirio Díaz to the back streets of Chinatown. The relocation of "gambling houses and dance halls" had been "predicted for some time," according to the *Calexico Chronicle*. As an editorial stated, "I don't like the things Mexicali tolerates any place, but we have a clean town here now and if they are going to have these things over there I hope they will keep them back and not plant them up right under our noses on the border."[30]

The Owl relocated its business from Ave. Porfirio Díaz to Chinatown, where a larger and more ambitious building was constructed in 1916. Architectural descriptions of Mexicali's new red-light "restricted area" evoke a defensive, confining design that reaffirmed the notion that sex commerce had to be strictly controlled. One early settler of Mexicali remembered that officials kept the prostitutes (*las filipinas*) "in a building entirely separated from the pueblo and enclosed by a high wall."[31] Judging from the following press description of the restricted zone, las filipinas may have been working at the Owl, which along with other like establishments, was to be "located within a high-fenced enclosure." Months later, a second article predicted that the "restricted district . . . will be entirely fenced in." Perhaps as telling as the order to zone Mexicali's red lights away from the conspicuous Porfirio Díaz location was the installation of a "string of lights" that led visitors from the port entrance to the "new restricted district."[32] The lighting both guided tourists to the zone of debauchery and led the way back. For tourists, the organized lighting provided a crucial security measure. And tourism objectively benefited from just these details: good roads, electrification, personal security, and spatial differentiation. (Slumming couples and private parties enjoyed booths and a special entrance to the Owl, just as there was a special entrance, bar, and casino for *gente de color.*)

The construction of Mexicali's first public secondary school, Escuela Cuauhtémoc, enhanced the differentiation of civic space. Its construction also added another compelling reason to segregate the vice business to Chinatown. Education, not debauchery, would symbolize the Cantú legacy. The relocated students and their parents would be spared a close-up of vice commerce because the school "command[ed] a general view of the main street in Mexicali." A later article reiterated the idea that "amusement resorts" were to be "isolated" away from the new school, "which will house Mexican children from all over Lower California."[33] Soon, children were transferring out of American schools in Calexico and crossing the border to attend Escuela Cuauhtémoc.[34] This constituted a major change in migratory patterns, as prostitutes now faced a de facto demobilization of sorts while quartered at the Owl. Baja California's federal school inspector emphasized the importance of setting a civic and moral example for the children. Before completion of the new school, schoolroom capacity was so limited that some students had to share space with municipal treasury officials. The inspector objected to the rather unseemly lesson in civics that the students received when prostitutes made their weekly visit to the building to pay taxes. Until the situation could be resolved, the inspector urged police to ensure that Owl *meretrices* dressed less meretriciously when in public.[35]

Regardless of whether Mexicali's Chinatown proved to be a desirable zone for the red lights, Ave. Porfirio Díaz would become a "strict business section . . . devoted entirely to mercantile establishments" and saloons providing exclusively "bar service." Indeed, an advertisement from 1922 for the Vernon, a new resort with a "modern air," exemplified the social tenor planners had in mind for Porfirio Diaz. Highlighting its location in a "quiet section" near the Cuauhtémoc preparatory school, the Vernon catered to "the best trade," a real "first-class grill making a specialty of family trade—*The Best Stock, Best Service, and Best Surroundings.*"[36]

Mexicali's regulated prostitution program added the final polish to the image of order buttressing the Cantú government's vice-tourism policy. Soon, Ensenada's ayuntamiento requested a copy of the policy to use as a model in regulating Tijuana's disorganized sex commerce.[37] In typically draconian fashion, Mexicali's regulated prostitution ordinance tracked prostitutes through a *registro de meretrices,* which contained front and profile photographs, the woman's demographic profile, and her fiscal standing with the municipal treasury. The program defined "public women" in terms of sexual relations of exchange, but Mexicali's councilmen exhibited the same policing paranoia over independent working women in Mexicali as they did elsewhere.[38]

An urban census conducted in 1918 and the Owl's concession contract both clearly illustrate how prostitution left its own particular institutional and architectural imprints. The Owl's contract stated in unequivocal terms that prostitution services would be central to its business. The fact that the sex workers lived at the brothel distinguished it from most cantina or assignation operations, a feature that owed to the social threat posed by unfettered prostitutes to civic patriarchal sensibilities. The Owl initially featured seventy-five rooms, to be expanded "if the number of prostitutes required it." Apparently demand had increased by 1918, because the Owl had expanded to 104 rooms.[39]

Historical source materials typically offer very limited information about prostitutes as individuals. Clearly, however, prostitutes at the Owl exhibited the racial and ethnic diversity to accommodate the equally varied phenotypic and national background of the Owl's clientele. Kenamore's comment that the Owl's "dance-hall girls [came] from the four quarters of the world" provides a colorful entry description.[40] The sample presented here corroborates her observation and highlights those registered prostitutes who recorded the longest labor stints at the Owl. This sample, taken from two volumes of Mexicali's registro de meretrices (1919–1922), also elucidates the demographic breakdown of prostitutes by color (race), nationality (ethnicity), and birthplace (citizenship). The subjective nature of these categories is reaffirmed through several examples that establish the descriptive variation in sociopolitical categories used to classify race, ethnicity, and nationality.

Grace Clark, who first registered in room 16 in 1919, when she was twenty-seven years old, logged the longest stint at the Owl (see figure 2). Her demographic profile reflected statistically dominant categories, ones that reaffirmed the foreign-enclave profile of Mexico's border.

Clark's color profile lists her as white (*blanca*), as was 77 percent of the sample. Like 89 percent of the 312 registered women, Clark was born in the United States; and like more than half of the *Americanas*, she came from a western state, with her birthplace of San Francisco, California, ranking the highest among cities (12 percent) and states (53 percent).[41] Mexican-born prostitutes constituted only 6 percent of the registered women sampled. They evinced a variation in color codes that undermines the notion of a singular *raza mexicana*. Of the nineteen women born in Mexico, eight were categorized *blanca*, seven *morena*, two *mulata*, one *trigueña*, and one was uncategorized. Sara Soto, characterized as *blanca*, registered with the program around the same time as Grace Clark and had the second longest labor stint (see figure 3). Like Soto, Rosario Mendoza came from Sonora which, together with Sinaloa and Baja California Sur, were the most highly represented Mexican states in the sample. Mendoza, who fell among the 6 percent of women who were classified as *morena*, spent the sixth longest stint at the Owl.[42]

Figure 2. Grace Clark, from San Francisco, California, Owl room #16. (Courtesy of Archivo Histórico del Estado, Baja California Norte)

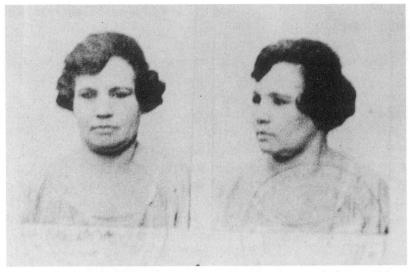

Figure 3. Sara Soto, from San Antonio de la Huerta, Sonora, Owl room #10. (Courtesy of Archivo Historico del Estado, Baja California Norte)

Comparing Mexicali's prostitution registry of 1919–1922 with the ad hoc registries generated by Mexican immigration officials in 1909–1914 generates a striking picture of how shifting and arbitrary social and political categories could be. Several prostitutes who were deported from Mexicali only to return years later to the Owl offer an opportunity to cross-check official perceptions of race, ethnicity, and nationality. One Mexican immigration inspector gave Beatriz Smith, Le Roy Fensley, and Susie Roundtree the rather distinguishing national moniker *negra-americanas* when they worked at Mexicali's second-class house of prostitution in 1912. The same immigration inspector listed Madge Evans as *norteamericana*, a noteworthy contrast to the dubious color-coded nationality given the other women. Years later at the Owl, the municipal registry listed all four as *americanas*, but each one received a slightly different color category. Smith and Roundtree, who shared Louisiana birthplaces, were now considered *mulata* and *trigueña* (or wheat-colored) like 5 percent and 2 percent of the registered women, respectively. And finally, only the Memphis-born Fensley remained *negra*, a color code reserved for 2 percent of the women registered between 1919 and 1922. When Madge Evans first registered at the Owl, she was first considered white but later received the novel description of dark hazel (*castaño obscura*). Ethel Clifford received a split *blanca-mulata* color description. Clifford was one of four Owl women to evince phenotypic ambivalence and a further reminder of how phenotyping race was subject to such slippage.

Further examination of birthplace and nationality reveals how the language of identity confounded ethnicity and citizenship. Even at thirty-nine years old, Ana Mendez was not the oldest prostitute at the Owl, but the Cape Verde native must have traveled the farthest to reach Mexicali (see figure 4).[43] Classified as *mulata*, Mendez's *portuguesa* nationality speaks of proscribed colonial identities that played off linguistic attributes. Rosena Childs was born in Los Angeles, but her nationality was Spanish. The Canadian-born Lula Fredricks listed an English nationality. May Steel, born in New York, was one of three Owl women to list Italian nationalities; the other two were born in Italy. The pattern of women who were born in the United States but were not classified as *Americanas* was most pronounced among Mexican women. Pauline Le Mar of Riverside, California, and Phoenix-born Carmen Morales and Alice Ward were among the fifteen women who were born in the United States but retained Mexican nationality. Furthermore, hyphenated nationalities were used for two women born in the historically fluid border town of El Paso: Mable Smith (Mexicana-Americana) and Babe Carrillo (Mexicana-Tejana). The political weight that nationalism and citizenship acquired with the institutionalization of the revolution reached its maximum expression in the 1930s, when Baja California's officials initiated a policy of Mexicanizing the prostitution sector by making *tolerancia* permits contingent upon proof of national citizenship.[44]

Figure 4. Ana Mendez, from Cape Verde, Owl room #15. (Courtesy of Archivo Historico del Estado, Baja California Norte)

*The Owl and Governor Cantú's Collaborative Relationship
with the United States, 1916–1920*

Coercive policies such as de facto extradition and forced repatria-
tions of socially marginal foreigners helped engender the stern face of
order worn by the Cantú administration. Not long after Cantú had risen
to power, he ordered the expulsion of twenty-six people from Mexicali.
"Mexicali Scum Dumped onto Calexico," read the *Calexico Chronicle*
headline. The Calexico paper seemed to echo Cantú's dislike for "the
chocolate-colored race, the majority of immigrants being dusky-hued
and walking with a shuffle, which indicated that most of them were
used to looking straight ahead for fear a guard would give them a demer-
it mark. The Ethiopians were not alone in their abdication of the Mexicali joy palaces, being accompanied by several Asiatics, among whom
figured Chinese and Hindus. Among the polyglot crew was found a
Hungarian who had got lost in the shuffle. The Negroes were all cooks
out of a job. They all hailed from the sunny south."[45]

Faced with the option of spending time in a Mexicali jail, the *Chronicle* observed that the majority preferred to cross the line and perform
police-supervised roadwork. The *Chronicle* delighted in the civic utility
of the forced repatriation. "Free labor was in great demand," and Calexico's authorities offered the "polyglot crew" a chance to "reflect on
past opportunities" through labor drafts. It is worth noting that only
one year previously, the Automobile Club of Southern California had
announced its support for the "institution of convict labor" to construct
roads. Subsidized labor costs from corvée and immigrant laborers were
instrumental in the arduous task of extending transportation infrastructure through the punishing desert. Indeed, Mexicali's "scum" were
helping to make automobile tourism a reality.[46]

Whether regulating Mexicali's commercial sex industry or Chinese
casinos and opium dens, Mexican officials demonstrated a policy awareness of the centrality of race or color in public perceptions. The notion
of race configured the only social demand made by Governor Cantú in
the Owl concession contract. According to the concession contract,
Owl management were to allow only "whites and the games to which
they are accustomed."[47] Alternative documents referencing the Owl
expose the limits of relying solely on documentary source material and
clearly adjust the "whites only" implication of the Owl's contract. After
all, considerations of race must not be forgotten when creating the
social ambience for slumming, one that could attract the disposable

income of an upwardly mobile tourist without blanching the déclassé fun expected from a "wide-open" Chinatown vice district. One journalist sounded the threat to racial purity posed by the Owl's clientele: Americans, Germans (*reservists*), Chinese, Japanese, Hindus, Mexicans, Indians, and a "few other breeds, unclassified, for many of the ghastly drug users who gather there have lost their racial traits."[48] The Owl's clientele occupied a segregated space, with a separate cantina, gaming parlor, and entrance for gente de color. According to the local press, the "Little Owl" was located to the rear of the building and "set aside for colored people."[49]

The shared social and political goals of U.S. governmental officials and the Cantú administration led to a collaborative relationship that both impressed and alarmed citizens from both countries.[50] The informal relationship that emerged between local law-enforcement agencies on both sides of the border, however, was not without its disappointments. Following a mutiny in Algodones instigated by the purported lynching of a Chinese worker, Governor Cantú exhibited the classic martial defense reflex by closing down the Owl and other high-profile establishments in the border region. Governor Cantú met with local officials from the Imperial Valley to discuss the removal of foreign pariahs holed up in Mexicali's underworld. Expecting some two hundred "pernicious individuals" to be deported, Calexico's sheriff expressed dismay when only thirteen Owl *cantineros* were handed over. The Los Angeles–based *Heraldo de México* vaguely claimed that the men made "undesirable" livelihoods, a thinly veiled insinuation of dealings in drugs or prostitution.[51] Threats of jail and the chain gang sounded in the press, but no labor value could be extracted from the men because officials vouched for their social status. Calexico's sheriff, Dick Applestill, stated that that he knew the bartenders personally. "All [were] men of work, and some are of good standing." They were family men "disposed of means and not given to drugs." It probably did not hurt matters when Frank "Booze" Byers, Owl principal and the letter *B* in the ABW Syndicate, arrived on the scene to arrange for their release.[52]

Although foreign workers held positions at the Owl that Mexicans coveted, vice-trade workers typically enjoyed a marginal status at best. The Owl orchestra, "famous through-out Southern California," inspired dancing and listening pleasure, but it was "composed of persons who dared not, for various reasons, cross the line to the American side."[53] Crossing the border from Mexicali was neither a privilege nor a right extended to all U.S. citizens, as Calexico's law enforcement at times welcomed the socially marginal with levees on the chain gang. Tenney, the composer of "Mexicali Rose" and bandleader at the Owl and Pablo Chee's Imperial Cabaret throughout the 1920s, reaffirms the marginal social status of Mexicali's red-light workers:

> Generally speaking, the Americans who worked in Mexicali, such as bartenders, musicians, and dealers, were not exactly acceptable socially by the elite of Calexico and the Valley. I was an obvious exception. I was a member of the Calexico Lodge of the Benevolent and Protective Order of Elks and a member of the Calexico Post of the Veterans of Foreign Wars. The latter organization included membership from a majority of Immigration and Customs officials stationed at the border.[54]

Collaborative relations between the United States and Governor Cantú were manifest in what was probably the most controversial and exaggerated crime to strike at the symbolic heart of the turn-of-the-century international audience of reformers, white slavery.[55] In a move not unrelated to wartime hysteria, U.S. Justice Agent Fred Bowden stormed the Owl in 1918 on the pretext that underage girls were working at the brothel. Bowden encouraged Mexicali authorities to "cooperate" before removing three underage prostitutes and one pimp from the Owl. "The saddest case" was sixteen-year-old Vista Key, "a rather pretty blonde girl" in the *Chronicle*'s aesthetic judgment, whose face already wore "the stamp of the scarlet sisterhood." Authorities sent Key to a correctional home in Dallas. Curiously, Mexicali's judicial authorities had already arrested Key only one month prior to Bowden's intervention, but they failed to specify the charges or conditions for her release.[56] Accused of living off his wife's prostitution earnings, Fred Bowden turned Dr. Stewart Napoleon Coleman, a World War I draft dodger, over to local police. As for Agent Bowden, little else is known of him except that he was present at the opening of the Tijuana racetrack in 1916, when he joined Charlie Chaplin and other distinguished guests of honor alongside Governor Cantú.[57]

Bowden surely violated Mexico's sovereignty, but such interventions were common on both sides of the border and may even have been consistent with the spirit of a verbal agreement negotiated in 1918 between Governor Cantú and U.S. Naval Intelligence Agent Joseph Hutchinson. The United States agreed to lift trade restrictions imposed during World War I in exchange for Cantú's willingness to monitor slackers, white slave traders, and drug commerce as well as to investigate

pro-German sympathizers. This concession was owing to the fact that
the U.S. State Department closely monitored the governor's in-laws,
especially his Austrian-born father-in-law, Paul Dato Sr. Once Cantú left
power in 1920, United States authorities arraigned Paul Dato Jr. on
charges that he violated the Mann Act by taking Billie Palermo, an
eighteen-year-old cigar concession worker in Mexicali, to Tijuana for
"immoral purposes." Meanwhile, his brother Fred was arrested for neutrality violations due to arms purchases.[58]

Scandals at the Owl seem to have been silenced fairly well, but below
the veneer of the "amusement resort" carnival excitement flowed a
more turbulent and lurid stream of human activities that were not
entirely recorded for posterity's sake. After First Sergeant Miguel Hon-
norat and Private José M. Valenzuela became embroiled in scandalous
incidents, district officials found it necessary to remind military personnel that the Owl and other like establishments were off-limits. Perhaps explaining why military tours of the border did not become a
factor until World War II, U.S. Navy personnel received a similar prohibition order for Tijuana from the upper brass.[59] Antonio Gerardo, a
norteamericano, offended somebody by taking pictures in the Owl's
salon without a permit and was fined by the local government. In a case
possibly unrelated to Gerardo's, one year later municipal authorities
charged Fred C. Espinosa with being the ringleader of a "gang of licentious men and women who trafficked in obscene pictures and literature." Espinosa sent nude photographs from Mexicali to his son in Los
Angeles.[60]

THE SOCIAL AND CULTURAL GEOGRAPHY
OF RED-LIGHT DISTRICTS

The nineteenth- and early-twentieth-century popular lexicon of
"wide-open" and "Chinatown" conditioned the U.S. cultural perception of Mexicali as a center for vice tourism. These popular idioms
derived from the largely U.S. western urban geography, but transcend
the level of mere association and perception in that they accurately refer
to the similitude of Mexicali's red-light district and the social geography it contained. While foreigners supplied much of the vice-tourism
capital in the Baja California border, the political practices and institutional developments crafted by district and municipal governments did
not develop in a vacuum. Regulated gambling, public entertainment,

and inebriants ranging from alcoholic beverages to elixirs sporting cocaine and opiates had been a part of Mexico's national and colonial history. The *barrio de tolerancia* formed Mexico's counterpart to the segregated prostitution district in the United States.[61] The rise of industrial capitalism and international market integration in the late nineteenth century created the same social dislocation and subsequent amassing of single male workers in the United States as it did in Mexico. Across Mexico's rough-and-tumble mining districts (Parral and Cananea), provincial cities, and metropolitan centers (Guadalajara, Oaxaca, and Mexico, D.F.) officials regulated and zoned vice commerce.[62] Despite this, the symbolic power of sex, gaming, and drug commerce in *gringo*-contaminated Mexicali aroused nationalist indignation, reflecting the border's cultural power and symbolism.

Mexicali as a Wide-Open City

"Wide-open" described morally permissive political economies in U.S. urban settlements in the nineteenth and twentieth centuries. In wide-open cities, authorities regulated gambling and prostitution, or at least tacitly accepted the "inevitable evil."[63] Lurid journalistic accounts often depicted foreign criminal syndicates that, in collaboration with corrupt local officials, forced morally depraved commerce on the community, prying open the city and sundering civic tissue. Conversely, "closed cities" resolutely resisted the corruption of their local political economy. The open-closed opposition emerged from the latent reservoir of sexist metaphors confounding female virginity with virtue. Not unlike the more familiar duality of dry versus wet cities, the open versus closed dichotomy recalls the culturally and politically lopsided struggles between "civilization and barbarism" across the frontier zone of the Americas. The *Calexico Chronicle* summed up this duality of civic morality in the twin-city complex. "Paris has her Versailles, El Paso her Juárez, Detroit her Windsor, Calexico her Mexicali, and now comes Yuma with Algodones."[64] Signaling the public relations efficiency of Constitutionalist diplomatic machinery, American observers expected the revolution to close the "wide-open towns which were so popular under Huerta."[65] Following the lead of the activist Treasury Department, U.S. Customs took an aggressive prohibitionist approach to foreign relations at the border, urging President Carranza "for the benefit of California" to end Mexicali's "wide-open gambling," drug traffic, and

prostitution commerce.[66] Expressing the point with the promotional
color that became characteristic of the nascent marketing industry of
the twentieth century, an advertisement for Antonio Elosua's "Typical
Mexican Fair" illustrated for vice reformers the corrupting influence of
Mexico's border towns: "We Never Close, Always Open—WIDE
OPEN. There's no place like Tijuana. Something doing 24 hours a day.
See how they do things in Mexico." The way they did things in Tijuana was not very different than in Mexicali. "For concentrated wicked-
ness and vice," Claire Kenamore wrote in 1917, Tijuana's hippodrome
and casinos could not "compare with Mexicali."[67] And while Tijuana
and its high-profile Hollywood crowd attracted greater press attention
than did Mexicali, there was something unique about the cultural geography of Baja California's new capital that set it apart on the touristic
map.[68]

Red-Light Social Geography: Chinatown-Chinesca

If a binational public began to associate the name Mexicali within
this cultural geography of fast capitalism and promiscuous commerce,
Chinatown provided another social plane onto which popular associations of urban sexual geography were grafted. The derivative language
used in H. A. Houser and F. A. Henderson's proposal for a brothel and
casino featuring *diversiones chinescas* in Mexicali suggests the power of
orientalist idioms for evoking notions of depraved leisure services. The
Distrito Federal had its Calle Dolores, and Mexico's Pacific coast nest-
ed several of its own Chinatowns, but only Mexicali seemed to use the
term *La Chinesca*. In his well-known article "Hell along the Border,"
Hal Aikman identified Asiatica as the defining ingredient that distinguished Mexicali from the standard Mexican border town. Aikman
considered the reputation that Mexican border cities had earned for
debauchery and old-world piquancy to be largely the fantastic work of
tourism literature and railroad guidebooks. The only exotic elements were
the "Spanish-speaking brown skinned inhabitants, adobe architecture,
and the occasional visitor from the interior flourishing a serape or the
high-peaked sombrero by which Mexicans may be recognized in the
movies." Mexicali was different, Aikman conceded, for the presence of
"turbaned Hindus and black-pajammaed Chinese."[69]

Popular associations of Chinatown elevated the permissive moral
economy of wide-openness to the level of racialized ethnic difference.

Segregated to the extent of a ghetto, Chinatown nevertheless had a combination of erotica and exotica that attracted a racially, ethnically, and economically diverse clientele. Most tourism literature identifies tourists as (auto)mobile, bourgeois sightseers in search of pleasure, adventure, and experiences. Historically, vice-based leisure services have not repelled tourists. The inspiration to sightsee did not exclude the morally repugnant. Conservative observers were shocked at the "morbid curiosity" that attracted people to Chinatown and the segregated vice district: "By the turn of the century, 'slumming' had become a popular form of middle-class entertainment as respectable citizens sought cheap, but socially acceptable, visual thrills."[70] By 1913, U.S. tourists began visiting opium dens and casinos in Mexicali's nascent Chinatown. Mexican officials expressed concern that the once submissive and silent Chinese community showed signs of actively soliciting this type of tourism.[71]

Chinatown and downtown entertainment districts enriched the standard menu of visceral attractions in most red-light zones in the U.S. West with an exotic cultural component. Besides the Owl, La Chinesca housed opium dens, cantinas, and restaurants that endowed Mexicali with an unrivaled tourism geography. An urban census of Mexicali's first block of real estate (*sección primera*) conducted in 1918 provides a revealing look at red-light attractions and related commercial services of La Chinesca.[72] At least half of the fourteen cantinas listed in the survey featured rooms for hospitality. Having said this, it must be pointed out that the Owl commanded a near-monopoly on prostitution services in Mexicali, with some 96 percent of the 312 municipally registered prostitutes working at the Owl between 1919 and 1922.[73] Despite the global origins of the Mexicali prostitutes, no Chinese women registered as prostitutes at the Owl or elsewhere. Rather predictably, the *Heraldo de México* editorialized about the continued clandestine sale of opiates, cocaine, and marijuana to Owl prostitutes and the Chinese.[74] Located across the street from the Owl on Ave. Juárez, Jim Man Uon's Gran Hotel Peninsular offers a clear picture of the commercially diverse yet intertwining activities that scholars have noted in Chinese settlements of Southeast Asia (the Malaysian *kangkar*) and the U.S. West. A billiards parlor, the Black Cat Cabaret, and a restaurant graced the hotel's bottom floor. Prostitutes and johns made use of the twenty-seven rooms on the top floor. Besides hospitality services, the property included the Casa Colorado, described by one U.S. customs agent as a coolie labor recruitment center, general store, and opium business.[75]

Restaurants, hotels, tailors, and other small commercial establishments functioned symbiotically with Chinatown red-light districts. Laundromats cleaned the daily cargo of soiled laundry. The few tailors and the hat maker located near the Owl may well have produced eye-catching uniforms for entertainers, dancers, and prostitutes. The Owl had its own barbershop, and several *peluquerías* offered depilatory and grooming services in the surrounding blocks. Finally, a photography studio provided portraiture and image memory making for special occasions and tourism. These commercial services were central though not exclusive to Chinatown and the red-light district.[76]

Mexicali's Chinese restaurants followed the pattern of other Chinatown culinary merchants, in that they struggled to rise above the (*tong* controlled) menu of vice attractions but endured as primary touristic attractions for both foreign and national clientele. At one corner of the Owl, Hop Lee's Chinese restaurant served hybrid Asiatica-Americana to the hungry, curious, and no doubt, inebriated. Nearby, Wing Lee, Tuy Hing, Jim Man Uon, and Spaniard Benigno Barreiro had restaurants listed in the urban census.[77] Advertisements make explicit the Chinese import and distinction. "Expert" Chinese chefs offered "American food and Chinese dishes" at both the Cosmos Café and the San Diego Café ("for those who craved something different"). A popular "*chale*," Carlos Au Lam, invited the *Heraldo de México*'s readership to the inauguration of his new casino in Mexicali. Located on the second floor of the Estrella Azul, across from the Owl, the attractions included Chinese food, live music, and gaming for "friends of the house." To this day, Mexicali's most famous Chinese restaurant was the Callejón 19.[78]

Mexicali's Chinatown became a popular tourist attraction for the first organized tours that visited the agricultural facilities of the Imperial and Mexicali Valleys, sponsored by firms such as the *Los Angeles Times* and the Southern Pacific Railroad that had economic interests in the area. At a time when wartime demand stimulated the rapid expansion of cotton acreage in the valleys, the agricultural work tour functioned as a promotional campaign to increase investor interest in the area. After touring the cotton gins, irrigation systems, and shops in the Imperial and Mexicali Valleys, the *Times* tour group feasted on a "Chinese luncheon" in Chinatown. The guests amused themselves with what the *Calexico Chronicle* obliquely characterized as "novel features."[79]

International Harvester sponsored a work tour that included a visit to Mexicali and Chinatown. "Like all visitors," the *Chronicle* observed, "they were anxious to cross into Baja California."[80]

The inassimilable Chinese experienced similarly hostile treatment in Mexico as they did in the United States. District and municipal governments taxed Asian immigrants and subjected them to an alien registry much as they did with prostitutes. The hygienist who examined sex workers for venereal disease, Dr. Ignacio Roel, was also in charge of inspecting the tunnels, basements, and interior patios of La Chinesca for disease and insalubrious conditions.[81] The Cantú administration decreed the *salón de recreo chino,* or opium den, off limits to the *raza nacional,* reserving it for the hopelessly addicted "yellow" and "black" races.[82] Federal officials in the Obregón administration advanced this logic in Mexicali, as well as in Ensenada and Tijuana, establishing the *casino chino* as a segregated space where Oriental vice could be contained and the pernicious contagion of race degeneration was prevented.[83] By the 1920s, calls for segregationist measures against the Chinese echoed from the populist ranks of labor. But Mexicali did not experience violence and anti-Chinese campaigns like the ones that rampaged across the Mexican northwest during the 1920s. Nor did the "native" merchants boycott Chinese commerce, as those in Ensenada did.[84]

Slumming and Working at the Owl

If Mexicali was "wide-open" and "Chinesca," then the Owl Café and Theatre centered this reputation. "When the [Owl's] gambling concession was open at its widest extent, more than sixty girls appeared nightly in the dance hall and among the tables. A gallery, used exclusively for 'slumming parties,' was rarely empty as tourists from the American side of the line were always present."[85] This *Los Angeles Times* passage from 1919 speaks to the Owl's two most publicized attractions, gambling and prostitution. It also plainly illuminates the cross-class digressive behavior of "slumming." An advertisement for Mexicali's nightlife from 1922 reaffirms the voyeuristic potential and centrality of digressive behavior: "The Owl is of special interest to those who desire to go slumming. A private entrance for private parties is afforded and booths are arranged along the side of the dance floor, which give seclusion to those who merely wish to look in." According to this advertisement, the Owl was the "oldest and most famous resort on the other side of the line," and a visit there implied crossing to the "other side," a symbolic but no less real alteration in social mores and role inversion.[86]

Shrewd promotional strategies framed the Owl alongside the popular "wide-open" vice district of San Francisco. Six years earlier, Harry Carr had also placed the Owl at the center of Mexicali's "red-hot red-light district" and compared it to San Francisco's "dives that flourished on the Barbary Coast." But Carr could reassure his reading public that the "old Gold field days" made Mexicali appear tame by comparison. "Your life is safe in Mexicali at any time of the day or night."[87] This type of promotion in local print media was simply unheard of during the period when Mexicali was absolutely too "wild and uncut" for delicate tastes. As vice-based leisure services became increasingly prohibited, nostalgia and curiosity drove sightseers to visit the Owl and other "famous resorts" on the U.S.–Mexico border. Following the promotional tip that *No Trip to Mexicali Is Complete Without Visiting This Famous Resort*, let us descend into the Owl's smoky, jazzy, and gas-lit interior.[88]

One article described the Owl as a "handsome building," and the property spread out over an entire block. A different description emerges from the oral history of Jack Tenney. Tenney described the Owl as "a large, rambling building on a back street in Mexicali." Considering the moral activism in California, it was no coincidence that Tenney had worked at a dance hall and casino named the Owl in the Nevada mining town of Ely before setting foot in Mexicali. "It was a rough, unattractive place, reminiscent of many such places I had seen in Nevada." The "profuse display of large potted imitation palms" not only made it "culturally distinctive," but the contrived interior designs were "an obscure preview of what would happen one day in Las Vegas."[89] Commercialized leisure services and rapid economic growth formed the proximate linkage between the mining center of Ely—the workers' camp that was Las Vegas in the 1920s—and the agricultural region of the Imperial and Mexicali Valleys.

The superlative promotional voices boosting Mexicali's Owl also resembled the later advertisers for the casinos and resorts of Las Vegas. It was commonplace to claim the Owl casino as "the largest gambling house on the American continent."[90] Indeed, gamers could choose from six roulette and faro wheels, keno and monte tables, and thirty-five card tables for poker. Legendary fortunes made were matched by tales of even larger losses in the same evening. Ten bartenders served alcoholic drinks to the Prohibition-afflicted at the "longest [bar] in the world"—a title also claimed by Tijuana's Ballena Azul.[91] Free silent movies and "the best vaudeville acts" established the Owl's location in popular culture.

Jazz music provided the Owl and Mexicali's Chinatown with the essential sonic sizzle to animate dance and Eros. Mapping jazz and its transcultural musical exchange forces us to look to the Mexican border, where jazz poured forth from dance halls and cabarets in the post–WWI era. Tenney led a so-called Dixie combination at the Owl and later at the ABW Club. Reflecting popular notions of jazz and aesthetics, Tenney characterized the music as more "raucous rhythms than musical excellence."[92] Jonnie Beauvais "[had] them all swinging to fast music at the ABW Club," where Miss Alva Smith, "that red-headed star who makes it a stack up proper" and "her beauty chorus of three Oklahoma queens, Babe, Mary, and Peggy," performed their "latest songs and dances."[93] The house band at Mexicali's Cosmos Café featured the Kings of Syncopation and invited its patrons to "Fun, Frolic and Dancing" with a catchy advertisement spelling the establishment's name: "Oh, you Jazz Fiends, Something doing all the time, Mexicali's finest and most refined cabaret." A smoking jazz band, judging from the heat blown from an illustrated sax player, performed at the Black Cat, "the liveliest place in Mexicali."[94]

Press renderings of prostitutes, management, and tourists at the Owl evoke popular notions of labor, leisure, and morality. The Owl had a reputation for "brilliant gaiety."[95] Suggestive of the euphoria and maniacal frenzy of pleasure seekers, gaiety describes only half of the affective equation. Hangovers, venereal disease, and fantastic gambling losses must be figured into the equation as likely consequences. Moreover, if there are consumers of alcohol, companionship, and games of chance, there must be those who produce this level of visceral experience. The *Los Angeles Times* summed up the equation in a Victorian formulation of supply and demand, casting the Owl as both "amusement place" and jail, where prostitutes lived as "inmates." Juxtaposed to the fettered "inmates," an estimated one thousand mobile tourists sought "amusement."[96] Was the "amusement" found in the thirty gaming tables "going full blast"? Or did the "amusement" come in the form of "one hundred girls in the back part of the hall" who were captivating "the attention of the crowds"? Covering the Owl fire of 1920, the *Chronicle* stoked the flames of sensation by focusing on the fleeing prostitutes. The scene in the cribs "was a wild one, with the lights out and the frightened inmates rushing madly hither and thither getting their effects together and donning street clothes."[97] The *Los Angeles Times* shared the same sexualized lens: "Two of the girls, scantily clad, were caught in great licks of flame when they attempted to get out through the back door and were slightly burned."[98]

Common opinion held that the 1920 Owl fire was an act of arson. Witnesses identified a "well-dressed Mexican and a peon" slashing the fire hoses.[99] Ironically, only a year before the fire, the ABW Syndicate had donated what would be Mexicali's first fire truck.[100] As fire raged inside, Owl manager Sid Coubern must have had the *Titanic* catastrophe in mind when he ordered the house musicians to "play on." "They stuck to their job until the last minute consistent with safety and had to race for the exits, leaving most of their instruments behind them."[101] Except for the Owl's cribs (brothel annex) and the section for non-white patrons, the entire Owl building was destroyed, including the barbershop and Hop Lee's restaurant. The fire broke out in the musicians' room, where it was discovered by a "celestial." The press foregrounded the orientalist optic to configure the humor from predictable phonetic material. Crowds understood "fight," but the Chinese man had really shouted, "fire."[102]

The Owl flew high at top speed and with great endurance. In 1920, the Owl witnessed one of the craziest New Year's Eve celebrations ever seen, with festivities winding down only as the sun was coming up.[103] At times the Cantú government did shut down the party, especially during times of acute political crisis. Thus, the Owl acted as a political barometer for local and national events. When the Algodones mutiny shattered the political tranquility of the northern district during the 1919 harvest season, Governor Cantú wasted no time in closing the Owl and the entire red-light district. "Year in and out, until closed by order of Cantú, the doors of the establishment were never shut," claimed the *Los Angeles Times*. Management even crafted the Owl's 24/7/365 "wide-open" access into a slogan: "the house was never closed and advertised, 'both night and day, across the way, you will never find closed, the Owl Café.' " Anti-Chinese sentiment fueled the Algodones mutiny, but not surprisingly the *Los Angeles Times* suppressed mention of the Chinese labor issue. Instead, the paper attributed the Owl closure to a groundswell of nationalism among Mexican gaming interests whose cry of "Mexico for Mexicans" punctuated their protest of the Owl's exclusive concession for gaming. The *Times* article advanced spurious claims about Mexican cultural and racial affinity for gaming. "Gambling in Mexico is a national pastime and the love of gambling is inherent in all Mexicans." Alcoholic excess, also apparently "inherent," triggered insubordination, and Governor Cantú decided to close "every saloon and resort in Mexicali to prevent Mexicans from obtaining liquor." Cantú made this decision on the "premise that a Mexican under the influence of liquor is a good fighter, but rather uncertain as to whom he owes allegiance."[104] When the Sonoran revolution forced Cantú's ouster and flight to Los Angeles on August 20, 1920, the interim government of Adolfo de la Huerta closed the Owl. The astonished Chinese patrons "couldn't believe their ears." Indeed, as if horses caught in a fire, they sensed that danger lurked close by and "stampeded wildly through all the wide doorways and ran for the Chinese quarter."[105]

The Owl after the Agua Prieta Revolt, 1920–1925

Economic recovery, state construction, and nation building constituted the primary goals of the Sonoran Constitutionalists. In the spring and summer of 1920, the Kingdom of Cantú remained an elusive yet attractive booty. The Sonoran clique made a few vain attempts to extend to Governor Cantú an olive branch, but not even his old friend Vito Alessio Robles could reconcile their differences.[106] In Los Angeles awaiting orders for the Constitutionalist invasion of Baja California in 1920, and quite possibly entertaining illusions of personal political power, Rafael Conrado Silver wrote Obregón of the "hellish underworld" that had become Baja California. The din of roisterers could be heard from the port of Ensenada to Mexicali: the whirring of the roulette wheels, the bridle jangle of thoroughbred racing, and hoarse cries of drunks rolling on the floor with bottle in hand shouting "vivas" for Governor Cantú.[107]

The federally mandated closure of the Owl in September 1920 freed the prostitutes from their "house arrest." Not surprisingly, Mexican and U.S. officials parroted the imperative for strict surveillance and control over prostitutes. Calexico's city marshal returned prematurely from a San Diego court appearance to ensure that the Owl women would "leave town" in an orderly fashion. The *Calexico Chronicle*'s take on the scene was a curious mixture of panic and amusement. "Women habitues" had been "turned loose on the town and the hotels . . . literally spread all over the place."[108] The freely associative sex workers subverted the social tranquility of civic space. Conrado Silver traveled from Los Angeles to Mexicali, where police led him on a vice tour of Chinatown. Despite his condemnation of Cantú's political economy as "reactionary depravity," Silver expressed a predictably regulationist position toward prostitution. Prostitutes would be "segregate[ed]," and he expected that a new Owl would reopen with "several women placed under strict police supervision."[109]

While the Sonorans reaffirmed state authority over property relations and the power of the Church, the vice-tourism economy invited largely discursive and symbolic attention. The Owl provides an illustrative case in point of how the Sonoran dynasty—known to be against such licensed vice concessions—deferred ideological concerns to the economic imperatives posed by reconstruction, slumping commodity prices and recession (1921–1923), mounting foreign debt, and the de la Huerta revolt of 1923. "Gradually the conviction has grown that the end of the big attractions at Mexicali and Tia Juana is close at hand and the Mexican cities over the border will have to depend on other attractions than those for their influx of visitors."[110] Whereas other casinos and cabarets in the border reopened shortly, the Owl remained closed while the ABW Syndicate negotiated with the Sonorans. Reportedly the ABW Syndicate offered "fabulous and unbelievable sums" of money to the central government for the right to continue the Owl operation. Apparently, it was an "open secret that the Mexican Government need[ed] the money," but de la Huerta refused the money, at least for the time being.[111] The Sonorans disliked the ABW Syndicate, if for no other reason than Carl Withington's active support of the unsuccessful Cantú rebellion of 1921. And while Article 27 of the Constitution of 1917 generated the primary source of this opposition to *constitucionalismo*, the ABW Syndicate reflected the gaming sector's resentment of Obregón's *programa moralizador*. As a Tijuana concessionaire exclaimed, they preferred that "business [be] shot to pieces by Cantú than wrecked by the Obregón laws."[112]

The Owl reopened after the federal closure and soon regained its dominance in prostitution and gaming until a second fire devastated the building in 1922. President Obregón received petitions from fifty-two people seeking to prevent the reconstruction of this "frightful and deplorable center of vice."[113] Representative of this epistolary protest, George Jayne's petition informed Obregón that if he failed to stop the "moral and physical ruin the Owl wreaked on young lives," there would be an "awful curse to both countries . . . [that] will bring the judgement of God upon us."[114] José Inocente Lugo, Baja California's third governor in two years, tried to allay Obregón's fears and assure him that these evangelical protestors were entirely mistaken about the new Owl. In his argument, Governor Lugo articulated a much-overlooked distinction between legal and illegal gaming. Lugo conceded that the Owl had been every bit the center of scandalous passions and vice during the Cantú period. The new Owl, which probably was renamed the ABW Club to dissociate it from its tainted past, featured only games permitted by law. This legalistic distinction guaranteed that morality and order would characterize the new casino's operations. No longer the rapacious and crooked casino, the Owl would now prevent disorder and scandal through legal gaming. He made no mention of the fact that the Owl continued commercial sex transactions in its crib operations.[115]

Legal gambling, private social clubs, and Chinese casinos became buzzwords for officials and promoters seeking to restore an element of legitimacy to the high-roller hospitality sector of the 1920s. The legitimacy itself hinged on the expectation that Mexico's working class and public at large would be protected from the casino complex and the "speculative capitalism" it fostered. One editorial from Mexicali's labor press denounced the reopening of the Casa de Lenocionio in 1923, arguing that the $40,000 in monthly tax revenue the ABW Syndicate agreed to pay the local government merely recycled the millions of dollars that management extracted from the "sweat of workers and other social clases."[116] The general tenor of vice-tourism policies witnessed during the Rodríguez governorship suggests that continuity rather than change characterized the regime. That the Owl weathered the moralizing storm brought on by the Sonoran clique in the 1920s irresistibly leads to the conclusion that things changed little. However, this seamless picture of regime transition belies the fact that organized labor, a relatively new political actor in the Baja California border zone, contested the liberty and privilege given to foreign capital.[117]

The ABW casinos in Tijuana, Mexicali, Algodones, and Tampico avoided permanent closure because of the powerful connections they had forged in the Obregón and Calles administrations. On the eve of the de la Huerta revolt in 1923, the ABW's Carl Withington donated some $80,000 dollars to General Rodríguez in exchange for a provisional extension of the syndicate's gambling permits. Observers noted that the provision had expired long after the rebellion, yet the ABW casinos continued to absorb the disposable income of flappers and Hollywood stars. Juan R. Platt and Francisco Javier Gaxiola lent their services in securing the good graces of Obregón and Calles. Platt had negotiated the "loan" between Withington, Governor Rodríguez, and the Obregón administration in 1923, and was guest of honor at an ABW Club banquet in 1929. Gaxiola served as a lawyer, along with Edmundo Guajardo, who later became vice president of the ABW Club. The changing of the guard could be seen in 1924 when the Owl reformulated its constitution and changed its *razón social* to the ABW Club. Carl Withington died a year later, leaving Marvin Allen and Frank Byers to control operations and marking the end of the ABW Syndicate's reign over Tijuana and Mexicali.[118]

Withington had been the negotiating cornerstone of the ABW Syndicate, but Wirt Bowman turned out to be a great replacement. Upon Withington's death, Bowman was quick to reject his press coronation as the new "King of the Border." With investors such as Rodríguez, Calles, Platt, and Gaxiola, his control over Tijuana's Foreign Club and Agua Caliente resort enjoyed unrivaled protection. Bowman was a natural fit because of his close business relations in Nogales and Guaymas, and family ties with Obregón and the Sonoran clique.[119]

Governor Rodríguez took cues from popular demands for employment and the groundswell of nationalism that characterized much of the 1920s. He decreed that all businesses employ at least 50 percent Mexican nationals. However, Mexico's enterprising generals strategically harnessed nationalism and wisely appropriated working-class mobilization. Rodíguez and his protector, President Calles, directly benefited from Mexicanization, as they acquired controlling shares in the ABW Syndicate's premier casinos following direct actions in Tijuana. In investing in Tijuana's Agua Caliente Resort, Rodríguez and Calles were merely following the example of Governor Cantú. Likewise, President Miguel Alemán became an investor in the nationalized Agua Caliente *hipódromo* in the 1940s. Lázaro Cárdenas understood the economic and political power that the border casinos produced for Calles and his addicts. And considering its austere social demeanor, it was no surprise that Constitutionalism reached its denouement with the closure of the casinos at the ABW Club and expropriation of the Agua Caliente Spa and Resort in 1936.[120] ✤

Notes

I wish to thank my wife, Lucía Avilés Schantz, for photographic reproduction help and for her assistance with the photo layouts. The pictures of the prostitutes are from the Archivo Historico del Estado, Baja California Norte, Fondo, Gobierno del Distrito, Sección: Ayuntamiento, *Registro de Mertrices,* *1919–1922.* The photo of the Owl is located in the Archivo Historico del Estado, Baja California Norte, Fondo, Gobierno del Distrito, Sección: Fototeca. An extensive bibliography on this topic can be found in my doctoral dissertation, "The Mexicali Rose and Tijuana Brass: Vice Tours of the U.S.–Mexico Border, 1910–1965" (University of California at Los Angeles, 2001).

1. In the unpublished manuscript "Reinventing the Border: From the Southwest Genre to Chicano Cultural Studies," Hector Calderón perceptively notes that at the turn of the century, M. L. Holt coined the names of the twin cities Calexico and Mexicali as a reflection of their economic interpenetration. For a refined discussion of regions, see Eric Van Young, ed., *Mexico's Regions:* *Comparative History and Development* (San Diego: UCSD Center for U.S.- Mexican Studies, 1994). The introduction offers a useful critical assessment of theories and a bibliography on regions, regionality, and regionalism. The best discussion of regional concepts for the border is Ellwyn R. Stoddard, "Frontiers, Borders, and Border Segmentation: Toward a Conceptual Clarification," *Journal of Border Studies* 6, no. 1 (Spring 1991): 1–21. Also see Don Coerver and Linda B. Hall, *Revolution on the Border: The United States and Mexico* (Albuquerque: University of New Mexico Press, 1988); Paul Ganster and Alan Sweedler, "The United States–Mexican Border Region: Security and Interdependence," in *United States-Mexico Border Statistics since 1900,* ed. David Lorey (Los Angeles: UCLA Latin American Publications), 419–41; Oscar Martínez, *Border Boom Town: Ciudad Juárez since 1848* (Austin: University of Texas Press, 1975), 6, 7, 31, and *Troublesome Border* (Tucson: University of Arizona Press, 1988); Ellwyn R. Stoddard, "Border Studies as an Emergent Field of Scientific Inquiry: Scholarly Contributions of U.S.–Mexico Borderlands Studies," *Journal of Borderland Studies* 1 (Spring 1986): 1–33. Daniel D. Arreola and James R. Curtis offer an excellent study of border geography in *The Mexican Border Cities: Landscape Anatomy and Place Personality* (Tucson: University of Arizona Press, 1993), 21, 22.

2. Quotation from Archivo Fernando Torreblanca (hereafter AFT); fondo 11, serie 030400, gaveta 17, exp. C-7 and E-03/104, inventario 2120, Calles, P. E. Leg. 1/2 and 2/2, fojas 1–71/138, 1920, México D.F.; Hermosillo and Nogales, Sonora; Chihuahua, Chihuahua; Culiacán y Mazatlán, Sinaloa; and Torreón, Coahuila. Correspondencia entre el Gral. P. E. Calles, Srio. de Guerra y Marina y el Gral. A. Obregón. An eclectic body of musical references to Mexicali may be witnessed in Jack Tenney's waltz "The Mexicali Rose (Mexicali Rosa)"; Frances Dailey's "Mexicali Moon" (1961); Horace Silver's "Señor

Blues"; and the Grateful Dead's "Mexicali Blues." On tourism see Dean Mac-Cannel, *The Tourist: A New Theory of the Leisure Class* (New York: Schlocken Books, 1989), 40–44. For detailed review and analysis of MacCannel's theoretical framework, see Georges Van den Abeele, "Sightseers: The Tourist as Theorist," *Diacritics* 10 (Winter 1980): 2–14. Arreola and Curtis offer similar observations and provide a sound discussion for examining ideas of touristic notoriety and the distorted cultural perceptions of authenticity; see *Mexican Border Cities*, pp. 79, 84, 90–96.

3. Ivan Light gives an example of how anti-Chinese campaigns increased the interest of middle- and upper-class whites in "From Vice District to Tourist Attraction: The Moral Career of American Chinatowns, 1880–1940," *Pacific Historical Review* 43 (1973): 367–94. The standard work on the Progressive Era mentality remains Richard Hofstadter, *The Age of Reform: From Bryan to FDR* (New York: Alfred Knopf, 1959). For border-area studies, see Vincent C. de Baca, "Moral Renovation of the Californias: Tijuana's Political and Economic Role in American-Mexican Relations, 1920–1935" (Ph.D. diss., University of California, San Diego, 1991), 70–109; and Kendel Croston, "Women's Activities During the Prohibition Era Along the U.S.-Mexico Border," *Journal of Borderlands Studies* 8, no. 1: 9–111.

4. The black legend refers to the myopic history depicting Spanish colonialism in the Americas as exceedingly brutal and cruel, which was produced by English, Dutch, and sometimes French artists and historians. On Rodríguez, see Gobierno del Distrito Norte de la Baja California, *Memoria administrativa, 1924–1927* (Mexicali: Gobierno del Distrito Norte, 1928), 23, 33, 34; and Carlos Martínez Assad et al., *Revolucionarios fueron todos* (México: SEP/80, Fondo de Cultura Económica, 1982), 324–35. A distilled discussion of the Constitutionalists may be found in Alan Knight, *The Mexican Revolution*, vol. 2., *Counter-Revolution and Reconstruction* (Lincoln: University of Nebraska Press, 1986), pp. 494–516. The argument about Progressivism and Constitutionalism is drawn out more fully in Knight, *U.S.-Mexico Relations, 1910–1940* (La Jolla: Center for U.S.-Mexican Studies, University of California, San Diego, 1987).

5. A succinct description of moral reform in California and its push effects on the saloon milieu is contained in Edwin Grant to Secretary of State Charles [Evans] Hughes, October 14, 1924, Records of the Department of State, Internal Affairs of Mexico (hereafter cited as RDS-IAM), 812.40622. Tourists began visiting Mexican border cities before national prohibition in 1919 due in part to the fact that more than 23 percent of the United States was dry before 1900. See Martínez, *Border Boom Town*, 6, 7, 31.

6. Mexicali figured in the Municipality of Ensenada de Todos Santos until 1915. The municipal area had a population of 7,583 (4,327 males; 3,256 females). *Censo: División territorial del territorio de la Baja California* (México: Imprenta de la Secretaría de Fomento, 1905), 8. Mexicali proper and its municipal area (formalized in 1915) evinced rapid growth between 1900 and 1920. Population grew from 462 males and 1,417 females in 1910 to 6,782 males and 14,599 females in 1921; David Lorey, ed., *United States–Mexico Border Statistics since 1900* (Los Angeles: UCLA Latin American Center Publications,

1990), 11; see also Jerry Ladman, *The Development of the Mexicali Economy* (Tempe: Bureau of Business and Economic Research, Arizona State University, 1975). Edna Aidé Grijalva Larrañaga, "Colorado River Land Company," in *Panorama histórico de Baja California,* ed. David Piñera Ramírez (Tijuana: Litográfica Limón, 1983), 350–61.

Research on class and gender has produced recent advances in our understanding of commercialized sex and regulatory practices across the Americas. See, e.g., William French, "Prostitutes and Guardian Angels: Women, Work, and the Family in Porfirian Mexico,*" Hispanic American Historical Review* 72, no. 4 (1992); Andrew Grant Wood, "Viva La Revolución Social! Postrevolutionary Tenant Protest and State Housing Reform in Veracruz, Mexico," in *Cities of Hope: People, Protests, and Progress in Urbanizing Latin America, 1870–1930,* ed. Ronn Pineo and James A. Baer, 88–128 (Boulder: Westview Press, 1998); Ivan Light, "From Vice District to Tourist Attraction"; Lucie Cheng Hirata, "Chinese Immigrant Women in Nineteenth-Century California," in *Women of America: A History,* ed. Carol Ruth Berkin and Mary Beth Norton (Boston: Houghton Mifflin, 1979); Ruth Rosen, *The Lost Sisterhood: Prostitution in America, 1900–1918* (Baltimore: Johns Hopkins University Press, 1982), 4–18; Jeffrey Weeks, *Sex, Politics, and Society: The Regulation of Sexuality Since 1800* (New York: Longman, 1981), 61–81.

Quotation from *Los Angeles Times,* "MEXICAN MONTE CARLO SHUT UP. The Owl, Internationally Famous, Closes Its Doors. Political Agitation Forces the Governor to Act. Mexicali Resort Had History of Brilliant Gaiety," September 27, 1919.

7. Andrew Wood, "Writing Transnationalism: Recent Publications on the U.S.–Mexico Borderlands," *Latin American Research Review* 35 (Fall 2000); Kerwin Klein, "Frontier Products: Tourism, Consumerism, and the Southwestern Public Lands, 1890–1990," *Pacific Historical Review* 62, no. 1 (February 1993): 39–71; Jack D. Forbes, "Frontiers in American History," *Journal of the American West* 1 (July 1962): 62–73.

States covet border relations and typically provoke center-periphery antagonisms because of their obsession with boundary maintenance. Foreign enclaves and company towns provoke similar nationalist indignation. See Stoddard, "Frontiers, Borders, and Border Segmentation"; Knight, *Mexican Revolution,* 1:144; Knight, "Peasant and Caudillo in Revolutionary Mexico, 1910–1917," in *Peasant and Caudillo in the Mexican Revolution,* ed. D. A. Brading (Cambridge: Cambridge University Press, 1980), 19, 20; "Revolutionary Project, Recalcitrant People: Mexico, 1910–1940," in *The Revolutionary Process in Mexico: Essays on Political and Social Change, 1880–1940,* ed. Jaime E. Rodríguez O. (Los Angeles: UCLA Latin American Center Publications, 1990), 228, 236, 237; Mark Wasserman, "Provinces of the Revolution," in *Provinces of the Revolution: Essays on Regional Mexican History 1910–1929,* ed. Mark Wasserman and Thomas Benjamin (Albuquerque: University of New Mexico Press, 1990), 1–14.

8. John Price argues that the ABW relocated to the border after being forced out of Bakersfield in *Tijuana: Urbanization in a Border Culture* (Notre Dame: University of Notre Dame Press, 1973), 51. A photograph from 1914

shows the first Owl located on Avenida Porfirio Díaz. Archivo Histórico del Estado de Baja California (hereafter cited as AHE), fondo *fototeca*. Controversy plagued the public administration of Mexicali's vice tourism from the Porfiriato until the end of Huertista rule.

9. IIH, UABC-UNAM 1909.41 [40.41]; AGN, fondo Gobernación, exp. 10, 1909–1910, Baja California Distrito Norte, "Denuncias e informes de vecinos y autoridades sobre la existencia de cantinas y burdeles en Mexicali, Baja California." "Varios vecinos de Mexicali manifiestan que el expresado lugar es un centro de depravación y vicio, 30 de agosto 1909, Mexicali"; Colorado River Land Company, Anderson's Portfolio no. 37, Anderson to Chandler, September 1909; Sherman Library, general archives, box 287, Bowker to Chandler, September 6, 1909, cited in Dorothy Kerig, "Yankee Enclave: The Colorado River Land Company and Mexican Agrarian Reform in Baja California, 1902–1944" (Ph.D. diss., University of California at Irvine, 1988), 119–22. For a later source, see IIH, UNAM-UABC 1914. 14 [8.4]; AGN, ramo Gobernación, fondo Período Revolucionario, caja 116, exp. 28, "Negativa a la propuesta de Francisco Vázquez, Jefe Político de la Baja Calif., de suprimir la planta de empleados de inmigración de Mexicali." AHE, fondo Gobierno del Distrito Norte; sección Hacienda del Distrito; serie Tesorería General; exp. s/n, "Catastro" 1917–1918, Lote #9, Celso Vega #111, 113. El Hotel Emporio: *Construcción de ladrillo, adobe, y madera con 2 salones y 9 cuartos.*

For information on Celso Vega's rather unspectacular career, see Francoise-Xavier Guerra, *México: del antiguo régimen a la revolución*, 2 vols. (Mexico City: Fondo de Cultura Económica, 1988), 451. For historiography of the social and political standing of the Porfirian jefe político, see Paul Vanderwood, "Explaining the Mexican Revolution," in *The Revolutionary Process in Mexico*, 107–10, 112; Knight, *The Mexican Revolution*, 1:15–30; Guerra, *México*, 1:124. For accounts of corruption and opposition to mayors and other local executives of law and order, see, e.g., Rosen, *Lost Sisterhood*, 14–37; James A. Sandos, "Prostitution and Drugs: The United States Army on the Mexican-American Border, 1916–1917," *Pacific Historical Review* (November 1980): 629, 631.

10. IIH; UABC-UNAM 1909.41 [40.41]; "Denuncias e informes." Sierra's concern was not without some degree of foundation considering the chilling of bilateral relations following Díaz's attempt to favor European over U.S. capital, and especially the persistence of annexationist sentiment in the United States Congress. See Eugene Keith Chamberlin, "The Japanese Scare at Magdalena Bay," *Pacific Historical Review* 24 (November 1955): 345–59; Michael C. Meyer, "Albert Bacon Fall's Mexican Papers: A Preliminary Investigation," *New Mexico Historical Review* (April 1965): 165–74; Joseph Werne, "Esteban Cantú y la soberanía Mexicana en Baja California," *Historia Mexicana* 1 (July–September 1980): 1–30; "WAR TO THE KNIFE," *Calexico Chronicle*, August 5, 1909.

11. *Calexico Chronicle*, September 30, 1909, June 3, 1909.

12. Within the Progressive Movement, the eugenics movement strongly influenced medical and legal opinions about the impossibility of redemption of certain racial and social groups. David Starr Jordan, a leading eugenicist and

anti-imperialist, showed keen interest in sealing the U.S.–Mexico border to prevent further contamination of the white American body politic. See Alexandra Minna Stern, "Buildings, Boundaries, and Blood: Medicalization and Nation Building on the U.S.–Mexico Border, 1910–1930," *HAHR* 79, no. 1 (1999): 41–81. Quotations from *Calexico Chronicle*, June 3, 1909, and November 21, 1909.

13. *Calexico Chronicle*, September 21, 1909.

14. *Calexico Chronicle*, May 21, 1910.

15. "High-Priced Lid on at Mexicali," *Los Angeles Times*, January 2, 1915.

16. The Cantú government made its intentions clear in the case of regulated opium. In discussing a tax increase on the opium den (*salón de recreo chino*), the district government emphasized the need to discourage national working classes from following the same "hopeless path to addiction" that mired the yellow and black races. Taxes on opium dens, laboratories, and import houses rose steeply during the first two years of Cantú's administration to make the drug prohibitively expensive to the working class while maximizing tax revenues. An incipient prohibitionist state in Mexico and the United States, it must be stressed, objectively contributed to the rise in taxes. AFT, fondo Alvaro Obregón, serie 010302, inventario 57, exp. "2", "CONCESIONES" OPIO. Derechos de importación, de patente, etc., impuestos a dicha droga, foja 20, sección III, Jefe Político Provisional (Francisco Maytorena B. a las Aduanas del Distrito), 12 enero 1915, sección I, El Coronel Jefe Político Esteban Cantú, 23 de septiembre, 1915, foja 25. "Cantú Says No Export Duty on Cotton—Finances Sufficient Without Taxing of Cotton Planters. No Need to Take Such a Step, Mexicali May Have Higher Moral Tone," *Calexico Chronicle*, January 5, 1915.

17. "Need U.S. Money. Saloons Re-Open," *Calexico Chronicle*, January 9, 1915. Afterwards, Mexicali's "pleasure resorts" remained closed due to a boycott staged by the "sport concessionaires." However, local government exercised greater resolve and slowly the commercial vice establishments began to conform to the new tax schedule

18. James A. Sandos, "Northern Separatism during the Mexican Revolution," *The Americas* 41 (1984): 191–214, 209, states that the most obvious source of Cantú's income was the Tecolote or Owl. Sandos's limited documents do not allow him to see the full quantitative picture as to prostitution, gaming, and drug revenues.

19. Werne, "Cantú y la soberanía mexicana"; Sandos, "Northern Separatism."

20. Harry Carr, "The Kingdom of Cantú: Why Lower California Is an Oasis of Perfect Peace in Bloody Mexico," *Sunset* 37, no. 3 (April 1917): 66–67. Two sets of quantitative data on tax revenues exist: external sources from consular and customs correspondence; and internal sources, such as tax schedules and regulatory decrees. Werne, "Cantú y la soberanía mexicana"; and Sandos, "Northern Separatism," employ external sources. Linda Hall, "El liderazgo en la frontera," *Boletín* 21 (Fidecomiso Archivos: Plutarco Elías Calles y Fernando Torreblanca): 1–30, uses internal sources.

American ranchers claimed that "old Pablo Dato can invent more unheard [-of] kinds of tax on short notice than any other financial advisor alive." Dato no doubt acquired valuable commercial experience and acumen from having lived abroad in China as well as Mexico (Guaymas, Son.) Moreover, before Esteban Cantú even reached Mexicali in 1911 and married Ana Dato Félix in 1913, the "shrewd old German" shows up in notarial records (1907–1912) as translator and bondsman for individuals operating in Mexicali's red-light district; see Archivo Notarías del Estado (hereafter cited as ANE), Libro 1: 6/12/08–3/3/10, Libro 2: 3/2/10–2/38/12.

21. Edward Simpich to Secretary of State, April 16, 1917. RDS-IAM; 812.113/6580.ʹ Subject: Political Conditions in Lower California. Answering Instructions. Dollars used to pay taxes were often recorded as pesos, which at an exchange rate of 2:1 offered plenty of opportunity for embezzlement and skimming. Officials in Ensenada complained about the graft by tax collectors in Mexicali. AHE, *Periódico Oficial,* 20 de febrero, 1914, Sesión Ordinaria Ayuntamiento, 27 de mayo, 1913; diciembre 10, 1914, Sesión Ayuntamiento, 16 de noviembre, 1914. Carr "Kingdom of Cantú," 65.

22. AFT; Fondo 11; Serie 010302; Exp. 2; "Concesiones;" fojas 37, 38; inventario: 57. "Casino en Mexicali: Concesión provisional otorgada a C. Withington. Simpich estimated Owl gaming taxes as between $13,000 and $15,000 dollars in 1917; Simpich to Secretary of State, April 16, 1917. RDS-IAM; 812.113/6580. The upper figure was cited by Claire Kenamore, "The Principality of Cantú," *The Bookman* 66 (1917): 25–28; and Sandos, "Northern Separatism," 209. The *Los Angeles Times* estimated that the Owl paid $14,000 dollars in monthly gaming taxes to the district government in 1919. "MEXICAN MONTE CARLO SHUT UP," *Los Angeles Times,* September 27, 1919. Walter Boyle described district revenues as "immense." He listed $3,000,000 dollars collected from land, labor, and vice taxes in 1920. The value of the cotton crop for 1920 was $16,000,000, generating $2,000,000 from cotton export taxes. U.S. Consul Walter Boyle (Mexicali) to Secretary of State, August 25, 1920. RDS-IAM, 812.00/24495.

23. Prostitution generated an average of 25 percent ($2,600) of monthly municipal income in 1915, before declining to 4 percent ($750) in 1920 and reaching its lowest figure of 2 percent ($1,100) in 1922. Sex commerce then recovered and increased from 8 percent ($1,700) in 1924 to 14 percent ($3,500) in 1926. Tax revenue for *tolerancia,* or prostitution, collected by the Ayuntamiento of Ensenada, principally from Tijuana, constituted a trickle of total revenue. Tijuana's gaming industry, principally the hippodrome and ABW casinos (Monte Carlo, Sunset, and Tivolí) produced greater revenue than the sex industry. Gaming taxes in Mexicali averaged 8 percent ($800) of revenue in 1915, before reaching a low of 1 percent ($300) in 1920. Then gaming revenue rose precipitously in 1922 to 20 percent ($4,000) of municipal income, increasing in 1924 to 30 percent ($6,800), before resting at 12 percent ($3,000) in 1926. Alcohol barely contributed to municipal income in 1915 at 2 percent, expectedly rose in 1920 when it led in fiscal contribution among the big three (6 percent), rose to 7 percent in 1923, reaching 12 percent in 1925,

before dropping to 10 percent in 1925. AHE, fondo Gobierno del Distrito Norte, sección Gobernación, Serie Asuntos Administrativos, 1917–1926, exp. s/n, "Desconocimiento del Presidente Municipal Otto Moller por parte del Ayuntamiento de Mexicali." See Marco Antonio Samaniego López, "El desarrollo económico durante el gobierno de Abelardo L. Rodríguez, 1924–1928," in *Mexicali: una historia*, vol. 2 (Mexicali: UABC, 1991), 11, 18–26.

24. Carr, "The Kingdom of Cantú," 66.

25. Harry Carr, "Border: Mexicali Is Tingling with Rumors of War. Warm Reception Planned for First Chief's Army if It Gets There," *Los Angeles Times*, November 19, 1916.

26. "Money Tied up by Injunction. Governor Cantú Made Defendant by Carranza Agent," *Los Angeles Times*, October 24, 1915, p. 3; "CANTU PROTESTS LEVYING OF TAX. ALLEGES COTTON INDUSTRY WILL BE SERIOUSLY AFFECTED THEREBY," *Los Angeles Times*, July 25, 1915, p. 2. Active in opposition politics, Cantú conspired with Manuel Pelaez and Felicista rebels in Sonora. Cantú also met with Senator Albert B. Fall and key representatives of the oil sector (William Buckley, Harry Sinclair, and Edward Doheny) in Los Angeles and Washington, D.C., to coordinate logistics and financing for his 1921 revolt. Considering that Frank Byers had "large" oil interests in Texas, it is not surprising that the ABW Syndicate backed the rebellion, which was largely supported by oil interests. Retired Col. Ben Franklin Fly to Captain McNamee (Naval Operations Bureau, Washington, D.C.). Admiral Fullam to the Secretary of the Navy, May 29, 1918. RDS-IAM 812.00, Cantú's Detention, Miscellaneous Papers. Carl Withington financially supported the Cantú rebellion in exchange for assurances regarding the ABW's gaming operations in Tijuana, Mexicali, and Algodones. Archivo Plutarco Elías Calles (hereafter cited as APEC), gaveta 9, exp. 16, inventario 569, leg. 1, foja 24, 1922. San Diego y México, D.F. Memorandum F. W. Becker. Asunto: F. W. Becker informa de las actividades de Carl Withington y Frank Byers en Tijuana y Mexicali, durante el período de E. Cantú." "MEXICAN MONTE CARLO SHUT UP," *Los Angeles Times*, September 27, 1919.

27. U.S. Consul Walter Boyle (Mexicali) to secretary of state, August 25, 1920. NA-RDS, 812.00/24495. Joseph Werne was the first historian to bring Boyle's report to historiographic light: see "Esteban Cantú y la soberanía mexicana en Baja California"; and Evelyn Hu-DeHart, "The Chinese of Baja California Norte, 1910–1934," *PCCLAS Proceedings* 12: 9–30.

28. "Carta que dirige E. Cantú al director de *El Heraldo de México*, desmiente declaraciones que fueron atribuídas a su hermano, J. T. Cantú, relativas al movimiento revolucionario en Baja California." APEC, gaveta 11, exp. 185, inventario 812, leg. 1, foja 3, 1921–22.

29. Jack Tenney stated that he had never been paid so well as he had working at the Owl and later at Pablo Chee's Cabaret Imperial. For well-documented antagonisms resulting from the highly segregated labor market in the border region, see Jack B. Tenney, oral history transcription, UCLA, URL Special Collections (1966), 162. See C. de Baca, "Moral Renovation of the Californias"; Samaniego López, "El desarrollo económico," 18–26.

30. "To Clean Front Street of Mexicali. Order Enclosure in New Plan," *Calexico Chronicle,* April 16, 1916; "Rumor Reports Casino to Get Choicest Site," *Calexico Chronicle,* June 12, 1919; "Casino en Mexicali: Concesión provisional otorgada a C. Withington," AFT, fondo 11, serie 010302, exp. 2, "Concesiones," fojas 37, 38, inventario 57.

31. Pablo Herrera Carrillo, "Historia del Valle de Mexicali contada por sus viejos residentes, 1938," in *Mexicali: escenarios y personajes,* ed. Gabriel Trujillo Muñoz and Edgar Gómez Castellanos (Mexicali: UABC, 1987), 47–48.

32. "To Clean Front Street of Mexicali," *Calexico Chronicle;* "Mexicali Move Made Tonight. Main Street Will Now Be Converted to Thoroughfare for Business Houses," *Calexico Chronicle,* June 1, 1916.

33. David Piñera Ramírez's oral history of Dr. Francisco Dueñas Montes tells us that Cantú imported the latest in building design and materials for the secondary school. "Testimonios de personas que vivieron la época," in *Panorama histórico de Baja California,* 421–23; Rolando Modesto, *Informe sobre el Distrito Norte de la Baja California* (México: SEP, 1993), 160, positively assessed Cantú's expansion of public education; see also Carr, "The Kingdom of Cantú," 34. Quotations from "To Clean Front Street of Mexicali" and "Mexicali Move Made Tonight," *Calexico Chronicle.*

34. "Niños americanos que van a la escuelas de México. Los de Calexico pasan diariamente a recibir instrucción en Mexicali. Es quizas el único caso en que los niños de una nación reciben instrucción en las escuelas de otra," *El Heraldo de México,* March 4, 1920. This fact is supported by the oral history of Dr. Francisco Dueñas Montes. Interview conducted by Eric Schantz, May 12, 1997.

35. AHE, *Periódico Oficial,* 11 de mayo 1916, Ayuntamiento de Mexicali, sesión extraordinaria, 28 de marzo 1916.

36. "Rumor Reports Casino to Get Choicest Site," *Calexico Chronicle;* advertisement for the Vernon, *Calexico Chronicle,* May 10, 1922.

37. AHE, *Periódico Oficial,* 2 de octubre 1915, sesión ordinaria; Ayuntamiento de Mexicali, 4 de septiembre 1915.

38. Reglamento de sanidad para el Distrito Norte de la Baja California, sección 7, número 8, Ayuntamiento de Mexicali, B.C., 1915. Copy obtained from Ing. Adalberto Walter Meade and his generous staff at Centro de Investigaciones Históricas, UABC, Mexicali; "Reglamento para las casas de tolerancia de la ciudad de Mexicali, Baja California," decretado por el ayuntamiento de dicho municipalidad y aprobado por la Jefatura Política del Distrito, por oficio de 13 de septiembre 1915. Obtained from Lic. Ignacio Guajardo. Reglamento de Sanidad para el Distrito Norte de la Baja California, sección 7, número 8, Ayuntamiento de Mexicali, B.C., 1915, artículos 14 and 25. The Municipal Sanitation Police could force women who "exercised licentious acts," or who were diagnosed with venereal disease and unmarried to submit to medical examinations. Brothel madams (under the age of thirty) and maids (under the age of thirty-five) were also subject to medical inspections. Mexicali's cabildo amended the ordinance in 1916 to include performers (*artistas*) suspected of moonlighting in the sex trade. AHE, *Periódico Oficial,* 10 de julio 1916, sesión ordinaria, Ayuntamiento de Mexicali, 20 de mayo 1916.

39. AFT, fondo 11, serie 010302, exp. 2, "Concesiones," fojas 37, 38, inventario 57, Casino en Mexicali: Concesión provisional otorgada a C. Withington; AHE, fondo Gobierno del Distrito Norte, sección Hacienda del Distrito, serie Tesorería General, exp. s/n, "Catastro" 1917–1918, Manzana 9, nota sobre los lotes números 1, 2, 24, 25, 26, 27, y 28, se encuentran localizadas en la casa de juego y anexas conocidas por "El Tecolote"; "Owl Gambling House Is Destroyed by Fire Last Evening. Loss $25,000.00," *Calexico Chronicle,* February 10, 1920; "Women Are Ordered to Leave Owl," *Calexico Chronicle,* September 20, 1920; Edwin Grant to Charles [Evans] Hughes (Secretary of State), October 14, 1924. RDS-IAM, 812.40622.

40. Ivan Light, "From Vice District to Tourist Attraction," 371; Kenamore, "Principality of Cantú," 27.

41. According to the less-than-precise registration dates on Clark's profile, I calculate her total sojourn at the Owl at 741 days; the average was 98 days. Of the 277 U.S.–born women, 148 were born in the western states (in descending order of rank): California, Washington, Oregon, Texas, Utah, Arizona, Oklahoma, Nevada, and Colorado. Los Angeles (10 percent) was the second most heavily represented city within California. AHE, fondo Gobierno del Distrito Norte de Baja California, sección Ayuntamiento, Registro de Meretrices, 1919–1922.

42. Soto, who logged 557 days, came from San Antonio de la Huerta, while Mendoza was born in Alamos, Sonora. AHE, Registro de Meretrices, 1919–1922.

43. Evans worked at Ben Hodges's cantina, a first-class *casa de asignación,* offering exclusively "white" prostitutes. For color references and prostitution registry, see IIH UNAM-UABC, 1912.117, AGN, fondo Gobernación, Período Revolucionario, Oct. 31, 1912, El Subinspector de Inmigración en Mexicali de Norte, B.C. For tax rates on *casas de asignación,* see AHE, fondo Distrito del Norte, sección Ayuntamiento, serie Tesorería, exp. 31, Ensenada 18 de enero de 1913, "El Sub-Colector de Mexicali dejar de cobrar las cuotas correspondientes a bailes públicos por el mes de noviembre del ppdo." The two first-class cantinas paid a monthly tax of 150 pesos; the only second-class establishment paid 100 pesos, and the three third-class shacks paid 50 pesos.

44. Doris Jayne, 44, Wellion Thomas, 41, and Alice Pates, 40, were the oldest women registering with the municipal prostitution program. AHE, Registro de Meretrices, 1919–1922.

45. AHE, Registro de Meretrices, 1919–1922; AHE, fondo Gobierno del Territorio, 1938–1965, caja 247, Impuestos sobre Alcoholes, Ingresos Ordinarios, 852/411.9/3188 Casa de Tolerancia Graciela Adalco 852/411.9/3189 Consuelo Monreal, casa de asignación, 852/411.9/3229, Cabaret "California" Casa de Asignación. 1938.

46. "MEXICALI SCUM DUMPED ONTO CALEXICO," *Calexico Chronicle,* February 16, 1915. Cantú displayed unusual interest in the presence of African Americans in the PLM-IWW invasion of Baja California Norte, 1911. See Adalberto Walther Meade, *Coronel Esteban Cantú Jiménez* (Mexicali: Instituto de las Américas, 1993), 77.

47. "MEXICALI SCUM DUMPED ONTO CALEXICO," *Calexico Chronicle;* see the following supportive articles in the Automobile Association's

travel magazine, *Westways-Touring Topics:* "Convict Labor May Solve California's Road Problems," January 1914; "Convict Road Building Proved Economic Advantage," July 1914; "Convict Labor Lowers Highway Cost," December 1914.

48. AFT, fondo 11, serie 010302, exp. 2 "Concesiones." The text reads, *"Que el casino o salones que establezca para explotar los juegos, serán atendidos por individuos de raza blanca y con juegos que esta misma acostumbra."*

49. Kenamore, "The Principality of Cantú," 27; "Three Shot as Dash to Grab Coin Follows Gambling House Fire," *Los Angeles Times,* February 10, 1920, sec. 1, p. 1; "MEXICAN MONTE CARLO SHUT UP," *Los Angeles Times,* September 27, 1919; "Owl Gambling House Closed. Its Doors Are Tightly Locked on Order from Mexico City Last Night," *Calexico Chronicle,* September 8, 1920; "Owl Gambling House Is Destroyed by Fire," *Calexico Chronicle,* February 10, 1920.

50. For published accounts on Cantú's collaborative relationship with the U.S. government and foreign capital, see Werne, "Esteban Cantú y la soberanía mexicana"; Linda Hall, *Oil, Banks, and Politics: The United States and Postrevolutionary Mexico, 1917–1924* (Austin: University of Texas Press, 1995), 54–57.

51. "Cantú prometió deportar 200 perniciosos, pero solo entregó 13 y no eran vagos. Comprometiose con las autoridades de Calexico a 'limpiar' Mexicali," *El Heraldo de México,* November 11, 1919. The text reads, *"Una de las explicaciones del caso es la de que los hombres en cuestión eran 'cantineros' en le Tecolote, pero que vivían de manera que hacía su presencia poco deseable del lado mexicano."*

52. "MEXICAN MONTE CARLO SHUT UP," *Los Angeles Times,* September 27, 1919.

53. Ibid.

54. Tenney, oral history transcription, p. 164.

55. Much of the academic work done on the topic suggests that racial and cultural prejudice conspired to create public hysteria over the procurement and deepening commercialization of prostitution. See Donna Guy, *Sex and Danger in Buenos Aires: Prostitution and Nation in Argentina* (Lincoln: University of Nebraska, 1991), chap. 1; Rosen, *Lost Sisterhood,* chap. 7

56. "16-Year-Old Girl Taken by Officer. Young Wife of USC Graduate Rescued from Sad Life of Mexicali Also," *Calexico Chronicle,* January 8, 1918. *Periódico Oficial,* 2 de diciembre 1917, Del Juez de Primera Instancia, Oficio #281 2 del actual, acusando recibo del oficio de consignación de la detenida Vista Key.

57. "Slacker Charge Given Coleman," *Calexico Chronicle,* January 8, 1918. The photograph showing Agent Fred Bowden appeared in "Tijuana Race Track Opens with Blazing Crown of Success. 10,000 Cheering Fans Attend First Contest; Many Women Among Spectators; Ovation Given Cantú, Staff," *San Diego Union,* January 2, 1916, sports section, p. 1.

58. Joseph K Hutchinson, voluntary aide to the Director of Naval Intelligence, Washington, DC.NA-RDS, 812.00, Cantú's Detention, Miscellaneous Papers. "History of relations with Gov. Cantú of Baja California, Mexico"; José

Vasconcelos, *Memorias. Ulises Criollo. La tormenta* (México: Fondo de Cultura Económica, 1983), 864–65. Admiral Fullam to the Secretary of the Navy (Operations), May 29, 1918, RDS-IAM 812.00, Cantú's Detention, Miscellaneous Papers; "PAUL DATO CASE UP IN U.S. COURT," *Calexico Chronicle*, October 4, 1920; "Brother-in-Law of Former Governor Held as a Slaver," *Los Angeles Times*, November 2, 1920, p. 14; "Arrest Fred Dato. Man Lately Convicted for Neutrality Violation Must Now Face Accusation under Espionage Act," *Los Angeles Times*, April 2, 1918, sec. 2, p. 5; "Troops Are Being Moved Against Cantú Regime," *Los Angeles Times*, August 13, 1920; Hall, *Oil, Banks, and Politics*, 166, 167.

59. *Periódico Oficial*, 1916, Ayuntamiento de Mexicali, 20 de mayo 1916; 10 de julio 1916; Ayuntamiento de Mexicali, 20 de mayo 1916; Bascom Johnson, "What Some Communities of the West and Southwest Have Done for the Protection of Morals and Health of Soldiers and Sailors," *Social Hygiene* 4 (October 1917): 487–503; "El Vicio también evoluciona," *El Heraldo de México*, January 29, 1920.

60. On the Gerardo case, see *Periódico Oficial*, 21 de noviembre 1916, #30, Ayuntamiento de Mexicali, sesión ordinaria, 23 de Septiembre, 1916, Del Gobierno Político del Distrito; on Espinosa, see *Calexico Chronicle*, March 17, 1917.

61. William Taylor, *Drinking, Homicide, and Rebellion in Colonial Mexican Villages* (Stanford: Stanford University Press, 1979), chaps. 1 and 2; Juan Pedro Viqueira Albán, *¿Relajados o reprimidos? Diversiones públicas y vida social en la ciudad de México durante el Siglo de las Luces* (Mexico City: Fondo de Cultura Económica, 1995), chaps 1, 3, and 4; William H. Beezley, *Judas at the Jockey Club, and Other Episodes of Porfirian Mexico* (Lincoln: University of Nebraska Press, 1987); "The Porfirian Persuasion: Sport and Recreation in Modern Mexico"; Knight, *Mexican Revolution*, 1:443–44, 2:247, 250, 462–64, 501–33; Luis Astorga, *El siglo de las drogas. Usos, percepciones y personajes* (Mexico City: Espasa, 1996), 11–38. The interest in physical, institutional, and cultural space of *zonas de tolerancia* by geographers is exemplified by Daniel D. Arreola and James R. Curtis, "Zonas de Tolerancia on the Northern Mexican Border," *Geographical Review* 81: 333–46.

62. Archivo Histórico Municipal de Oaxaca, Ramo de Tolerancia, Registros de Prostitución, offers complete volumes from 1892 to 1957, a promising data series awaiting analysis; Alberto Trujillo Bretón, "La prostitución en Guadalajara durante la crisis del porfiriato, 1894–1911" (Tesis profesional para licenciatura en historia, Universidad de Guadalajara, 1994); French, "Prostitutes and Guardian Angels"; Sandos, "Prostitution and Drugs."

63. Neil Larry Shumsky, "Tacit Acceptance: Respectable Americans and Segregated Prostitution, 1870–1910," *Journal of Social History* (Summer 1986): 665–66; Rosen, *Lost Sisterhood*, 30, discusses the tendency to describe the moral latitude of cities during the progressive reform campaigns using the terms "open" or "closed." Essentially, cities that allowed prostitution, either through de jure or de facto regulation, were considered "open" or "wide-open"; cities where progressive reformers repealed or eliminated red-light districts similarly became "closed." Las Vegas, Reno, and Virginia City registered use of the term. For Tijuana, see Curtis and Arreola, *Mexican Border Cities*.

64. Klein, "Frontier Products: Tourism, Consumerism, and the Southwestern Public Lands, 1890–1990," *Pacific Historical Review* (February 1993): 39–40. Algodones, Mexicali's border-town cousin to the east, began attracting similar vice-tourism investment, including a replica of the Owl. Quotation in "YUMA WILL HAVE YOUNG MEXICALI. ALGODONES THREATENS MUCH IN WAY OF DIVERSION. YUMA IS HALF WAY DELIGHTED," *Calexico Chronicle*, January 28, 1915.

65. "Villa May Visit Baja California. Colonel Cantú Likely to Be Appointed Military Head in Troublesome Mexicali," *Calexico Chronicle*, September 1, 1914.

66. U.S. Collector of Customs (Los Angeles) to Hon. William McAdoo (Secretary of the Treasury), January 4, 1916, RDS-IAM. 812.4065/15.

67. Excerpt of advertisement from *San Diego Union*, July 7, 1916; Kenamore, "The Principality of Cantú," 27.

68. Hollywood left its mark in Mexicali too. The marriage of Rudolph Valentino to Alice Hudnut (AKA Winifred de Wolf, Natacha Nambova) at Otto Moller's house in 1922 stands out as the most celebrated early instance. The restaurant-cantina El León de Oro also attracted its own Hollywood milieu, including John Wayne, Lana Turner, Humphrey Bogart, Gary Cooper, Ava Gardner, Bing Crosby, and Liz Taylor. Gabriel Trujillo Muñoz, "Quinteto," in *Mexicali, escenarios y personajes*, 204; Natacha Rambova, *Rudy: An Intimate Portrait of Rudolph Valentino by His Wife Natacha Rambova* (London: Hutchinson and Co., 1926), 51. Francisco Rodríguez remembers Charlie Chaplin, Gloria Swanson, and Jean Harlow. Benjamín Serrano González recalled that Rita Cansino [Hayworth] worked at the ABW Syndicate's Foreign Club, then later at the Agua Caliente, where she engaged in the Tarde Mexicana, a strange spectacle where Cansino paraded on top of a burro, accompanied by women dancers. Piñera Ramírez, *Panorama Histórico de Baja California*, 454–56.

69. AFT, FAO, serie 010302, inventario 57, exp. "2," "CONCESIONES," copia certificado del contrato de concesión otorgada a los señores H. A. Houser y F. G. Henderson, para el establecimiento de un Casino o Casinos en Mexicali, B.C., fojas 39–41. The text reads, *"Además el que se necesite para la construcción de los alojamientos de los empleados y personas que concurran a distraerse a los dichos lugares, obligándonos a pagar una cuota mensual de $4,000 mil dolares y $3,000 mil dolares mensuales si llegaremos a explotar juegos, loterías y diversiones chinescas,"* 4 de octubre 1915. On the use of La Chinesca, see Carleton Beals, *Brimstone and Chili* (New York: Alfred A. Knopf, 1927), 310–15; Hu-DeHart, "Chinese of Baja California Norte"; Astorga, *Siglo de las drogas;* Vasconcelos, *Memorias;* Duncan Aikman, "Hell along the Border," *American Mercury* 5 (May 1925): 17–23.

70. Quotation from Light, "From Vice District to Tourist Attraction," 383; Shumsky, "Tacit Acceptance," 666; MacCannel, *The Tourist*, 41–52; John Jakle, *The Tourist: Travel in Twentieth-Century North America* (Lincoln: University of Nebraska Press, 1985), xi–xiii; Klein, "Frontier Products," 39; Arreola and Curtis, *Mexican Border Cities*.

71. IIH 1913.90, "La Administración de Aduanas en Mexicali informa acerca de las condiciones que prevalecen en esa población," 1913; 108 "El

General comandante Militar de la Baja California a Gobernación, 1 de agosto 1913," exp. 88/4 "Averiguaciones sobre las denuncias presentadas por Esteban Cantú, jefe de la guarnición de Mexicali, B.C., en contra Enrique Tejedor Pedrozo, subprefecto político, por permitir la explotación de vicio . . .", 1914.15 [8.5]. "Jefe Político del Distrito Norte de la C.C. propone de suprimir por inecesario los empleados Agentes de Inmigración," 10 de marzo 1914.

72. Mexicali's urban residential layout was divided into three sections. *Sección primera* was inhabited "en su mayoría por individuos de nacionalidad china" (mostly by people of the Chinese nationality), while *sección tercera* (the third section) was populated "por el elemento obrero en general" (by the general working class). *Sección segunda* was zoned for government buildings and, ostensibly, the non-Chinese and non-working-class elements. Such a deduction is borne out by the average real estate values extrapolated from the governor's report: sección primera, $6,464.89; sección segunda, $10,100.69; and sección tercera, $462. Gobierno del Distrito Norte de la Baja California, *Memoria administrativa.*

73. AHE, Registro de Meretrices, 1919–1922. Municipally registered prostitutes used the rooms offered at the Cantina Monte Carlo, Hotel and Café Paris, Cantina 5 de Mayo, Hotel Emporio, Cantina Swiss-Italiana, Cliff House Café, the Hotel Pullman, and the Gran Hotel Peninsular. AHE, "Catastro."

74. "Noticias de Mexicali," *El Heraldo de México,* December 19, 1919.

75. Carl Trocki defines the commercial center of the kangchu as having "usually a couple of rows of shop houses near a landing or dock. The shops included gambling and opium dens, a pawnbroker, a pig farm, a small temple or shrine, a couple of general provision shops, and a few residences." See Trocki, *Opium and Empire: Chinese Society in Colonial Singapore, 1800–1910* (Ithaca: Cornell University Press, 1990), 242; advertisement for the Black Cat, *Calexico Chronicle,* May 13, 1922; AHE, "Catastro" 1917–1918. Manzana 8: Ave. Juárez: Lote #13: 787.26 meters. Jim Man Won y Cía. # 70, 72 [also Azueta]. Construcción ladrillo y adobe. 2 pisos; Gran Hotel Peninsular. Planta baja: billares, cantina, restaurant. 4 salones; 5 piezas. Planta alta: 27 cuartos. Renta estimada: dls $420.00/$840 mn. Construcciones con 3 piezas. Tienda (Casa Colorada) Renta: $100dls./200 mn.

Pablo Chee and Mariano J. Uon appeared in Treasury records as representing Wing Hie in receiving 587.600 kilos of imported refined opium. They paid $58,770 pesos in importation taxes. AHE, fondo Gobierno del Distrito Norte, sección Hacienda Federal, serie Aduana Marítima, exp. Oficina Recaudora, Correspondencia Recibida (6/19/17), tesorero General del Distrito (Mexicali), Marzo 29, 1917, Oficio: #2337. Deputy Collector GS Quate to Collector of Customs (Los Angeles), RDS-IAM 812.114/Narcotics/22. January 15, 1918.

76. Shumsky, "Tacit Acceptance"; AHE, "Catastro." Manzana 8. Lot #8, #63, #65, #9, #67, #10, #69, #11, #73, #4, #90, #86–88, #84, #36–38.

77. In "From Vice District to Tourist Attraction," Light argues that Chinese restaurants constituted the vanguard of a petty-bourgeois campaign to rid Chinatown of vice and the tong wars and hoodlum delinquency it begat. The census of restaurants is in AHE, "Catastro."

78. *Calexico Chronicle,* May 13, 1922; *El Heraldo de México,* 14 de diciembre 1919; interview with Fernando (Man Gun) Lee, proprietor and grandson of the original owner of Callejón 19, Mexicali, Baja California, August 7, 1997.

79. MacCannell, *The Tourist.* 36, 58; "Imperial Valley Lands Will Give Bumper Yield," *Los Angeles Times,* March 24, 1914; Kerig, "Yankee Enclave," 128–79; Ladman, *The Development of the Mexicali Economy* (Tempe: Bureau of Business and Economic Research, Arizona State University, 1975); "Happy Crowds Seeing Valley Enjoy Selves," *Calexico Chronicle,* March 31, 1917.

80. *Calexico Chronicle,* February 18, 1919.

81. For tax decrees, see *Periódico Oficial,* 3 de febrero 1915, Ayuntamiento de Mexicali, 10 de enero 1915. Reforms in the municipal budget raised the trimestral taxes from six to twelve pesos (divided equally for public education and assistance). For hygiene inspections of the *barrio chino,* see *Periódico Oficial,* 10 de octubre 1918. Ayuntamiento de Mexicali, sesión ordinaria, 19 de abril.

82. AHE, *Periódico Oficial,* 20 de julio 1915. Ayuntamiento de Mexicali, sesión ordinaria, 12 de junio 1915. *"El 7 de julio, los señores Wing Lee and Tay Chan han obtenido el permiso para la exclusiva de juegos chinos y un Salón de Recreo."* AFT, Fondo Alvaro Obregón, serie 010302, inventario 57, exp. "2," CONCESIONES": OPIO. Derechos de importación, de patente, etc., impuestos a dicha droga. Sección I, El Coronel Jefe Político Esteban Cantú. 23 de septiembre 1915, foja 25.

83. AGN, grupo Presidentes, fondo Obregón-Calles, Gobernador del Distrito de Baja California Norte, J. I. Lugo to Sr. Presidente, 10 de febrero 1922, 13 de marzo 1922, Presidente Alvaro Obregón to Gobernador José Inocente Lugo, exp. 425-B. Lugo's report is published in *Mexicali. Una historia,* vol. 2 (Mexicali: UABC, 1991), 9; "El Informe de José Inocente Lugo al Presidente de la República, Alvaro Obregón." Also, see AGN, Presidentes Gobernador E. Ibarra to Presidente de la República, exp. 425-T, 11 de enero 1922 (re: el Casino Chino de Ensenada).

84. Samaniego López, "El impacto de la gran depresión, 1929–1933," in *Mexicali. Una historia,* 34. Despite the Asian head tax, calls for segregation, and other forms of de facto racism, Mexicali never witnessed the anti-Chinese campaigns of the north. In fact, the migration of Chinese to Mexicali after 1920 seemed to destabilize the economic relations for the established brotherhoods, leading to gun battles by rival brotherhood or tong associations at the Casino Chino in 1922 and 1924. The pioneering article by Charles C. Cumberland, "The Sonora Chinese and the Mexican Revolution," *HAHR* 40 (February 1960): 191–211, sets out the essential political and social antagonisms as they related to the revolution. However, the article wrongly gives the impression that Governor Cantú canceled the importation of Chinese laborers in 1919. In fact, Chinese tended to migrate to Baja California in increasing numbers as revolutionary violence and despoilment afflicted northern settlements between 1915 and 1920. Hu-DeHart, "Chinese of Baja California Norte." For a summary of popular Sinophobia during bouts of revolutionary violence, see Knight, *Mexican Revolution,* 1:8, 146, 152, 207–8; 2:44, 50, 148, 279, 331, 416, 462.

85. "MEXICAN MONTE CARLO SHUT UP," *Los Angeles Times.*

86. "Carnival Saturday Night," *Calexico Chronicle,* May 13, 1922. Social and cultural role inversion is discussed in the literature of leisure, carnivals, and public festivals. Many of the ideas about role inversion and the liminality of spatial boundaries come from Victor Turner, *The Ritual Process: Structure and Anti-Structure* (1969; reprint Ithaca: Cornell University Press, 1977); and Turner, *Dramas, Fields, and Metaphors: Symbolic Action in Human Society* (Ithaca: Cornell University Press, 1976).

87. "Carnival Saturday Night," *Calexico Chronicle;* Carr, "Border: Mexicali Is Tingling with Rumors of War"; Carr, "The Kingdom of Cantú," 66.

88. "Carnival Saturday Night," *Calexico Chronicle.* "Jazzy" refers intentionally to both the hybrid music that became popular following WW I and the ambience of sonic sexualization that stimulated red-light commerce; David Meltzer, ed., *Reading Jazz* (San Francisco: Mercury House, 1993), 41–70, covers the written history of the musical idiom, especially the coinage or etymological origin of jazz.

89. "MEXICAN MONTE CARLO SHUT UP," *Los Angeles Times.* Tenney, oral history transcription.

90. "MEXICAN MONTE CARLO SHUT UP," *Los Angeles Times;* Kenamore, "Principality of Cantú," also repeated assertions of "the Tecolote gambling house, proudly proclaimed the largest in the world."

91. "MEXICAN MONTE CARLO SHUT UP," *Los Angeles Times.* Acevedo Cárdenas, Piñera Ramírez, and Ortiz, "Semblanza de Tijuana," 437.

92. Jack Tenney unequivocally places jazz as a popular music form on the border; Tenney, oral history transcription. Advertisements also make the preeminence of jazz clear; see *Calexico Chronicle,* May 13, 1922. Tenney worked at the Owl from 1921 until it was destroyed by fire in 1922. Then he worked at Pablo Chee's Imperial Cabaret, where he composed "Mexicali Rose." When business dwindled during the era of early border closing, Tenney returned to Los Angeles, where he worked at Metro-Goldwyn-Mayer film studios in 1925. He then returned to the Owl, which had been rebuilt and renamed the ABW Club, although official documents in Spanish continued to call the establishment El Tecolote.

93. San Diego Historical Society (SDHS), Border Issues, *The Rounder,* "The Rounder's Page of Hammer-Tongs Events" [1927].

94. Carnival advertisements, *Calexico Chronicle,* May 10 and 13, 1922.

95. "MEXICAN MONTE CARLO SHUT UP," *Los Angeles Times.*

96. "Three Shot as Dash to Grab Coin Follows Gambling House Fire," *Los Angeles Times,* February 10, 1920, sec. 1, p. 1.

97. "Owl Gambling House Is Destroyed by Fire Last Evening," *Calexico Chronicle,* February 10, 1920.

98. "Three Shot as Dash to Grab Coin Follows Gambling House Fire," *Los Angeles Times.*

99. The Owl fire was preceded by a fire that destroyed the Teatro Mexicano. Political origins of the blaze may discerned from its proprietors: Enrique Terrazas and Eustacio Angeles, brother of General Felipe Angeles. "Un gran incendio en Mexicali a punto de destruir la ciudad. Amparito Guillot sufrió la

perdida de todo su vestuario," *El Heraldo de México,* December 18, 1919; "Fire In Mexicali," *Calexico Chronicle,* January 2, 1920; "Owl Gambling House Destroyed by Fire," *Calexico Chronicle.* Uninsured and perhaps uninsurable, the Owl was reduced in minutes to "a tangled mass of wreckage," with damages estimated at around $250,000.

100. "Mexicali Has a Fire Truck," *Calexico Chronicle,* January 7, 1919. Sources attributed the donation to Mayor Bórquez's outreach efforts. The article refers to the Owl ownership as the "ABW owners (Marvin Allen, Frank Beyer and Carl Withington)."

101. "Three Shot as Dash to Grab Coin Follows Gambling House Fire," *Los Angeles Times.*

102. "Owl Gambling House Destroyed by Fire," *Calexico Chronicle;* "Three Shot as Dash to Grab Coin Follows Gambling House Fire," *Los Angeles Times.*

103. "Gran fiesta de fin de año hubo en Mexicali," *El Heraldo de México,* January 2, 1920.

104. "MEXICAN MONTE CARLO SHUT UP," *Los Angeles Times.*

105. "Owl Gambling House Closes," *Calexico Chronicle.*

106. Sandos, "Northern Separatism," 211.

107. AFT, FAO, fondo 11, serie 030500, gaveta 31, exp. 1441, inventario 4314, Rafael Conrado Silver to General A. Obregón, 6 julio 1920. Silver to Sr. Don Adolfo de la Huerta (Presidente de la República Mexicana), 8 de julio 1920.

108. "Owl Women Ordered to Leave City," *Calexico Chronicle,* September 17, 1920.

109. "Mexicali 'Clean Up' Is Carried to Opium Dens: Drugs and Men Taken," *Calexico Chronicle,* September 22, 1920.

110. "Governor Salazar Revokes Owl Close Order," *Calexico Chronicle,* August 31, 1920; "Gambling Houses below Border Ordered Closed September 1 Is Report. The Owl Will Close," *Calexico Chronicle,* July 8, 1920.

111. *Calexico Chronicle,* "Owl Gambling House Closed. Its Doors Are Tightly Locked On Order From Mexico City Last Night," September 8, 1920.

112. APEC, gaveta 9, exp. 16, inventario 569, leg. 1, foja 24, 1922. "Memorandum F. W. Becker. Becker informa de las actividades de Carl Withington y Frank Byers en Tijuana y Mexicali, durante el período de E. Cantú. Incluye una breve lista de mexicanos sobornados para beneficio de los primeros"; Hall, *Oil, Banks, and Politics,* 54–58.

113. AGN, Grupo Presidentes: Obregón-Calles, 425-M, December 1922–January 1923. A letter from Ann Waite carried eighty signatures from the Long Beach Central Methodist Church. Dr. Charlotte J. Baker (San Diego Women's Civic Center) to President Alvaro Obregón, September 19, 1922; Anne Waite et al. to Hon. Alvaro Obregón, January 6, 1923.

114. AGN, grupo Presidentes: Obregón-Calles, 425-M, George E. Jayne (Salt Lake City) to president of Mexico, December 19, 1922. One Laguna Beach resident remarked that his interest in Mexico's "highest welfare" compelled him to protest not only as an American but "as a representative of Christ, the Saviour of the World," and to implore Obregón to prevent the Owl

from causing further "sin and ruin to the Mexican people." AGN, grupo Presidentes: Obregón-Calles, 425-M, Peter Reef (Pastor, Farmington, ME, Church) to Hon. President Alvaro Obregón, December 9, 1922.

115. AGN, Grupo Presidentes: Obregón-Calles, 425-M, J. I. Lugo to Fernando Torreblanca (secretario particular del presidente de la república), January 8, 1923. Lugo concluded by emphasizing that scores of missions and tours led by evangelical ministers had witnessed firsthand how the government's new moralizing policy had eliminated the "centers of vice" in Baja California. Edwin Grant to Hon. Charles [Evans] Hughes, secretary of state, October 14, 1924 (RDS), 812.40622.

116. "Otra vez el fatídico Tecolote," *El Regional,* May 1923. IIH: UABC-UNAM, 11 [3.51], fondo Dirección del Gobierno, serie D.22.550.197, caja 9, exp. 197. "Protesta por la reapertura de El Tecolote, garito de Mexicali, Baja California."

117. IIH UABC-UNAM 25.19. AGN, fondo Dirección General de Gobierno, serie 22.362 (301) 1, caja 24, exp. 14. José Bermejo al Srio de Gobernación, 28 de diciembre 1928. IIH UABC-UNAM 25.7. AGN, fondo Dirección General de Gobierno, serie 2.362 (2-1) 1, caja 24, exp. 1. "Solicitúd del Sindicato de Filarmónicos de Mexicali, Baja California, para que el estado unidense Dave Gussin sea expulsado del país." "Sebastian Armenta (Sindicato de Filarmónicos de Baja California, CROM) a Srio de Gobernación," June 3, 1929. IIH UABC-UNAM 2.55. AGN, fondo Departamento de Trabajo, caja 1171, exp. 9, "Denuncia de Federico Ramírez, hijo, contra el ABW Club de Mexicali, por despedido injustificado." Cayetano Pérez Ruiz (inspector federal de trabajo) al jefe, Departamento de Trabajo (Reynaldo Cervantes Torres), 5 de marzo 1927, 31 de marzo 1927. José Gascón, Federico Ramírez, y Sebastián Armenta (El Sindicato de Filarmónicos) a jefe de Departamento de Trabajo, 7 de abril 1927. IIH UABC-UNAM 25.19. AGN, fondo Dirección General de Gobierno, serie 22.362 (301) 1, caja 24. exp. 14. Informe del gobierno del distrito sobre los extranjeros Mike Miller y William Hoots, 14 de agosto 1929; "Los empleados del 'ABW Club,' " 18 de junio 1929.

118. AGN, grupo Presidentes (Obregón-Calles), exp. 425-T, Gabriel Muñoz (presidente, Comité de Trabajadores a Presidente Obregón), 4 de septiembre 1923. IIH UABC-UNAM, 5.47. AGN, fondo Dirección General de Gobierno, serie C.251.183, caja 25, exp:183, "Solicitúd de extensión del pago de impuestos federales al donativo hecho por Carl Withington al gobierno del Distrito Norte de Baja California, a cambio de un permiso temporal para explotar juegos de azar." AGN, grupo Presidentes (Obregón-Calles), exp. 425-B, President Obregón to José Torres, José García y demás firmantes (Los Angeles, California), March 24, 1924. AGN, Grupo Presidentes (Obregón-Calles), exp. 425-T–7, Governor Rodríguez to President Obregón, March 7, 1924. AFT, fondo FT, serie 010207, gaveta 40, exp. "259"/201, inventario 652. Juan R. Platt, leg. 1, foja 8. 1928, *Asunto Hipódromo.* AFT, fondo Soledad González, gaveta 82, exp. 632, inventario 560, Juan R. Platt. APEC, gaveta 61, exp. 8, inventario 4533, Juan R. Platt, foja 74, 1924–1936. Francisco Javier Gaxiola, *Memorias* (México: Editorial Porrúa, 1975), 139–47,

163–75. "El Sr. Juan R. Platt fue ofrecido con un Banquete," *La Gaceta* (Mexicali), 20 de julio 1929. On the ABW Syndicate's deal with Platt, see AGN, grupo Presidentes (Obregón-Calles), exp. 425-T–7, Governor A. L. Rodríguez to President A. Obregón, March 7, 1924. Registro Civil de la Propiedad, Mexicali #111–130, ABW Acta Constitutiva, 28 de febrero 1930. El primer testimonio de la escritura de modificaciones a la constitutiva de la Sociedad A.B. y W., pasada ante el not. Lic. Roberto Rosado Domínguez #105. Marvin Allen, con el carácter de presidente de la referida sociedad, comprobó con el testimonio de la escritura pública número 3050, 4 de marzo 1924. Notario lic. Manuel Jiménez, con el libro de Actas y Acuerdos (interprete Edmundo Guajardo). Francisco Javier Gaxiola (como apoderado de la ABW SA) en el que manifiesta que dicha sociedad se constituyó el 4 de marzo 1924.

119. "King of Border Story Refuted by Nogales Man," *Los Angeles Times,* November 19, 1925. Bowman argued that playing bridge with his wife and investing with a syndicate of San Diego businessmen did not amount to heading up a gambling ring. "Death Comes to Withington. Southland Millionaire and Sportsman Succumbs," *Los Angeles Times,* October 24, 1925; "Withington's Funds Tied Up. Property Worth $3,000,000.00 in Receiver's Hands," *Los Angeles Times,* October 14, 1925; APEC, gaveta 31, exp. 8, inventario 1970, Facultad de Medicina, fojas 102–151/202, 1933; Gral. P. E. Calles to Foreign Club, September 19, 1933; Wirt G. Bowman to Gral. P. E. Calles, September 21, 1933, gaveta 10, exp. 156, inventario 709, foja 17, 1921–1936; Wirt G. Bowman (Agua Caliente, Baja California) to General P. E. Calles. AFT, Fondo Alvaro Obregón, serie 060200, gaveta 38, exp. 34, inventario 5086, Negocios Testamentaria: Bowman, Wirt G., leg. 1, foja 46, 1930–34. Fondo 11, serie 030400, gaveta 17, exp. 88, inventario 2104, Bórquez, Flavio A., leg. 1, foja 27, 1920. Bowman apparently did Governor Rodríguez the favor of depositing earnings from gaming and prostitution revenue in his own account, but allegedly took a giant tax hit that left him in ruins. Juan Andrew Almazán, "Memorias de Juan A. Almazán," *El Universal,* January 20, 1959.

120. Marco Samaniego López, "El desarrollo económico durante el gobierno de Abelardo L. Rodríguez, 1924–1928," in *Mexicali. Una historia* 2:6. "Las épocas de Cantú y Rodríguez. Semblanza de Tijuana," in *Panorama histórico de Baja California,* 438; Martínez Assad et al., *Revolucionarios fueron todos.* Cantú acquired or was gifted 1,000 shares in the Lower California Jockey Club. Rodríguez became a principal stockholder in the Agua Caliente Casino and Spa, which took over the Lower California Jockey Club's hippodrome concession. For Calles's involvement in the Agua Caliente, see the telegram that Wirt G. Bowman sent to General Calles on January 28, 1931, APEC, gaveta 10, exp. 156, inventario 709, Bowman, Wirt G. Lugar: Nogales, Son. México D.F.; Agua Caliente, Tijuana, El Sauzal, Baja California Norte. El Paso Tex., Los Angeles, Palm City, Cal., EUA, foja 17, 1921–1936; IIH; UABC-UNAM: 4.3. AGN, Ramo Presidentes, fondo Lázaro Cárdenas, Francisco Cervantes (Unión de Empleados de Restaurantes) al sr. presidente, 5 de enero 1935, 15 de Febrero 1935. For Cárdenas' closure and expropriation of Agua Caliente Casino in Tijuana, see C. de Baca, "Moral Renovation," 163.

The "Shame Suicides" and Tijuana

VINCENT CABEZA DE BACA AND JUAN CABEZA DE BACA

Thomas M. Peteet, his wife Carrie, and their daughters (twenty-six-year-old Clyde and nineteen-year-old Audrey) presented refined and cultured airs to new acquaintances. The Peteet family claimed "the best Southern blood" from New Orleans, Louisiana. Middle-aged Mr. Peteet wore a dignified gray flannel suit on his long, lean frame and a hat on his balding head when in public. Mrs. Peteet appeared matronly, robust, and genteel. The attractive daughters studied classical music: Clyde performed on the violin and Audrey played the piano. The girls declared that their father had been a doctor in New Orleans until Carrie's and Audrey's sicknesses caused the family to seek healthier climes. It would have been improper to inquire about the nature of a lady's illness. They presented a solid image of decent, God-fearing folks.

Private detectives later discovered that, after leaving Louisiana, Thomas Peteet worked as a sales agent for a Chicago slot machine company, while his family lived in Mount Washington, Missouri. The family had also lived in Omaha, Seattle, Portland, and San Francisco. Thomas and Carrie had married, divorced, and remarried over the years. In fact, brunette Clyde was Carrie's daughter from her second marriage and, therefore, Thomas's stepdaughter. The blonde daughter, Audrey, was born after the couple's remarriage.[1]

In September 1925, the family arrived in San Diego, California, and rented a small house at 4423 Arch Street in the Hillcrest community (see figure 1). On December 9, fifty-five-year-old Thomas opened a lucrative popcorn and peanut stand in San Diego's renowned Balboa Park. His business partner, Dan Conlogue, said that "Peteet was a very honest and upright man. . . . He was a hard worker and . . . never drank until this Tijuana trip. He seemed to be quite religious and would not work Sundays. . . . He intended to take a trip into Mexico, to Ensenada, I believe."[2] That was the last conversation Conlogue had with his partner before the family's intended trip. Neighbors also believed the Peteets were every bit as respectable as they appeared. Yet the family had another side. The Peteets told neighbors about being homesick and bored in San Diego.

Figure 1. The Peteet family home in San Diego. (Courtesy of San Diego Historical Society)

On Saturday, January 30, 1926, the Peteets drove to Tijuana, Mexico, and rented a pair of modest rooms there at the San Diego Hotel, beginning a week-long, south-of-the-border vacation. Each day, Thomas crossed the border, drove twenty miles home to feed his cat, and then returned to Tijuana by late afternoon. They spent the remainder of the day eating, drinking, gambling, and carrying on in a manner unfit for polite society. Come evening, witnesses saw the family drinking excessively in shabby saloons along infamous Revolution Avenue or at the popular Agua Caliente racetrack (see figure 2).

After four days of such high life, at 4:00 P.M. on Wednesday, February 3, Thomas Peteet called a Mexican physician; Carrie had taken ill. A doctor examined her and prescribed "some morphine to quiet her nerves, which at the time were rather unstrung," as Thomas later told U.S. Immigration Officer-in-Charge Harry B. Hannah.[3] Other witnesses speculated, however, that her condition resulted from a bad hangover. While their mother remained in her hotel room, Peteet took the two daughters into various Tijuana saloons searching for cold beer and Hawaiian music.

At 8:00 P.M., Peteet and his daughters entered the Oakland Bar and drank several beers. Bar owner Luis Amador introduced them to the Tijuana police chief, who was drinking in the cantina. The chief had one dance with young Audrey; afterward, he joined them at their table. In a February 5 written deposition, Thomas Peteet claimed that he bought only one last round of drinks and "the Chief did the same." However, the daughters told Officer Hannah that Thomas invited the chief to

Figure 2. Map of modern Tijuana. From the San Diego Union.

join them for several rounds of beer. The volume of liquor may have been in question, but two things were clear: Amador offered them a "new drink," and the Peteets drank it.

According to their best recollection, sometime about 9:00 P.M., the mysterious new drink caused Thomas, Clyde, and Audrey to lose control and fall into a "drugged stupor." For his part, Mr. Peteet swore in his February 5 deposition:

> After I had taken that drink I remember nothing until I found myself in bed in the [San Diego] Hotel, it is my belief that I was drugged, my wife said I had been taken there by a man about Ten O' Clock, then my wife said she left to go and look for the girls but could not find them, as soon as it was Daylight we went again to look for the girls and I reported the matter to the Police but could get no assistance.[4]

A published newspaper account explained the sequence of events differently. The *San Diego Union* reported on February 7 that the ailing Carrie Peteet became so concerned about her missing family that she got out of bed and searched the border town for them. She found her husband lying in an alley behind the Oakland Bar. He was in a "horrible condition," and she helped him back to their hotel room. Frantic, she hired a cab to search for Clyde and Audrey in the saloons on Revolution Avenue. She went to the Hot Springs Hotel, four miles east of town, but the hotel staff refused to let her search the premises. Reluctantly, Mrs. Peteet returned to her husband's bedside and waited for word about the missing girls.

The family's official depositions set the record straight on some basic facts. Audrey, the younger daughter, recalled drinking at the Oakland Bar with the Tijuana police chief (later identified as Zenaido Llanos). She swore that Llanos, not Amador, ordered the small "new drink" that they swallowed. Hands trembling as she wrote, Audrey swore that, "After that I remember nothing until I woke up partly undressed. I know I was ravished by the Chief of Police. Then I was put in a car, and taken to room no. 6 Sandiago [*sic*] Hotel to my mother."[5] Audrey elaborated on the details to Officer Hannah, who later told local reporters that "she awoke in a strange place with the chief of police and realized that he was attacking her. She struggled against him but was so weak physically that her attempts to free herself were futile. In about two or three hours the chief put her into an automobile," and Audrey was returned to her parents' hotel between midnight and 1:00 A.M.[6] Adding to the confusion, the *San Diego Union* attributed Audrey's affidavit incorrectly to her older sister, Clyde.

In her deposition, Clyde described a similar fate that evening. She recalled the drink and remembered "Louie" (Luis Amador, the bar owner) abducting her. Louie drove her through Tijuana, covering her mouth with one hand as she screamed for help. He stopped and dragged her into a hotel room. Given her lingering stupor, Clyde wrote an awkward deposition in which she swore:

[He] then dragged me into hotel and then into a room and on to a bed, then he forced me, all the time I was calling for help. Hotel National? After Louie left he send up two men, first man I put out of room, then about 4 o'clock another man came said he was sent by Louie said I ought to have some whiskey to quiet me, after drinking, I was out, when I came to he was in the bed with me. My father came with a Policeman and found me in this room.[7]

Later, Officer Hannah told the press that Clyde verbally elaborated that the first man was Asian and that the second man, who drugged and raped her, looked American. The *San Diego Union* initially confused the facts, reporting that Mexican police returned Audrey, not

Clyde, to her parents' hotel, on February 4 at 11:00 A.M. The initial horror of the family's "lost weekend" ended with their reunion.

Before Clyde's reappearance, at 8:00 A.M. on Thursday, Thomas Peteet approached U.S. immigration officers at the border for help. Clearly, U.S. agents had no jurisdiction south of the border, and they told Peteet to return when their superior arrived. At 12:00 P.M., the family left Tijuana, crossed the border, and registered at the Derby Hotel in nearby San Ysidro. The father returned to the port of entry and spoke to Officer-in-Charge Harry Hannah for the first time. Peteet and Hannah crossed the border together at 1:00 P.M. and met with Tijuana Mayor Federico Palacio, to whom Peteet recounted the incident. They agreed on a second meeting in Hannah's office, at 2:00 P.M., so the Peteet girls could tell Mayor Palacio their stories. However, they failed to meet the Tijuana mayor, who waited two hours before returning to Mexico. At 4:30 P.M., Officer Hannah interviewed the Peteet women at their hotel room, when he collected written depositions from them.

At this point, American and Mexican officials had the victims' statements. They promised full investigations and said they hoped to bring charges forward eventually. After the trauma of being drugged, kidnapped, and raped, the Peteets were understandably impatient with the bureaucratic pace of border justice. In frustration, Thomas Peteet told investigators that he wanted to get his pistol and take personal revenge on the guilty parties. The despondent family received no legal or medical help from U.S. border officers and were left to cope with their emotional pain on their own.

That evening, at 7:30 P.M., police stopped Thomas Peteet, who was driving his family car north on old Highway 101 headed for San Diego. The police found Thomas, Carrie, and Clyde thoroughly intoxicated and seized three bottles of whiskey in the car. They deemed Audrey sober enough to take her mother and sister home to Arch Street in a taxi. But they arrested Thomas, impounded his car, and took him to the San Diego jail. After his release, on Friday morning, February 5, neighbors saw Peteet at home watering his yard.

On Saturday afternoon, February 6, Dan Conlogue went to the Peteet home, concerned that Thomas had missed so much work. Conlogue found a note in the mailbox on the porch, which read: "Please deliver these letters at once. Have the police open the house. *Beware of gas.*" He immediately rushed to the San Diego police station. Eventually, two rumpled flatfoots, George Cooley and F. W. Blacker, responded to the scene. Reluctantly, they tried the front and rear doors and peeked inside windows. The cops finally broke two windows to clear the gas before they covered their mouths and entered the Arch Street house.

Officers discovered the family on the kitchen floor, lying side-by-side upon neatly piled pillows and blankets, which reporters described as a "death couch."[8] An officer turned off the gas on the unlit stove. The mother and youngest daughter were initially supposed to be asleep, but were lifeless and deadly cold. The father's constricted face gave evidence of his painful last moments; an unfired pistol lay by his hand. The macabre serenity was disrupted only by Clyde, barely alive, frothing and unconscious. She lingered at Mercy Hospital for three and a half days before finally succumbing. The remains of the family's last meal were left on the kitchen table. Lastly, the wet, stiff carcass of their pet cat was found in a sack on the back porch. The jaded cops left the dead and barely living unattended and finished their business. They found Thomas's handwritten last will and two farewell notes, which failed to explain why the family had committed suicide. Peteet willed his possessions to Conlogue and ended the document by stipulating, "None of my kin folks are to get anything I have."[9] After the bodies were removed, the house was sealed. Neither police nor neighbors had any idea why the family took their own lives.

As the story unfolded, the American news media declared that the "innocent" Peteets were not responsible for their fate; Mexicans were to blame. The *San Diego Union* dispatched a wire service article and photos purporting to explain the Peteets' mental state:

> Forcing his wife and two daughters . . . at the point of a revolver to lie down upon the kitchen floor of their San Diego home, Thomas McConnell Peteet turned on the gas jets of the kitchen range and watched his victims slowly lose consciousness until he himself fell under the fumes. . . . The tragedy was the aftermath of a party held at Tia Juana. . . . According to reports, the girls, drugged by a drink from a man who was introduced to them as a Mexican official, were missing from their parents two days. The story told by them after their return, of being attacked, was so sordid, that it is believed the father decided to have them all die together because he could not bear the disgrace.[10]

The editors did not alert readers that the story was one of many possible scenarios. As a rule, the press needed sensational news to sell papers. In its first story, on February 11, the *Los Angeles Times* coined the phrase "shame suicides" to give a moral angle to the story. This article quoted a letter allegedly written by Thomas Peteet, which read, "We cannot stand the dishonor and the disgrace of what has happened and have decided upon the only course to follow."[11] The paper never explained how the letter was obtained, and no other paper ever cited the same letter. Furthermore, on February 11, the *Los Angeles Examiner* printed an editorial titled "Tia Juana Is a Disgrace to Mexico, a Menace to America." Editors of both papers blamed the incident on Mexicans in general and their government in particular. The editorial claimed that "the terrible outrage committed upon two innocent American girls, who were so overcome by their disgrace that they and their whole family committed suicide, must have reached the ears of the . . . President of Mexico." [12]

Such editorial commentaries were loaded with ulterior motives. The owners of California's three largest newspapers (John D. Spreckels of the *San Diego Union,* Harry Chandler of the *Los Angeles Times,* and William R. Hearst of the *Los Angeles Examiner*) had extensive investments in Tijuana, Baja California, and other parts of Mexico.[13] These three papers meddled in Mexican affairs when American interests were at stake. In contrast, journalist Henry Pringle challenged the prevailing media view of the Peteets' innocence, claiming they died "in a fit of remorse, rather than from shame."[14] Undaunted, most of the press corps quickly spread the sensational story far beyond the borderlands.

Overall, local public opinion squarely blamed the "shame suicides" on the purported immoral conditions in Tijuana. In particular, outraged San Diegans learned that among the seven men arrested for the Peteet daughters' rape were Tijuana police chief Zenaido Llanos[15] and Oakland Bar owner Luis Amador. When the incident became known, politicians, pseudo-patriotic clubs like the San Diego Law Enforcement League, and moralistic church groups quickly assembled to discuss the proper responses to the threat that Tijuana posed to innocent tourists.

American officials were indignant toward Mexico from the start. San Diego Coroner Schuyler O. Kelly played a crucial role in molding public opinion and directing the political events. On February 7, Kelly declared to the press that his examination revealed evidence that Audrey and Clyde Peteet had been raped. He called on the U.S. State Department to take appropriate federal action in the Tijuana tragedy. Secretary of State Kellogg responded that his office was investigating the case.

At his inquest, Kelly collected testimony from the autopsy surgeon, border officers, city police, character witnesses, a private detective, and a "mystery witness." Dr. John Shea said that he and other doctors, including two Mexicans, found "definite signs" that the Peteet girls had been raped. U.S. Customs Officer Fred Markley reported that over the years many American women had accused Tijuana police officers of sexual assaults, but he cited no specific cases. Kelly assembled the typed depositions for presentation to the coroner's jury.

The last inquest witnesses provided compelling testimony. Private detective Captain James M. Adamson of Atlanta had become tangled in the Peteet affair. The Catton Insurance Company had sent Captain Adamson to investigate a client's suspicious death in the Tijuana jail, and while there he heard of the Peteets' problem with Tijuana police. On the night before they died, the detective visited the family and took depositions similar to those taken by Officer Hannah. As the last person to see them alive, he was an inquest witness; he received a mailed letter from Thomas Peteet after his death. Peteet's letter from the grave read, "Push this case and, if you can, have the government avenge our wrongs. We will appreciate it where we go, maybe. Death was always preferred to dishonor to our women."[16] Taken as genuine, this letter provided a clear motive for the shame suicides. Adamson tried to establish that his client's injuries resulted from a pattern of abuse by the Tijuana police, and that the Peteet Case was just another example of such official corruption.

The most dramatic testimony was given by an unnamed "mystery witness" who saw the girls in the Oakland Bar on Thursday night. He recalled anxiously peeking through the bar's front window in fear for the girls' safety fifteen minutes before closing time. He testified that barkeeper Amador had doped other American girls in the past, but he could not provide names. The mystery man said he saw Chief Llanos's daughter wearing a large diamond ring the next day. He suspected that it was taken from Audrey Peteet. Lastly, the witness feared that if his name was revealed, "he would be shot and killed within 10 minutes."[17] His testimony provided crucial circumstantial evidence, yet, legally speaking, much of it was hearsay.

Despite the secrecy, the mystery witness was identified the next day, at the February 12 coroner's jury hearing, as Rudolph Bachman. He was an American bartender who worked at the Oakland Bar. Bachman failed to appear, but the coroner entered his deposition that Llanos and Amador took the girls from the bar and later bragged about their sexual conquests. Ultimately, Coroner Kelly's reports asserted the Mexicans' guilt and freed the Peteets of responsibility.

In a suspicious move, Coroner Kelly released all the depositions publicly on February 11, and the press published them before the coroner's jury actually read the testimony on February 12. Taking a cue from the coroner, the *San Diego Union* proclaimed the inquest's true purpose: "From behind the veil of death the Peteet family suicide after the daughters had been dishonored in the dens of Tijuana, yesterday pointed accusing fingers at the chief of police of the border town and demanded vengeance for the wrongs they suffered."[18] Americans cried out for justice but thirsted for revenge.

On February 12, the coroner's jury officially ruled that Thomas, Carrie, and Audrey died on Saturday, February 6. Clyde Peteet died of suicidal asphyxiation on February 9, "while despondent with grief and remorse over the fact that she had been outraged by Chief of Police Llanos of Tijuana, Mexico, said outrage having taken place in Tijuana."[19] The jury ruled that Audrey died in the same manner, but they named Amador her assailant.

Given this interpretation of the facts, Kelly said publicly that the suicides justified murder charges against the Mexican prisoners. More than a thousand angry citizens approved the coroner's opinion with a thunderous ovation. Anticipating the outcome, Congressman Phil Swing, Governor Friend Richardson, U.S. Consul Bohr, and Secretary of State Kellogg demanded that Mexico provide "delayed justice" for the Peteets by punishing the culprits and by solving border crime. Furthermore, Congressman Swing threatened federal action if Mexico failed to bring murder charges against all seven defendants to avenge the suicides.

The coroner's jury convened at the Johnson-Saum Funeral Home with 1,200 spectators attending. In an adjacent room, jurors and spectators could view the four family members on public display, lying on a large couch in solemn repose. Almost a week after their deaths, the morticians presented the Peteets lying with arms folded over their bodies in the same order as when they had been found (see figure 3).[20] Emotionally charged, the audience erupted with jeers as the jury blamed Llanos and Amador for the shame suicides. San Diego officials seemed to have forgotten, however, that they had no legal power to make the government of Mexico, a sovereign state, charge its own citizens with murder for a suicide pact that occurred on foreign soil. Armed with the coroner's ruling, American officials at the local, state, and federal levels planned retaliation against any party deemed guilty, regardless of whether this violated Mexico's sovereignty.

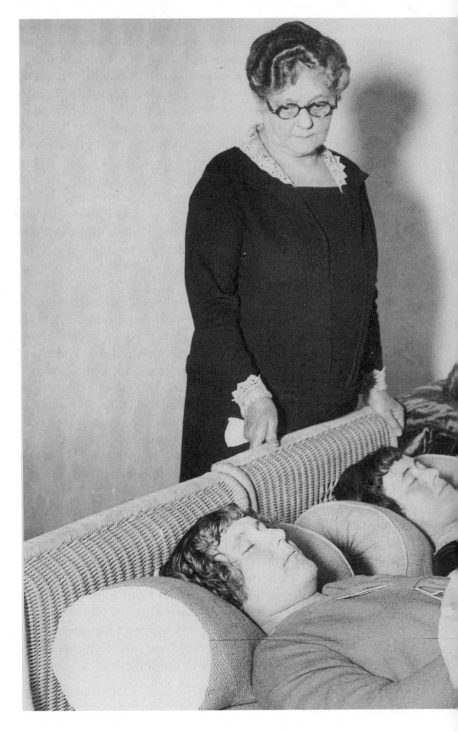

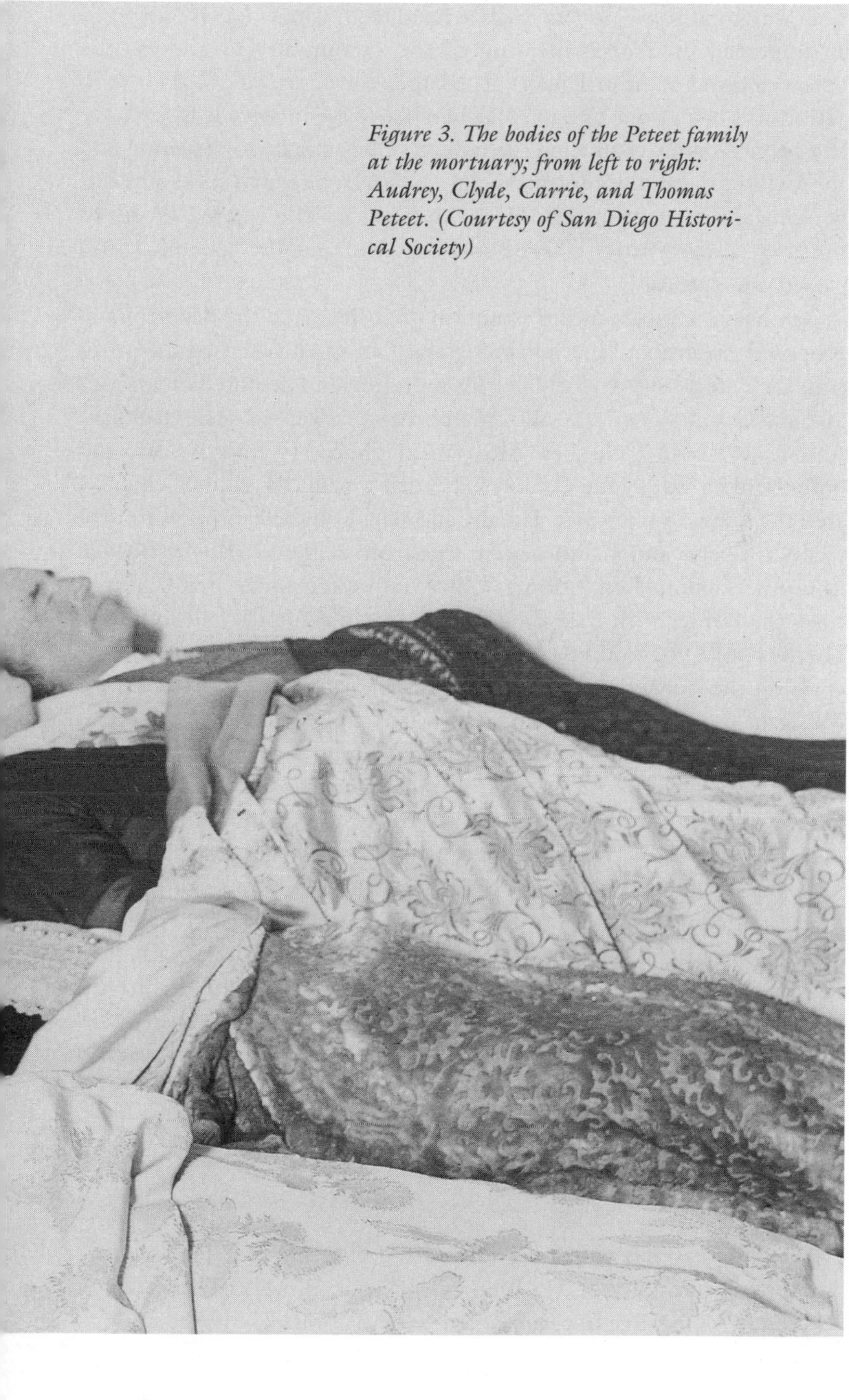

Figure 3. The bodies of the Peteet family at the mortuary; from left to right: Audrey, Clyde, Carrie, and Thomas Peteet. (Courtesy of San Diego Historical Society)

For example, on February 15, the San Diego City Council organized an unprecedented mass meeting of the community to address the Peteet case and crime in Tijuana. The large, unruly crowd called for mob action to burn down Tijuana and lynch anyone involved. Deftly, the city council barely channeled the collective hysteria by formulating and approving two resolutions marshaling federal, state, and local authority along the international border with Mexico. The council approved the first resolution by a three-to-two vote, and the second action passed unanimously.[21]

San Diego City Council Resolution #36808 stated the problem and proposed a solution: "Lawless individuals" in Tijuana caused the problem, the Peteet tragedy. San Diegans regretted and deplored conditions in Tijuana and along the California border that caused such tragedies. Americans would coax their Mexican neighbors to improve law and order on their side of the California border. Finally, the council empowered the mayor to convince Tijuana and Baja California officials to protect San Diego and California citizens from crime below the border. The other action, Resolution #36809, requested that federal officials close the border with Baja California between 5:00 P.M. and 8:00 A.M. Furthermore, it required the registration of all people and vehicles crossing the border. Americans cast down a gauntlet and waited for Mexicans to accept the challenge.

In word and deed, Americans disagreed among themselves about a proper response. On the one hand, some Americans wanted sanctions limiting border transit by imposing a dawn-to-dusk curfew and restricting Americans' right of free passage. On the other hand, curious American tourists flooded into the border town to take photos of the sites of the tragedy, including the Hot Springs Hotel, the Hotel Nacional, and the sealed Oakland Bar (see figures 4 and 5). "Voting with their feet," many Americans spent millions of dollars in Tijuana despite the moralistic, punitive sanctions proposed by other elements of society.

A few Americans consciously defended Mexico and placed the Peteet case in political and moral perspective. For instance, humorist Will Rogers used his popular newspaper column to mock self-righteous American attitudes belittling Mexico. In a lengthy article, Rogers sarcastically opined:

> Well, they were having a big stir out there, and in fact all over the United States, about Tia Juana and Mexicali, Mex. They want President Coolidge to clean these places up, or make Mexico do it,

Figure 4. The Oakland Bar, where Thomas, Clyde, and Audrey were drinking prior to the daughters' disappearance. (Courtesy of San Diego Historical Soci-

and if they won't, why, go to war with them and make 'em clean 'em up. It seems they sell drinks down there right over the bar. . . . that it is a disgrace to have these things done right there in Mexico, where the Americans can go right over and see all this.

Americans don't want to drink and gamble. They just go over there to see the mountains, and these scheming Mexicans grab 'em and make 'em drink, and make 'em make bets, and make 'em watch the race horses run for money. It seems that Americans don't know these places are over there at all, and when they get there these Mexicans spring on 'em and they have to drink or the Mexicans will kill 'em.

So Secretary Kellogg is going to send them another note. . . . We come nearer running Mexico than we do New York State. . . . For the love of Mike, why don't we let Mexico alone and let them run their country the way they want to! . . .

Suppose, for instance, when we had all our scandal in Hollywood, that Mexico had demanded that we clean up; that a lot of

Figure 5. Hotel Nacional, where Clyde Peteet was found by Mexican police. (Courtesy of San Diego Historical Society)

their Tourists were passing through there every day and that it was contaminating them. We would have laughed ourselves sober . . .

If we have to admit to the world, that we are raising people that don't know enough to take proper care of themselves, we will have to do it by another Amendment, as follows: "Americans are not allowed anywhere they will be subject to evil influences."[22]

Rogers's homespun political wit timelessly revealed the futility of legislating and imposing morality at home or in Mexico. As moral reformers increasingly dictated domestic and foreign policy, Americans repeatedly tried to force the Mexican government to conduct a moral cleanup of Tijuana. Ultimately, the United States threatened Mexico with punitive sanctions.

The monolithic Mexican government tried to prevent an international crisis. The territorial military governor of Baja California Norte, Major General Abelardo L. Rodríguez, met U.S. Consul Bohr and promised that Mexican courts would expedite their investigation of the family tragedy. Following Governor Rodríguez's meeting with the U.S. consul, news reporters stated that the Peteet case "has become perhaps the most important border event in the history of the southwest." Accommodating American concerns, Rodríguez pledged that the guilty would receive the "most severe punishment possible," including the death penalty. The governor stated his willingness to defend foreigners and punish Mexicans given the adverse publicity and American diplomatic-economic pressure.[23]

On February 9, under existing Mexican law, federal troops arrested Zenaido Llanos, Luis Amador, and five other men (see figure 6). The accused were jailed in Tijuana's military garrison. Territorial judicial officials immediately closed Amador's bar and relieved Llanos as police chief. While Llanos declared his innocence in preliminary court hearings, he admitted, "I accompanied the Peteet girls and their party to Tijuana Hot Springs. I left them there. I had nothing to do with them. But I accept full responsibility for what happened."[24] On February 13, Luis Amador, a founder of the local bartenders' union, attempted suicide by slashing his wrists in jail, but alert guards saved him from serious injury. A native-born U.S. citizen, Amador also had outstanding American arrest warrants for heroin sales and bail jumping, and he feared extradition to Los Angeles. In accord with American demands, on February 14, Mexican prosecutors filed first-degree murder, kidnapping, and rape charges against all seven defendants. Tijuana district attorneys announced publicly that they could sentence any defendants convicted of abduction to face a firing squad under Mexican law.[25]

Acquiescing to American protests, Governor Rodríguez (see figure 7) said that Tijuana vice activity would be cleaned up. On February 12, probably in response to the protests, Mexican President Plutarco Elías Calles ordered an anti-vice campaign in Tijuana. By February 15, the vice sweep had shut down fifty-two of the seventy-five saloons in the border town. The Mexican police deported more than five hundred foreigners (mostly American bar girls) who worked in Tijuana resorts. Officials announced that from now on, they would arrest and deport all undesirable aliens. Simultaneously, they sent twenty-five Mexicans to the infamous Islas Tres Marías penal colony without a trial or fixed terms of incarceration.[26] Mexicans acted swiftly to close saloons and protect foreign tourists. Meanwhile, the government changed Tijuana's official name to Zaragoza to avoid the border town's traditional stigma, with little effect. The Oakland Bar and the Hotel Nacional also changed their names. Cynical Americans wanted more proof that the border town would remain safe, since previous cleanup campaigns usually had allowed vice activity to start again soon after paying higher sin taxes. However, Mexican efforts never met American expectations.

In a February 17 pretrial hearing, Judge Saturnino Urías ruled on the charges filed against the seven defendants. To the chagrin of American reformers, the judge indicted Llanos and Amador only on rape, violent assault, and concealing a crime. He charged two other defendants with concealment of a crime and completely freed the last three defendants. Importantly, Judge Urías disagreed with Mexican prosecutors and American opinion when he decided that the evidence failed to sustain murder charges against Amador and Llanos under either Mexican or U.S. law.

The American government reacted immediately. Less than an hour after Judge Urías's ruling, the U.S. government announced plans to punish Mexico. On February 17, the U.S. Treasury Department ordered agents to close "the border at Tijuana between the hours of 6 P.M. and 8 A.M."[27] President Calvin Coolidge felt he had acted as far as federal law allowed. He could discourage tourists from going to Mexico but could not prohibit them from doing so. For his part, Congressman Swing wanted more; he planned to write a bill extending the curfew across the entire two-thousand-mile border until Mexico created a fifty-mile-wide vice-free zone along the border.[28] However, the U.S. president refused to act more forcefully over the shame suicides; he insisted that border conditions would improve when Mexican authorities

Figure 6. Six of seven defendants in the Peteet case, pictured in Tijuana. (Courtesy of San Diego Historical Society

*Figure 7. Baja Governor Abelardo Rodríguez, February 11, 1926.
(Courtesy of San Diego Historical Society)*

and American tourists forced changes. In the end, Coolidge suc-
cumbed to political pressure, imposing additional curfews at Mexicali,
Agua Prieta, and other border towns in quick succession. The curfew
satisfied few Americans and fewer Mexicans.

Unsurprisingly, the Mexican press criticized the American actions
against their nation. Mexico's foremost newspaper, *Excélsior,* pointed

out that the U.S. government had not punished American cities with worse crime problems than Tijuana had. The Mexicans characterized American border restrictions as childish and based on the incorrect assumption that passport laws and curfews would automatically moralize human beings. In an editorial titled "The Alarmists of American Puritanism," an *Excélsior* editor wrote:

> Certainly, the act is lamentable, and, according to wire service reports, Baja California authorities have already arrested culprits who will be punished to the fullest extent that the law requires. But the truth is that, in this case, no fault can be attributed to the population of Tijuana, nor to the officials that govern it, because there are criminals all over the world, and since Mr. Peteet was imprudent enough to have a "wild party" with his wife and daughters, he and he alone is responsible for the results.[29]

The Mexican press acknowledged that the accused would be prosecuted under the law. Blame rested on the Peteet family, not the Mexican people or their government, the paper claimed.

Just north of the border, on February 16, the San Ysidro Chamber of Commerce sent its own investigation of the Peteet case to Secretary of State Kellogg. The group worried that the U.S. government had merely consulted reports sympathetic to the Peteets and critical of Tijuana before ordering the curfew. Americans working in Tijuana testified before the chamber that the Peteets drank constantly and risked their own safety, and that bar employees repeatedly refused to serve them liquor at various establishments.[30] Chamber investigators presented testimony that Thomas Peteet used his daughters to get free drinks from men. Their investigation claimed to expose the Peteets' character flaws solely in the interest of justice without belittling the crimes committed against the family. Famous for confronting Mexico, Secretary Kellogg chose to ignore the chamber's report and continued to enforce the curfew.

Tijuana civic and business associations were nervous about the curfew. During the Prohibition Era, tourism provided Mexico with its second largest source of foreign exchange, and Tijuana businessmen feared losing millions of dollars of income. In addition, Mexican mining, lumber, agriculture, and oil exporters feared the potential ill effects of a threatened U.S. trade embargo. On the first day, tourists flooded back to the United States before the 6:00 P.M. border closing, and Tijuana resembled a ghost town that night. On February 18, the two hundred members of Tijuana's Chamber of Commerce, which mainly comprised American vice purveyors, met to devise means to counteract the sanctions.[31] Some businessmen were confident that the curfew would stimulate Tijuana's building boom, since tourist throngs would need more hotels, goods, and services during prolonged stays. American newspapers reported mixed results: sometimes Tijuana bustled with more tourists than ever, at other times Tijuana appeared empty and gloomy. One American newspaper concluded, "Tijuana is not dead, but it isn't so pert and chipper as it was a few days ago."[32] Throughout 1926, Tijuana's tourist income swung unpredictably.

Mexican officials felt the curfew was insulting after all the improvements undertaken to clean up Tijuana. They resented American attempts to intervene in Mexico's internal affairs and tired of anti-Mexican harangues in the American newspapers. They created special government committees to manage the crisis. Unofficially, government agencies encouraged anti-American protests conducted by labor unions and civic groups that sporadically blocked American tourists and trade goods from crossing the border.[33] Tijuana historians have described these protests as historic assertions of Mexican nationalism, but the protests were ineffective in protecting the local tourist economy and counteracting American diplomacy.

On February 24, an angry Governor Rodríguez declared:

Since some of our California neighbors and especially Los Angeles newspapers are exhibiting such a spirit of unfriendliness toward us, I have decided to recommend to President Calles the closing of Mexicali and Tijuana as ports of entry immediately. This would mean that no commerce could be transacted through these ports. . . .

It would seem that some California politicians in Los Angeles and the Imperial Valley are taking advantage of the Peteet case at Tijuana to make great capital out of it at this time.[34]

Although the governor lost patience with what he called yellow journalism, President Calles never authorized closing the ports to American trade goods or tourists. Periodically, local civic groups circulated petitions protesting the curfew and Governor Rodríguez dutifully forwarded them to Calles, awaiting federal action. The Mexican protests failed to stop the United States from extending the curfew to Ciudad

Juárez a month later.[35] Mexico had little leverage to block American sanctions effectively.

Meanwhile, the presiding judge in the criminal trial, Saturnino Urías, sifted through evidence while prosecutors revised the case against the defendants. At 11:00 A.M. on July 27, 1926, Urías started the public proceedings at the Zaragoza Mutualist Center in Tijuana before a nine-person jury. Press reports described an angry atmosphere in the courtroom. The small room held about fifty spectators who attended by invitation only. Americans present seemed confused by the Mexican judicial procedures, which differed dramatically from the American legal system. The marked informality of the trial surprised the foreign press. Mexican prosecutors had no obligation to produce a witness list, and Americans wondered if they would call James Adamson and Rudolph Bachman to testify in person.

The defense attorneys, four of whom were Mexican Americans, began their opening statements, followed by the defendants' testimony. All four defendants asserted their innocence. Significantly, Amador admitted that he had had consensual sexual relations with Clyde often between January 30 and the night in question. Allegedly, Clyde had told Amador that she loved him and hated her family. He adamantly denied drugging, kidnapping, or raping the young woman. The defendants contradicted the facts contained in the Peteet depositions. Llanos denied having had sexual relations with Audrey, citing two reasons. First, he said that he always became impotent when he drank. Second, she had passed out during the evening.[36] Lawyers asked whether he believed the girls were "professionally immoral," and Llanos answered yes. Next, three defense witnesses disparaged Thomas Peteet as a common drunk who used his daughters to get liquor, and they attacked the girls as carelessly flirtatious. At day's end, the defense lawyers said they planned to call more witnesses before they rested their case. The court then adjourned until the next morning.

Reporters noted the conspicuous absence of American officials at the trial, the only exception being a representative from the San Diego district attorney's office.[37] A Los Angeles columnist wrote accusingly that government authorities had "washed their hands of the affair and placed in the hands of . . . [Mexican prosecutors] the safety of all American tourists to the border cities of Old Mexico."[38] Likewise, the reporter predicted that the guilty parties would "go scot-free" due to the "sordid repetition of attacks on Peteet's morals." Since court testimony unfairly branded Clyde and Audrey as immoral, foreign journalists wrote that the trial judge had already determined the verdict from the start.

When the trial resumed on July 28, defense attorneys questioned the remaining Mexican and American witnesses. Seventeen additional defense witnesses corroborated the previous testimony about the Peteet family's wantonness. Procedurally, Mexican law did not permit cross-examination of witnesses by the state. In the people's case, prosecutors did not call witnesses, instead simply reading written testimony into the court record. The testimony included the Peteet depositions and findings from the San Diego coroner's inquest. As the prosecutor was reading, Thomas Peteet's former partner, Dan Conlogue, interrupted and gained permission to speak to the court. He testified about the family's good character and promised to finish testifying when the court resumed on the following day.

On July 29, prosecutors rested their case when Conlogue failed to appear at the trial. The state attorneys made their closing statements. For their part, the defense concluded by entering written testimony into the court record from pretrial witnesses who were not even present in the courtroom. Interestingly, defense lawyers admitted into evidence a statement written by Joseph W. Kelly, a private detective working for the American Federation of Labor (AFL). In an act of international labor solidarity, Mexico's national labor confederation apparently asked the AFL to investigate the background of the Peteet family. Kelly swore that he interviewed people in Kansas City who described the Peteet girls as "loose and that they had frequented disorderly resorts."[39] In the transcript, he deduced that the girls had histories as prostitutes. The labor investigator concluded, "The United States shouldn't try to regulate the moral behavior of other countries when it can't regulate its own."[40] Kelly also criticized America's "vicious propaganda" against Mexico in this case.

Once the jury got the case, they deliberated for two hours and twenty minutes. The jury voted unanimously to acquit the four defendants of all charges. Hundreds of Mexicans in the street outside the building cheered the verdict and congratulated the freed men as national heroes. Most foreign reporters considered the trial a travesty of justice for the victims and Americans in general. They called the celebration disgusting. Uncharacteristically, the *San Diego Union* conceded, "Those up on legal lore stated that if an American district attorney were given the same evidence that the prosecution in the Peteet case had, the matter would never have come to trial as no complaint would have been issued."[41] Some Americans accepted the decision, while others slowly burned with anger. The Peteet case had climaxed abruptly without achieving definitive moral, legal, or political closure.

After the trial, the two main defendants in the shame suicides faded into anonymity. Although initially celebrated, they never regained their former prestige, wealth, or influence in Tijuana. Zenaido Llanos returned home to Mexicali, but on Christmas Eve 1926, his wife divorced him, citing the Peteet case, his cruelty, and his death threats against her as just cause.[42] Luis Amador briefly reopened the Oakland Bar, but local authorities forced him out of business. He disappeared into southern Mexico, since arrest warrants still awaited him in California.

Under diplomatic pressure, the Mexican legal system ran its course. Mexican officials hoped that the United States would lift sanctions once the trial ended, but that did not happen. Mexicans won a symbolic victory over the Americans that cost the border town foreign respect and dollars in the end. Meanwhile, the proud U.S. government could not admit moral failure, and ineffective border controls remained in effect for many years.

Tijuana tourism achieved a golden age despite ineffective U.S. sanctions. From 1926 to 1935, American developers (known as Border Barons) built and operated the world-renowned and extremely profitable Agua Caliente resort complex (see figures 8, 9, 10). Tijuana high life attracted hundreds of millions of American dollars until the Great Depression slowly eroded tourist spending in the border town. In 1931, President Herbert Hoover's administration stubbornly reaffirmed the border curfew as a Republican diplomatic tactic. Many large holes cut into the eight-mile-long border fence allowed American tourists to enter Tijuana illegally and return home after hours without interference. Cynically, thousands of fence jumpers honored American moral laws and the border curfew in the breach.[43] After closing hours, the United States border resembled a leaky sieve, rather than a respected, impermeable political barrier. In 1933, after eight years, U.S. President Franklin D. Roosevelt lifted the curfew as an early token of his more friendly hemispheric strategy. In the same year, Tijuana lost major tourist appeal after the United States ended the prohibition of liquor. In 1935, newly elected Mexican President Lázaro Cárdenas banned Tijuana's gambling casinos, ending its golden age.

Postscript

In context, the perennial American campaigns to outlaw vice activity were most intense during the Prohibition Era (1920–1933). Literally millions escaped American laws in Tijuana saloons, casinos, brothels, and opium dens. During tourism peaks, 180,000 people a day swarmed Tijuana.[44] American vice purveyors capitalized on Mexico's tolerant vice laws, and Tijuana developed into a regulated vice haven catering to foreigners.[45] Mexicans denied that Tijuana represented national culture. Local residents worked directly or indirectly in the illicit economy while their hometown got a national reputation as "the mouth of Hell." American tourists were undeterred by the problems that typically befell the unlucky in such locales. To be sure, border scandals had

Figure 8. 1929 brochure advertising Tijuana's Hotel Agua Caliente and Casino. (Courtesy of San Diego Historical Society)

Figure 9. Parking area and walkway leading to the Hotel Agua Caliente, 1920s. (Courtesy of San Diego Historical Society)

drawn protests from moralistic American religious groups before the crisis.[46] Ironically, during the Roaring 1920s, the American press widely publicized the wide-open conditions along the border, but these reports only encouraged would-be tourists. Like so many other Americans, the Peteet family came to red-hot Tijuana like moths to a flame.

The rise of Las Vegas, Nevada, in the 1930s meant that Tijuana no longer had a West Coast monopoly on the forbidden fruit of liquor, gambling, sex, and drugs. The border town's attractions drew few Americans until World War II unleashed an invasion of U.S. military personnel seeking vicious pleasure every night.

Historically, Tijuana had problems protecting American tourists before and after the Peteet tragedy. In 1934, officials in Tijuana and San Diego covered up a scandal about young American girls recruited by the Ruiz brothers to work as prostitutes in Tijuana's Ben Hur Café. Proudly, Baja California's governor sent a top-secret, coded telegram to interim Mexican president Abelardo Rodríguez. The territorial official reported to Rodríguez that they had averted another crisis like the

Figure 10. Sunset Inn and race track in Tijuana, 1920s. (Courtesy of San Diego Historical Society)

Peteet case with direct help from U.S. authorities.⁴⁷ Mexican and American officials had learned the hard way how to avoid international conflicts by means of discreet cooperation.

Eventually, the Peteet shame suicides receded into the collective unconscious on both sides of the border.⁴⁸ The dead family faded from memory, the accused disappeared, and new sensations replaced Tijuana in popular culture. San Diego officials demolished or remodeled the Peteet home at 4423 Arch Street at some unknown time and eliminated the former address. Further study may reveal why the city tried to wipe out the memory of this sad incident.

Nevertheless, the Tijuana stereotypes created by American newspapers have subsided but have never fully disappeared. Tijuana residents and other Mexicans remain very sensitive about the border town's past and deny that vice activity played a role in the life of the city. American and Mexican newspapers, literature, films, businesses, and popular culture have had a mania about Tijuana's lurid mystique known as the black legend (*leyenda negra*). The "new" Tijuana promoted by boosters and politicians conflicts with the rough reputation and bad publicity the city still receives. ❖

Notes

1. Henry Pringle, " 'Shame Suicides' Throw the Spotlight on the Infamies of Tia Juana," *The World* (New York), February 21, 1926.

2. *San Diego Union,* February 10, 1926.

3. *San Diego Union,* February 7, 1926.

4. Thomas Peteet Deposition, February 5, 1926, Bishop Collection #88:17082, Research Archives, San Diego Historical Society.

5. Audrey Peteet Deposition, February 5, 1926, Bishop Collection #88:17081, Research Archives, San Diego Historical Society.

6. *San Diego Union,* February 7, 1926.

7. Clyde Peteet Deposition, February 5, 1926, Bishop Collection #88:17083, Research Archives, San Diego Historical Society.

8. *San Diego Union,* February 7, 1926.

9. Will of Thomas Peteet, February 5, 1926, County of San Diego, Record of Wills, vol. 15:299 #R3.5, Research Archives, San Diego Historical Society.

10. "Uses Gun to Force Family to Take Gas," *San Diego Union,* February 8, 1926, Bishop Collection #88:17077, Research Archives, San Diego Historical Society.

11. "New Suicide Seizures," *Los Angeles Times,* February 11, 1926.

12. Editorial, *Los Angeles Examiner,* February 11, 1926.

13. Vincent C. de Baca, "Moral Renovation of the Californias: Tijuana's Political and Economic Role in American-Mexican Relations, 1920–1935" (Ph.D. diss., University of California, San Diego, 1991), pp. 36–39.

14. Pringle, "Shame Suicides."

15. Pablo L. Martínez, *Guía familiar de Baja California, 1700–1900* (Mexico City, 1965), p. 880. Zenaido Llanos was born in 1881 in Ensenada, Baja California. His father was from Baja California Sur and his mother from Los Angeles, California. Ironically, Chief Llanos had been praised in American newspapers only days before the Peteet case occurred. He captured a twenty-two-year-old female Mexican American named Tessie Peña, who worked as a prostitute in Tijuana's Eden Bar. Peña was wanted in San Diego for murdering an elderly woman, and Llanos released her into the custody of Sheriff Roy Volk at the Tijuana port of entry. *La Prensa* (San Antonio, Texas), February 7, 1926.

16. *San Diego Union,* February 12, 1926.

17. Ibid.

18. Ibid.

19. *San Diego Union,* February 13, 1926.

20. Bodies of Peteet Family (photo), Bishop Collection #88:17088, Research Archives, San Diego Historical Society.

21. Resolutions #36808 and #36809, City Clerk of San Diego, Resolutions Book #45, Research Archives, San Diego Historical Society.

22. James M. Smallwood, ed., *Will Rogers' Weekly Articles,* vol. 2 (Stillwater: Oklahoma State University Press, 1980), pp. 164–65.

23. *San Diego Union,* February 12, 1926.

24. Ibid.

25. *New York Times,* February 14, 1926; *La Prensa,* February 16, 1926.

26. *San Diego Union,* February 16, 1926; *La Prensa,* February 17, 1926.

27. *New York Times,* February 18, 1926.

28. *San Diego Union,* February 18, 1926.

29. Editorial, *Excélsior* (Mexico City), February 13, 1926.

30. *San Diego Union,* February 17, 1926.

31. *San Diego Union,* February 19, 1926.

32. *San Diego Union,* February 20 and February 23, 1926; *New York Daily News,* February 18, 1926; Owen White, "Border Yearns to Lead Its Own Life," *New York Times Magazine,* March 21, 1926.

33. David Piñera Ramírez, coord., *Historia de Tijuana: semblanza general* (Tijuana: Centro de Investigaciones Históricas UNAM-UABC, 1985), p. 282. The author incorrectly writes that the Peteet case and the related Tijuana protests occurred in 1921.

34. *San Diego Union,* February 25, 1926.

35. White, "Border Yearns to Lead Its Own Life."

36. *Los Angeles Times,* July 28, 1926.

37. *San Diego Union,* July 29, 1926.

38. *Los Angeles Times,* July 29, 1926.

39. *Los Angeles Times,* July 30, 1926.

40. *San Diego Union,* July 30, 1926.

41. Ibid.

42. *San Diego Union,* December 25, 1926.

43. *La Opinión* (Los Angeles), March 29, 1931.

44. Pringle, "Shame Suicides."

45. Ramón Eduardo Ruiz, *On the Rim of Mexico: Encounters of the Rich and Poor* (Boulder: Westview Press, 2000), pp. 48–50. The author writes that the Peteet case occurred in 1924.

46. C. de Baca, "Moral Renovation of the Californias," pp. 45–47.

47. Telegram from Agustín Olachea to Abelardo Rodríguez, Mexicali, Baja California, May 5, 1934, Archivo General de la Nación, Presidenciales, Fondo Rodríguez, Exp. 622.2.

48. Richard Pourade, *The History of San Diego,* vol. 6, *The Rising Tide* (San Diego: Union-Tribune Publishing Co., 1978), pp. 83–84. The author writes briefly about the Peteet case, only mentioning the drugging and rape of the "disgraced" girls. See also David Piñera Ramírez, *Historia de Tijuana: edición conmemorativa del centenario de su fundación,* vol. 2 (Tijuana: Centro de Investigaciones Históricas UNAM-UABC), p. 169. The editor interviewed longtime resident Alejandro Appel, who placed the Peteets in the Klondike Bar in 1924 or 1925.

Low-Budget Films for Fronterizos and Mexican Migrants in the United States

María S. Arbeláez

During the 1980s and 1990s a new movie genre was mass-produced by the Mexican film industry. It incorporated the old *cabaretera* (dance hall) theme with contemporary topics of drug trafficking, police corruption, foul language, shootouts, road chases, and Mexico–U.S. border migration conflicts. This cinematic style can be broadly termed *narcofichera*. It became immensely popular throughout the country, in the border states, and among Mexican communities in the United States. It monopolized production, theaters, and public attendance. Many of these productions were low-budget 35-mm movies that were swiftly transferred to VHS format to be sold or rented outside the comparatively limited market of movie theaters. Given their immediate popularity among movie renters on both sides of the border, video productions by the Televisa conglomerate and its subsidiary, Telcvicine, dovetailed in an almost uncontested competition to mass-produce hundreds of these films.[1] The genre deals not only with drug trafficking, *ficheras* (prostitutes), and shootouts, but it also includes many of the themes and combinations common in action movies, romance, comedy, and old Mexican melodrama.

The purpose of this article is to review the themes contained in this new genre as broadly defined. A second purpose is to study its melodramatic character, assumed or present paradigmatic construction, ambiguous portrayal of gender roles, and irreconcilable differences between interpretations of acceptable morality and condemnable behaviors. Most significant here is the opposition between what is portrayed as permissible behaviors and themes that are purposely ignored or silenced.

Mexican scholars, filmmakers, mainstream producers, and critics have dismissed these movies from the canon. Currently, they center their attention on the new wave of Mexican cinema led by several graduates of the Centro Universitario de Estudios Cinematográficos (CUEC). One of the new members of the new cultural intelligentsia, film director Cristián González, appointed in 1989 as director of the Subdirección de Autorizaciones of the Dirección de Cinematografía, stated in an interview with Carl J. Mora:

> [Commercial films] touch the real feelings of people who can't
> afford other types of entertainment. They have no access to cul-
> ture; these are people who can't read, who don't wear shoes. They
> watch movies about violence, drugs, sex comedies—80 percent
> of Mexican movies are like this. If a woman is not a prostitute,
> she's being raped, or willing to have sex on the spur of the
> moment. Our policy is to try to influence the commercial produc-
> ers to return to family entertainment.[2]

González considers it imperative to "make Mexican movies in English with American actors," a move he considers necessary to recapture
the middle-class audience and provide a new life to the Mexican movie
industry.[3] Along the same lines, Alejandro Pelayo, another filmmaker,
older but yet still close to González's generation, acknowledged both
the declining quality of Mexican cinema under the pervasive domination of the narco-fichera genre and the social rifts among the Mexican
audience:

> There are two kinds of viewers: the mass working class public that
> goes to see comedies, actions, violence, drug smugglers. It coin-
> cides somewhat with the undocumented Mexicans in the United
> States, among whom the most popular stars are la India María
> and the Almada brothers. The middle class public . . . prefer to
> see *Rambo* and other American movies.[4]

Why is it that the narco-fichera movie genre and remakes of old-
fashioned melodramas, with their dreary subjects, impossible opposition between good and evil, themes of fall and redemption, moral
messages, and unfathomable inconsistencies, have achieved success in a
country that is considered Catholic, *guadalupano,* and prudish? Is its
subjectivity the opposite of that which is displayed? The point here is
that the Mexican film industry has been torn by its multiple roles. It
has been considered light entertainment, producer of mytho-histories,
alternative educator and forger of national identities, interpreter of
social problems, mediator of class conflict, and, above all, mediator of
social differences.[5] Others have seen the rise and demise of the contemporary Mexican movie industry in its affiliation to the state and its
inability to provide a critical stance to the "ogre" as defined by Octavio
Paz.[6]

The forerunners of narco-fichera movies were the cabaretera films, which were first mass-produced in Mexico during the late 1940s. The genre gained popularity with its depiction of sordid situations, crass corruption, female nudity, *albur* jokes,[7] and shabby sexuality. It focused on the underworld and the darkest sides of a modern, urban, impoverished, yet newly industrialized country. As the cabaretera films achieved center stage, socially provocative subjects and political criticism were pushed to the margins, censored outright, or ignored by both producers and audiences. The new policy was to produce what were expected to be commercial box office hits.

Still, narco-fichera movie subjects are omnipresent features of twentieth-century Mexican society. In this respect, they are not impervious to the tensions between traditional Catholic morality and the double standards that are deeply embedded in the national pathos. The movie themes are as ambivalent and contradictory as the society they are portraying and interpreting. The debut of the *comedia ranchera* genre in the aftermath of the Mexican Revolution epitomized the apparent contradictions between the rural and the urban milieu (e.g., *Allá en el Rancho Grande,* 1936). Gender roles, which had been subverted by women bursting onto the national stage as brave *soldaderas* during the revolution, were again stifled by idealized depictions of them as devoted mothers, wives, and defenders of Catholic family sanctity (e.g., *No basta ser madre,* 1937). Urban themes were not exempt from the intense cleavages in Mexican society and cultural mores inherited from many years of Porfirian rule, a regime that had regulated prostitution as a social need while at the same time bellowing for righteousness amidst the most extreme conditions of inequality and poverty. Movie producers nonetheless romanticized the era with comic nostalgia (e.g., *Ay, que tiempos señor Don Simón,* 1941). The emerging middle class of the 1930s and 1940s, under the leadership of a revolutionary elite of rural origin, subscribed to the ethos of social justice and egalitarianism and proclaimed new moral standards. However, they tailored their new value system by rescuing old patriarchal Catholic values of female chastity and loyalty to a family hierarchy (e.g., *Papacito lindo,* 1939). Many of the films produced during these years were notorious for their depictions of fallen and later redeemed women, filial betrayal, and forgiveness (e.g., *Santa,* 1931, *La mujer del puerto,* 1933, *Cuándo los hijos se van,* 1941). The melodramatic intensity of these movies was unexpectedly successful among the entertainment media's growing audience. It was also crucial to the expansion of an industry commanded by producers and directors drawn from the rich well of raw, middle-class sentimentalism, the hardships of rural dislocation, urban poverty, and the coarse rhetoric of the revolutionaries in power. It also provided the foundation for a series of stereotypical dramas in the cabaretera genre, a genre which reached the height of its popularity with the modernization frenzy of President Miguel Alemán's administration (1946–1952). The party atmosphere of the cabaret, with its purportedly egalitarian character, was in direct opposition to the current social commentary and political alacrity with which the regime moved to reinforce its presence in the moviemaking business.

The most notable movies of the cabaretera genre were *Sensualidad* (1950) and *Aventurera* (1952), both films by Alberto Gout starring Cuban *rumbera* Ninón Sevilla. However, it was the box-office success of *Aventurera* that crystallized the cabaretera genre as a true cinematic paradigm. Cuban music and the sensual dancing of the rumba, cha-cha, salsa, conga, and the favorite Mexican *danzón* created an alluring background for these films, which were all the rage among the viewing public. *Aventurera* was even more exhilarating because it featured Cuban Damaso Pérez Prado with his orchestra of bongos and timbales. Popular singer Pedro Vargas, an icon of the *ranchera* and *bolero* musical genres, sang the movie theme song. The lyrics were the creation of another beloved singer and composer, Agustín Lara.

Aventurera was about the fall from social grace of the good girl. Elena (Ninón Sevilla), the heroine of the film, like Dr. Faustus, descends into the underworld of corruption, prostitution, and degradation by deceit and betrayal. Ciudad Juárez, a city with a reputation as a "Babilonia pocha,"[8] served as an ad hoc background. More dramatic overtones were added by the fact that Elena was from ultraconservative Guadalajara. The seedy environment of the border town provided a metaphorical quality of a place that opens or succumbs to the other side. The United States is the other side of Mexico. Historically perceived as threatening, the United States is to be either loved or loathed. In the popular imagination, American society is modern, overly materialistic, decadent, and individualistic. It is in direct opposition to the imagined Mexican society, portrayed as familial, with atemporal characteristics of patriarchal order, deified motherhood, and Catholic purity. But this ideal society was the myth that *Aventurera* shattered by looking at its innermost layers. Still, if the plot revealed a deep-seated double standard and moral decay, all was resolved by redemption of the fallen and death of the doers of evil. Film scholars consider the movie the ultimate representation of the moral tensions in the new social standards of the emerging middle class.[9] *Aventurera*—admired and praised for its artistic qualities by producers, critics, and directors—became the template for successive films in the genre. It is comparable to Fernándo de Fuentes's *Allá en el Rancho Grande,* a film that set the stage for an endless sequence of comedias rancheras.

The audacity of *Aventurera* also launched the ascent of the fichera movie. Ficheras were based on the misfortunes and dramas of female escorts who worked at bars, dance halls, and cabarets. The women were called ficheras because they earned their money in *fichas,* or tokens. The girls would sit with a customer, and every drink he purchased meant a ficha or more; one ficha usually could buy a dance as well. At the end of the night, the bar owner or manager would exchange the women's tokens for cash. Several of these women engaged in prostitution as a side activity to pushing alcohol, small talk, and dancing. In the fichera movies, even if the girls were bad, they still had redeeming qualities. They were ficheras because they had been forced into it by a swindler who promised them stardom as dancers or singers, were single mothers, or were the only source of support for an ailing mother. The girl would manage to ascend or escape from her debased lifestyle and would either die, reform by casting out her demons in profound repentance, or obtain a new identity by forsaking the cabaret environment altogether.

The repetition of the original formula of *Aventurera* in the fichera film, and the paradoxical success of this genre at the box office, signaled the end of the mythical golden age of Mexican cinema. The industry, after the late 1950s, struggled with state protectionism, the invasion of Hollywood, attempts at independent moviemaking, actors' union strife, and the powerful private interests sheltered under the Banco Cinematográfico. When the state tried to curb the production of cabaretera films in both 1952 and 1960 by placing them on hold in a process called "canning," they were quickly replaced by comedies and horror films featuring the popular wrestler El Santo, El Enmascarado de Plata.[10] In the 1970s the genre came back and acquired a new life with *Tivoli* (1974), *Las ficheras* (1976), and *Muñecas de medianoche* (1979). These movies were instant successes due to their half-nudity, implied eroticism, musical backgrounds, sensual dancing, and foul language.

The Universe of the Mexican Movie
in the United States

Video stores serving the Mexican community in the United States carry hundreds of titles, mostly of the genres of drugs, violence, fichera, and bad but tough, kind-hearted, or deceived girls with no choices. A survey of rentals in two video stores located in communities where the majority of the population is either Mexican-born or of Mexican descent—communities in Homestead, Florida, and Omaha, Nebraska— showed that the most popular are movies with Rosa Gloria Chagoyan (*Lola, la trailera*), Jorge Luke, the Almada brothers (*El judicial I* and *II, La bronco gris*), Angelica Chain (*Camelia, la Tejana*), Claudia Bernal and Antonio Infante (*Laura Garza*), Valeria Palmer (*Perra maldita*), María Elena Velasco, La India María (*La presidenta municipal, Tonta pero no tanto, El miedo no anda en burro*), Gregorio Cassab, and Rafael Goyi (*Agarren al de los huevos*), among others. Hardly any of these actors and actresses are among the superstar list of movies considered serious or art films of the new wave. Three directors dominate the narco-fichera movie genre: Hugo Stiglitz, Alvaro Zermeño, and Alfonso Zayas.

Following in popularity are the classic movies with such luminaries as Cantinflas, Tin-Tan, Pedro Infante, María Félix, Dolores del Río, and Pedro Armendáriz. A distant third and spotty at best are movies, when they are stocked, like *La Tarea, Como agua para chocolate*, and *Danzón*. Other movies such as *Canoa, Frida*, and *Rojo Amanecer*, to mention just a few of the ones that critics have mentioned as worthwhile cinematography, are unknown to the owners of the video stores and do not appear in the distributors' lists.

I have chosen two films—*Laura Garza* (1996) and *La del moño colorado* (1997)—from among the 80 percent of films that Cristián González has defined as trash to illustrate how actors, scriptwriters, directors, and producers reweave topics contained in early movies, from comedias rancheras to cabareteras and the derivative ficheras, in order to mass-produce video successes. My choice, though arbitrary, still serves to illuminate the recurrence of popular themes and the reasons for their popularity among the Mexican community of movie fans.

Their overall structure is that of a collection of redundant sketches. *Laura Garza*, for instance, is advertised as a powerful melodrama, but it is far from having the emotional impact of the genre, instead delivering a farcical intertextuality. The film is an amalgamation of classical popular movie scripts. A follower of Mexican cinema can easily identify adaptations from several classic scripts of comedias rancheras, the urban comedies of Tin-Tan, Cantinflas, and film noir flashbacks. Meanwhile, *La del moño colorado* is a parody of organized prostitution and dance halls, a direct blast to middle-class double standards, and a mockery of the presumed naiveté of indigenous women.

In both movies, the actors are stiff and their performances amateurish. The scripts are simplistic and the narrative does not present a clear story line. Low-cost production is evident in shoddy stage settings and props, dull photography, and limited outdoor scenes. Low budgets are also clear from the absence of decorations, refined editing, and costumes. The dialogue is straightforward and closely resembles the plain lines and prompts of *telenovelas.* Background music conforms to the setting of each movie: mariachi and banda norteña. Awkward as the actors may be, the musicians who appear are even more tense, as if baffled by the presence of the camera.

In spite of their shortcomings, the films are still clever productions which, after all, are intended for a specific public: the Mexican migrant masses in the United States and the fronterizo population. The producers make no pretense of great cinematography or originality. What they have done well is to tap into an expanding consumer market that they have read and interpreted for decades. The producers elicit their films based on broad stereotypes of Mexican migrants. They know through simple marketing techniques that their consumers are mainly from rural or economically marginal urban areas, have low levels of education, and are concentrated in unskilled, low-paying jobs. They are also aware that high numbers of them are undocumented workers, mainly Spanish speakers, deeply attached to their Mexican identity, and politically disenfranchised.[11] This is the target audience of Televisa and Televicine's low-budget movie industry.

Laura Garza

Laura Garza. Directed by Jorge Manrique. Produced by Ramón Barba Losa. Alfa Audiovisual, Telestar Films. Released in 1996. Starring Jorge Luke, Toño Infante, Claudia Bernal, Gabriela del Valle, José Luis Carol, and Valentina Tinel.

In a nutshell, *Laura Garza* depicts the impossibility of conventional love stories in contemporary Mexico. It follows along broad lines the

CINEMA FILMS PRESENTA

LAURA GARZA

El odio y la muerte marcan el nacimiento de Laura Garza quien tiene que crecer sin su familia victimas de su orgullo y autores de propia tragedia.

Laura, entonces, se convierte en la joven más rica, poderosa y envidiada de toda la región y que, sin embargo, solo espera una vida llena de paz, felicidad y amor.

Eduardo será el encargado de fraguar el mayor de los engaños para deshacerse de ella y despojarla de toda su cuantiosa fortuna y compartirla con la mujer que despierta su mas profunda pasión.

Pero esta historia está escrita con sangre y nadie puede escapar del furioso poder del destino.

14712 PARTHENIA ST. "D" PANORAMA CITY, CA. 91402
Tel: (818) 830-8801 (1-800) 843-3618

Latin American romance depicted in early movies and derived from nineteenth-century novels. Its primer was *María* by the Colombian Jorge Isaacs, many times rewritten and adapted for radio and telenovela scripts. The story line depicts lovers from opposing social classes who are unable to overcome prejudice. They are socially rebuked, which can lead only to death. In this respect, *Laura Garza* rehashes a familiar theme in a present-day context. Consequently, it is a moral lesson with a series of atavistic epigrams and admonitions. The movie opens on the Mexican side of the border, on a city wall. It is filthy and dusty, and a stream of water runs down the broken, red, sandy ground. The Mexican side of the border is portrayed as ugly, dirty, and decadent. A navy-blue Chevy stops, and a man dressed in black and wearing boots gets out and walks toward the wall. A female narrator introduces the film as a story of impossible dreams, suffering, betrayal, and death. The man in black approaches a middle-aged man dressed in the typical outfit of a ranchero from the Mexican north, in jeans, a checkered shirt, beige drill jacket, and pointed cowboy boots. This is the prototypical outfit for *caciques* (political bosses), as they have always been represented in the movies. He hands the man in black a roll of pesos and asks him to do a good job. Immediately, the viewer knows the job is an execution or some sordid deal and the man in black is a hit man, a *gatillero*. In the following scene, the gatillero is killing a *presidente municipal* and two of his companions in an unspecified town in the north. He also kills some players in a card game when they catch him cheating (his hidden ace of spades falls onto the floor).

The scene then moves to the churchyard. Our heroine, Laura, accompanied by her Nana, Dolores, is coming out of Mass when our cacique approaches and asks that she reconsider his previous offer to buy her land. As she vehemently refuses, the narrator tells us that Laura Garza is an orphan and the wealthiest landowner around. A connection between wealth and surname is made, for she is a Garza, from the wealthy Garzas of Nuevo León. If she is not of that family, she must at least be related, as the surname is commonly associated with the powerful northern lineage.

In the next scene, Laura is seated on a park bench, reading. Dressed in tight jeans and a short blouse, she pores over (and reads aloud) a red, leather-bound book embossed with gold. It is none other than *Arabian Nights*. She muses over her reading and daydreams. She wants a husband who will give her what she reads in the book: sincere love, admiration, and care. Laura demands Nana's help, and it is obvious to viewers what kind of help is requested: Nana is a witch, the prototypical com- bination of *yerbera* sorceress, *cartomanciana* fortuneteller, and devot- ed guadalupana Catholic—no contradictions or innovations here, only a rather trite role. In Nana's room there are several altars with crosses, rosaries, saints, the Virgin of Guadalupe, candles, flowers, incense, and water vessels. Nana takes Laura to the forest and gives her a *limpia*. According to Nana, Laura embodies a fatal combination for possible suitors: rich, pretty, and independent. While Nana believes that women should be virtuous, to Laura purity might as well remain in Heaven because virtue is the source of her loneliness; what she wants is a reen- actment of her parents' love story.

This recollection is the perfect lead-in to a flashback. The love story of Laura's parents is a melodramatic depiction of class conflict with a tragic resolution. Laura's mother, a wealthy heiress, falls in love with Alvaro, the *caporal* (foreman) of the hacienda. In defiance of her role as a decent woman of status, she elopes with the *campesino*, a nobody, an opportunistic fortune-seeker, according to her father. Nana, of course, is an accomplice. The couple lives on the lam until Laura is born. When they are found by the hired hands that her father had on their trail, the father goes to the hut where the couple lives. He chides his daughter, also named Laura, about her lifestyle, which he sees as most improper for a woman of her class. He thinks she lives like a beggar. He takes baby Laura, his granddaughter, and demands that his daughter return home with him. When she refuses after a pathetic "it is him or me," he kills her. With Laura dead and mourned by Nana, Alvaro decides to con- front his father-in-law and retrieve baby Laura. Alvaro has to shoot his way into the hacienda, which he manages to do without a scratch. With the bodyguards dead, he faces the *hacendado*, who justifies killing his daughter as the only way to cleanse his stained honor ("betrayal had to be punished"). With no other way out because, as Alvaro states, "the world is as it is and not as one wants it to be," they kill each other. In a sorrowful voice, the narrator intones, "Blood purges sins but stains destiny."

This far into the movie, the discourse is translucent and readable. It articulates centuries-old themes that are commonly found in popular lore, novels, and romances. Rich girls cannot fall in love with and marry poor boys without paying a hefty price. Fate and unwritten moral codes are enforced against such a transgression. The class divide is unbreach- able, and the usual depiction of moral distance between classes surfaces unaltered. As in *Aventurera* or *Nosotros los pobres* (1947), the upper classes are portrayed as selfish, wicked, corrupt and as always having dirty little secrets.[12] Ranch hands, laborers, servants, and the underclass are essentially good, honorable, and compassionate. Class-crossing is forbidden, and trespassers of social boundaries are punished by death. Love across class causes mayhem; it is not an equalizer of social rifts, nor does it reconcile grievances. Blood is a purifier of contravention in the same way that water purifies original sin in baptism.

Laura flashes back to the present. The cacique, Don Arcadio (let's not forget the social standing of the don) is hiring the gatillero dressed in black to court Laura, marry her, and kill her. He concocts this scheme as the most feasible way to get hold of her land, which he is determined to possess. Land is wealth, prestige, and power. What would a provincial cacique be without large landholdings? Arcadio hands the gatillero, Eduardo, a bundle of money and a copy of *Arabian Nights*. According to the cacique, in order to rise to the challenge and beguile Laura, Eduardo must appear clean shaven, soft spoken, well dressed, and educated; that is, he has to transform himself into a middle-class suitor. After all, Laura is a high-class woman, a *mujer de categoría*. She reads only one book, but that is enough. A simple seduction followed by murder will not do. The book, literate demeanor, and bourgeois comportment are the perfect lures for Laura. Education is equated to high social standing.

When Eduardo, dressed in a two-piece suit, meets Laura at the park, he recites verses from *Arabian Nights*. That is charm enough. The message is that while Eduardo might be a low-class rogue, a hit man, and a schemer, he can nevertheless recite from memory excerpts from *Arabian Nights*. Does this make him less of a swindler, or does it imply that street-smart individuals can just as easily appear scholarly and resourceful, transforming themselves into educated members of high society? A more likely interpretation of this metaphor points to a deep-seated distrust many Mexicans have of the educated classes. There is no further elaboration, however, and what the viewer sees next is the wedding. In contrast to the happy newlywed Laura, Nana bemoans the ceremony because her "natural instinct full of premonitions" and card readings warn of upcoming misfortune.

What follows is a complicated tour de force in which a new character appears. It is a young woman, Amalia, a rival and pivot point for the story. Amalia is from town and has always been jealous of Laura's wealth, beauty, and good fortune. Amalia is depicted as an opportunistic social climber suffused with class resentment: "Laura always had everything, I had nothing." Amalia and Laura are social opposites, a point meant to be illustrated through their sexuality. Amalia is not above using her sexuality to seduce Eduardo. She is assertive; wears short, tight miniskirts, high heels, and low-cut blouses that provocatively reveal cleavage; and is confident that her advances will get her close to Eduardo. Unlike Amalia, Laura does not have to seduce Eduardo. Instead, he seduces her, not sexually but through his finesse and recitation of love stories, an imposture.

Gender constructs are never devoid of class leanings, nor are they unambiguous. Amalia states that she and Eduardo are both of low-class extraction; they cannot fool each other about passion and sex, for they have none of the libidinal constraints of the elite. The message here, of course, is that lower-class women do not need wit or education to survive in a classist society; their erotic instincts and their purportedly unrestrained sexuality enable them to rise above social inequality. What is seen as a solution, instead, condemns women. Open sexuality is chastised and cross-class sexuality is a punishable transgression. Amalia is assertive about her sexual superiority. She is not a fool because she knows that romantic love is a chimera. For her, what really matters is the free exercise of her sexuality. But erotic fulfillment is not enough, and she adds to it the power of knowledge because she knows about Eduardo and the cacique's complicated stratagem. Once caught in this trap, Eduardo has no choice but to join forces with Amalia; the seducer is seduced. The lovers execute Arcadio because he is no longer needed. He has become a nuisance. For Nana the complicity is casuistic; they were *mal nacidos y de mala entraña,* discreet metaphors for having been bastards and inherently corrupt. The stigma of Malinche is played out once again: illegitimacy, a sin, an indelible curse.

The conclusion is transparent. The lovers meet Laura at the house, ready to kill her, but Laura draws her gun first and shoots them both. In agony, Eduardo declares his eternal and undying love to Laura. This, of course, is to no avail. It is too late. Disillusioned but alive and triumphant, Laura rides into the sunset, never to be seen again. Rumor has it that she wanders the northern ranges as an *alma en pena* (suffering soul), leaving open the possibility of a sequel.

Laura Garza epitomizes the ranchera in particular, and Mexican melodramas in general. However banal the plot may be, it contains the basic formula: a familiar rural setting, sentimentalism, deception, class conflict, mariachi serenades, violent shootouts, and frustrated, unfulfilled characters. But are these elements enough to render the movie sleazy or trashy? The film lacks suggestive sex, nudity is tame, violent scenes are subdued, and foul language is moderate. At worst, *Laura Garza* as a story line might be considered merely thin and weak, its narrative unassuming and replete with commonplace, insipid dialogue, and clichés. However, it is precisely these characteristics—its allusion to popular themes—that make it successful. Indeed, these are the elements most easily identified by viewers on both sides of the border. Foremost is the geographical location, the attire, the accents, the wall, the *norteño* music, all especially familiar to fronterizos and popular in Mexican communities in the United States.

Still, there is an element of the movie that stands out: the striking absence of law enforcement. It is apparent that the people with guns (and certainly those with money) enforce the law. The police do not mediate or resolve conflicts; they simply are not present, physically or discursively. The police are never mentioned or even alluded to. Illustrative of this point is the scene where Laura's father is seen herding cattle. Suddenly, he is attacked by a group of gunmen and shoots all of them. This scene is a complete digression, for there is no explanation as to who these men are or where they come from. They could be rustlers, thieves, or drug dealers, among numerous possibilities. This does not matter in the plot, either. The caporal settles the affair with gun in hand. That is part of the job description of a caporal, to defend the life and property of the hacendado, an action for which he is handsomely rewarded (a bag of money). The implication is that there is no need to involve the law—doing so would complicate things. Another scene strengthens this point. When Eduardo, hired by the cacique, kills the presidente municipal and two of his aides, the police do not appear nor are they ever mentioned. Eduardo saunters away.

We can speculate on many reasons for the invisibility of the police. It may be an attempt to obliterate their corrupt character in present-day Mexico, to settle the score by erasing the institution altogether. Other determinations may have played a role in this omission, ranging from concerns about production costs to the director's antagonism toward the authorities. The point is that in several of these movies what is not shown often can be more telling than what is. Also meaningful is the indication of a profound rupture between Mexican law enforcement and a civil society today under siege by escalating crime rates. The corruption of law enforcement and the strength of drug trafficking criminal organizations have overpowered real-life events. Why should this not happen in films?

LA DEL MOÑO COLORADO

La del moño colorado. Directed by José Antonio Chávez Juárez. Produced by Blanca Isabel Samperio and Beatríz Pérez Negrete. Producciones Pirámide, Venus BB Business. Released in 1997. Starring Jorge Aldama, Valería Gallort, Ángel Camara, Alfredo Gutiérrez, El Chispita, and María del Carmen Reces.

In a male-dominated movie field, the most interesting and paradoxically intriguing facet of *La del moño colorado* is that the producers are women. Moreover, they employed other women to support the production. *La del moño colorado* is a farce of horrors, a hilarious comedy with an apparently guileless plot. The acting is dreadful, the film's low-budget production translates into lackluster scenery, very scarce technical props, and cheap costumes. It bears the same cinematographic deficiencies as *Laura Garza,* at times appearing as if it were made for fun by a group of friends experimenting with a home video camera, an effort better suited for private screening. The title itself, *La del moño colorado,* is asinine. In spite of all this (or perhaps because of it), the video is a popular rental.

La del moño colorado is the story of an *indita,* a young Indian woman with braided hair and a big red ribbon (*moño*) on top of her head. Francisca has left her home in San Juan Chamula for the city to work as a maid. When she arrives, she is immediately frightened by the intense city traffic and seeks the help of a policeman, who walks her to her new home. The stereotype of the naive Indian maid, prominent in movie and telenovela depictions, runs deep in Mexican society. As she speaks her lines, it is clear that Francisca is a takeoff of La India María, though not as witty or brassy. As with the character developed by María Elena Velasco, Francisca is gullible but sassy, childish but astute.

Francisca's new home is not a regular household. It is a *casa non sancta, una casa de citas,* a brothel in a middle-class neighborhood. The madam, a happy-go-lucky businesswoman, greets Francisca and introduces her to the *niñas,* the prostitutes. Francisca has no clue about what goes on in the house, and she never finds out. Her naiveté, however, is charming to the prostitutes. In both film narratives and telenovela scripts, the codification of indigenous and peasant women as dumb and naive servants is commonplace. The niñas, giggling constantly and always dressed in chiffon nightgowns with lace trimmings or electric yellow or pink baby dolls, embrace Francisca and name her Francis. After

LA DEL MOÑO COLORADO

"La Del Moño Colorado. " Una chica ingenua que decide irse a la capital de Mexico en busca de un futuro mejor.

Sin imaginarse que al llegar a su primer empleo como sirvienta, seria en una "CASA DE CITAS". Por lo tanto se ve envuelta en una serie de chistosas y confusas aventuras.

Salga Usted de la duda y vea esta simpatica y genial comedia. Apta para toda familia.

Tiempo de Duracíon 105 minutes

LIBRA PRODUCTIONS
1807 ...
Rosada, CA 91...
Tel. 1 800 711 ... (818) 724 ...
Fax (818) 772 ...

all, her name must not be out of step with those of the niñas: Didi, Nanette, and Bombom. The madam is not at all like the heinous *Poquianchis* characters of other films, and her clientele is not working class; they are lawyers, engineers, public officials, and a federal judge— middle-class professionals and upholders of the double standard, recreation at the brothel and reproduction at home.

The madam protects Francisca because "a maid is rarer and more valuable than a husband." Madam and prostitutes recoil at the thought of housework. This feeling, of course, holds true for both elites and the middle class, and the bluntness of its portrayal deserves consideration, particularly because similar comments are rarely voiced in public. Elite women have almost always relied on servants to do household chores, which in turn allowed them to engage in managing and supervising activities. In the aftermath of the Mexican Revolution, it was not the dividing up of domestic chores between husband and wife that allowed middle-class women to undertake economic, educational, or other activities outside their households. Usually, there was no such negotiation about gender roles. Instead, it was the maid who took up the slack. In this respect, the madam and the prostitutes are voicing the complaints of many women among the middle and elite classes who constantly bemoan the disappearing persona of the maid. They cannot hide their resentment at the modernization process, which has sent rural migrant women into commercial, service, and manufacturing jobs and away from domestic work.

Francisca is assertive as she confronts the *pelados*, the fruit and vegetable vendors at the market and in the streets. She fights their advances and gets physical in her defense. She enrolls in karate lessons to protect herself and the prostitutes. Francisca thinks that self-defense will prevent advances from street thugs. On one occasion she attacks clients of the brothel because she does not understand their getting fresh with the niñas. Francisca snaps at the women themselves, for being "half naked" and thereby encouraging the men to be "all hands." The commentary is meaningless to the niñas, who giggle because Francisca "does not know anything about real life in the city." Nonetheless, this scene is indicative of the popular perception that women invite sexual harassment through provocative clothing that exposes shoulders, breasts, and legs.

Francisca likes music and dancing, and on Sundays goes with the neighbor's maid to the California Dancing Club, where the scenes are filmed live with the regular clientele of the popular dance hall and the endorsement of the owner, Mariana de la Cruz. At the Califas, as the dance hall is popularly known, she meets a dance partner and reluctant suitor. But, under the dim lights of the hall and the loud norteño music of Los Elegantes, Francisca and her partner metamorphoze. She becomes the private secretary to the lady of the house, even wearing the madam's clothes and jewels. Meanwhile he, a *talachero,* a retreader of tires, wearing his best and only suit, becomes a certified public accountant. The scene is absurd and highly comical—but not impossible in a society whose members are constantly battered with media messages about desirable occupations that carry social recognition and prestige and about shunning low-skilled, menial work.

In the meantime, two voyeurs who regularly stalk the house plan to abduct the rich madam for a considerable ransom. However, they accidentally kidnap Francisca, who is mistaken for the madam because she is wearing her *patrona*'s clothes. She is taken to a shack on the outskirts of the city, from whence her boyfriend and a *diputado,* a congressman, rescue her. The madam and the prostitutes, dressed in faux leopard-skin tights and high heels, beat the kidnappers and tie them up. With this bizarre scene, the movie ends.

La del moño colorado is overtly racist and suffused with sexist remarks such as, "Hija de Tlaloc, ni que estuvieras tan buena" (roughly translated, "daughter of Tlaloc, after all you are not that desirable"). The expression has a double meaning, on one hand connoting Indianness in its most pejorative sense, while on the other disparaging a woman's sex appeal. Notably, the statement is not the invention of a scriptwriter but a part of Mexican vernacular.

The film contains suggestive sensuality and seminudity but no profane language or albures. Neither are there any audacious sex scenes, with the exception of some timid lovemaking and a suggestion of striptease. The movie makes no pretenses at moralizing nor is it intended to be a tearful, sentimental melodrama. The narrative develops in a social and political void, revealing a microcosm of middle-class mentality.

The movie distances itself from the depiction of the repentant and victimized prostitute of the cabaretera melodrama. The class system is never challenged, merely accepted and respected as the order of things. The prostitutes are street-smart women who nonetheless cynically prize the apparent innocence of the Indian woman. They express their sympathy while attempting to shelter her in the realm of primitive bliss.

Quite possibly, however, they do so not necessarily for Francisca's sake but to protect their own interests in keeping their maid, especially because she comes from a distant rural area.

CONCLUSION

From these two movies it is readily apparent that the plots of old melodramas and comedies need not be substantially changed. Dominant ideology structures the themes and mass-produces them for a public that has viewed and identified with them for generations. At the same time, the producers' reading of the Mexican public as undiscerning remains unchanged. Whether resurrected in the form of the realization of impossible love, contemptible melodrama, and insurmountable class barriers, as in the case of *Laura Garza,* or in the form of a blunt comedy of scathing banality, as in *La del moño colorado,* the early plots breathe a life of their own. These movies, and hundreds more like them, are a cauldron of degrading assumptions about the values and behavior of the Mexican popular classes. Replication and sameness continue with little resistance to historically accepted stereotypes.

It is noteworthy that many of the low-budget movies are not about raunchy sex, violence, or drug dealing. The themes of the movies capture existing stereotypes about popular classes, and there is no doubt that they are overtly racist, sexist, and classist. All of these elements are part of Mexican society and culture, however. Mexico is a class-based society in which discrimination does exist and is experienced on a daily basis. Most interestingly, these films do not shy away from this social reality and are not timid in expressing it crudely and bluntly. It is possible, then, to contend that such portrayals of the "popular" are what irritate filmmakers and critics like González and Pelayo. It is apparent that they are trapped in the contradictions of their middle-class mentality, which interprets the popular with an elitist dictionary. They criticize these productions as prejudiced and disdainful of the popular classes. Yet, at the same time, they are supercilious toward the same sector, whom they regard as barefoot illiterates with no artistic appreciation. In this respect, the remarks by Carlos Monsiváis seem appropriate:

> No one need concern themselves about ethical questions. After all, everything is resolved beforehand; everyone has his place on the ladder of command and everyone knows how to react to sex,

drink, food, and death. Producers, directors, scriptwriters, and actors take as their starting point traditional morality, in its most defensive version, and have the right wing in the forefront of their mind.[13] ❖

NOTES

1. Nissa Torrents, "Mexican Cinema Comes Alive," in *Mediating Two Worlds: Cinematic Encounters in the Americas*, John King, Ana M. Lopez, and Manuel Alvarado, eds. (London: BFI Publishing, 1993), 222–29.
2. Carl L. Mora, *Mexican Cinema: Reflections of a Society* (Berkeley: University of California Press, 1989), 182.
3. Ibid.
4. Ibid.
5. Carlos Monsivais, "Mexican Cinema: Of Myths and Demystifications," in *Mediating Two Worlds*, 139–46.
6. John King, *Magical Reels: A History of Cinema in Latin America* (New York: Verso, 1990), chapter 6.
7. *Albur* refers to a double entendre, usually of a sexual nature.
8. Oscar J. Martínez, *Border Boom Town: Ciudad Juárez since 1848* (Austin: University of Texas Press, 1978), 107.
9. Mora, *Mexican Cinema*, 85; Ana M. Lopez. "Tears and Desire: Women and Melodrama in the 'Old' Mexican Cinema," in *Mediating Two Worlds*, 158–59.
10. Carlos Monsivais, "Notas sobre la cultura mexicana en el siglo XX," *Historia general de México*, vol. 4 (México: Colegio de México, Centro de Estudios Históricos, 1976), 457.
11. Maurilio E. Vigil. *Hispanics in American Politics* (New York: University Press of America, 1987).
12. *Nosotros los pobres* was a box-office hit directed by Ismael Rodríguez. It featured Pedro Infante and Blanca Estela Pavón. See Emilio García Rivera, *Historia documental del cine mexicano*, vol. 3 (Mexico City: Ediciones Era, 1972), 274.
13. Mora, *Mexican Cinema*, 145.

Tex-Mex, Cal-Mex, New Mex, or Whose Mex? Notes on the Historical Geography of Southwestern Cuisine

Jeffrey M. Pilcher

Residents of the United States often have a peculiar view of Mexican food, drawn more from Mexican American restaurants or from fast food simulations than from actual experience south of the border. While the combination plates at local restaurants offer little of the rich complexity of Mexico's regional cuisines, they do have a history of their own, one that reflects the ongoing struggle of Mexican Americans to gain acceptance and citizenship in the United States.[1]

The cooking of the Southwest, like Mexican cooking in general, embodies a fusion of Native American and Hispanic influences, the legacy of three centuries of first Spanish and then Mexican rule. As examples of a common regional style, *norteño* cooking, the dishes from different parts of the borderlands resemble each other more than they do the foods of other parts of Mexico. One distinctive characteristic of northern Mexican cooking is the use of wheat flour instead of corn in making tortillas. The great herds of livestock raised along the frontier made norteños more carnivorous, in particular more fond of beef, than Mexicans farther south. On the other hand, the grassy plains and arid deserts of the north, well suited to cattle ranching and irrigated wheat farming, offered less variety in vegetables, herbs, and chiles, limiting the potential for complex sauces and soups. These common elements notwithstanding, considerable variety also exists within Southwestern cooking. Cheryl Alters Jamison and Bill Jamison, in their authoritative work *The Border Cookbook*, define four broad regions straddling the U.S.–Mexican border: Texas and northeastern Mexico, New Mexico, Sonora, and California. This essay will describe these differing cooking styles from a historical and geographical perspective.[2]

Native Americans and Hispanics in the Southwest already had long-established culinary traditions in 1848, when Mexico surrendered California, Arizona, New Mexico, and Texas to the United States in the Treaty of Guadalupe Hidalgo. The predominantly male fortune seekers who migrated to the region alternately looked down on the racially mixed residents and married into the more European-appearing elite, while grabbing land and wealth on an equal-opportunity basis. A peculiar gender dynamic emerged in which Anglo newcomers feminized the male inhabitants—think of stereotypes of passive Mexican men in dress-like serapes and big, gaudy sombreros—and sexualized the women as "hot tamales" and "chili queens." In this contentious environment, the women's work of cooking and the traditionally male task of grilling meat became sites of cultural conflict and accommodation. Simultaneously attracted to and repelled by the piquant stews of Hispanic women in San Antonio, Anglo males ultimately appropriated chili by taming the hot peppers into a mass-produced and easily regulated powder. Outsiders found some Mexican American dishes simply repulsive, most notably *menudo* (tripe), thereby making them powerful symbols of ethnic identity. Between these two extremes, most Southwestern dishes gradually entered the mestizo stew that makes up the cuisine of the United States, acquiring new tastes and forms but maintaining clear links to their ethnic origins.[3]

Corn Mothers and Animal Spirits

For more than a thousand years, cooks of the Southwest have taken inspiration from the civilizations of Mesoamerica. The agricultural complex of maize, beans, and squash, domesticated in central Mexico, gradually diffused through much of North America in the first millennium of the Common Era. The staple tortilla—made by simmering maize in mineral lime (CaO), grinding it into *masa* (dough) on a *metate* (grinding stone), patting it into a flat round shape, and cooking it briefly on a griddle—had also begun to arrive in the Southwest before the Spaniards, as had the more elaborate tamales, dumplings made of the same dough steamed in cornhusks. Justifiably proud of their elaborate cuisine, the inhabitants of the Valley of Mexico dismissed their northern neighbors contemptuously as Chichimecas (dog-people) for their scavenging ways. Nevertheless, the lack of large domesticated animals reduced even the haughty warriors of the Aztec Empire to considerable hunting and gathering to supplement their basically vegetarian diet, thus belying some of their claims to superiority over cooks from the northern frontier.

An assortment of wild plants and animals formed the common basis for human subsistence in the Southwest. With its large size and savory meat, the deer stood out as the favorite game animal for much of North America, although Indians hunted smaller game as well, including peccaries, rabbits, mice, rats, and snakes. Edible desert plants such as the prickly pear, mesquite bean pods, maguey, and a variety of roots, herbs, and *quelites* (greens) supplemented the hunt. In some areas nature provided so abundantly that the inhabitants had little incentive to undertake agriculture and instead could wander freely. For example, in the coastal regions of present-day California, acorns fell so profusely from the trees that the Indians could gather them as a daily staple, along with the plentiful fruits, berries, and game animals (see figure 1). The Seri Indians, living in what is now the Mexican state of Sonora, caught enough fish and sea turtles in the Gulf of California to feed themselves without agriculture. The Gulf of Mexico, particularly around the Rio Grande delta, yielded a similarly rich catch, although maize agriculture had begun to make inroads in this region when the Spaniards arrived. Even some inland areas, such as the confluence of the Rio Grande and the Rio Conchos, offered plentiful freshwater mussels and fish, but again not to the exclusion of floodplain agriculture.[4]

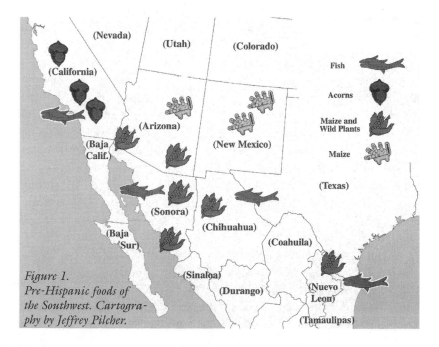

Figure 1.
Pre-Hispanic foods of the Southwest. Cartography by Jeffrey Pilcher.

The nomadic life of the California and Seri Indians contrasted sharply with the lifestyle in the Pueblo villages along the Rio Grande and the Little Colorado and Pecos Rivers. Irrigated maize agriculture supported large communities, in some cases numbering in the thousands and living in multistory mud-brick apartment houses. The Pueblo Indians consumed the staple corn in a variety of ways: toasted, boiled, and as gruel. In addition, the Spanish conquistadors described the making of tortillas and tamales; indeed, Coronado praised the Zuni tortillas as the best he had ever eaten. Nevertheless, the Spaniards did not mention the use of chiles, the principal flavoring of central Mexico. The Pueblo people also raised domesticated turkeys, but their sedentary life and advanced agriculture did not preclude hunting and gathering. Piñón nuts, gathered in the fall, added greatly to the Pueblo diet, and the Pecos Indians even ventured out onto the Great Plains to hunt bison. The people at Pecos may also have caught large amounts of trout, while the Zuni considered fish taboo.[5]

The majority of the Southwestern Indians were semi-sedentary, growing maize while still depending heavily on hunting and gathering. Called *ranchería* people by the Spaniards, they generally lived in bands numbering two or three hundred, spread out over considerable distances, and often migrating during the course of the year. The ranchería people comprised the Tarahumara and Conchos of the western Sierra Madre (Chihuahua); the Yaqui and Mayo, inhabiting river valleys of the same names, as well as their northern neighbors, the Lower Pima and Opata (Sonora), the Yuma in the Colorado River valley, and the Upper Pima and Tohono O'odham along various rivers in the Sonoran Desert (northwestern Sonora and southern Arizona). In addition, the Athabaskan-speaking people later known as Navajos and Apaches had recently migrated into the region from the north and were beginning to cultivate maize when the Spaniards arrived. While much of their harvest of corn, beans, and squash was simply roasted along with any game they may have caught, the ranchería people made *pinole* by adding toasted and ground maize seeds to water, and baked loaves of corn and mesquite bread. Some also drank a mildly alcoholic beverage of fermented cactus fruit.[6]

A common theme unified the lives of these otherwise disparate peoples, that of constant movement. Even the most settled Puebloans had to relocate regularly, rebuilding their adobe homes in the process, in order to find more fertile land in the arid climate. The agricultural Pueblo societies were matrilineal, and some authors have suggested that women may have fared better there than in the patriarchal hunter-gatherer societies of California. Moreover, the Pueblo Indians worshipped Corn Mothers as fertility symbols at the heart of their religious beliefs, while the ranchería peoples, who had adopted agriculture more recently, attached less religious significance to corn. But regardless of whether the Native Americans believed in animal spirits or corn goddesses, their encounter with Spanish priests changed their diet as well as their religion.[7]

FRONTIER FOODS OF NEW SPAIN

The conquistadors' mission of Europeanizing the Americas—literally founding a New Spain—required the simultaneous introduction of Old World plants and animals and the extirpation of native foods associated with heathen religious practices. Father Bernardino de Sahagún instructed the Indians to eat "that which the Castilian people eat, because it is good food, that with which they are raised, they are strong and pure and wise. . . . You will become the same way if you eat their food."[8] Yet his nutritional advice, like much of the Catholic doctrine, was accepted only halfway. Native Americans embraced some new foods, particularly livestock, while clinging stubbornly to their staple crops of maize, beans, squash, and chiles. A mestizo cuisine eventually emerged, combining foods from the Old World and the New, just as intermarriage between Spaniards and Indians produced Mexico's mestizo nation. These mixtures spread to the northern provinces as well, and on that distant frontier, mestizo society and culture were often mistaken for Spanish originals.

Catholic priests, whose evangelical mission to the Indians served to justify Spain's empire in the Americas, demanded radical changes in the lives of the new initiates. The European belief that civilization required permanent settlements brought an end to the nomadic or semi-nomadic lifestyle of many ranchería peoples, although the introduction of livestock compensated in part for the decline in hunting. Prohibitions on polygamy, together with the introduction of European diseases against which the natives had little resistance, decimated the indigenous social organization. Natives responded to these changes in different ways; the Yaquis embraced the missions, adopting far more of the newly emerging Mexican culture, including the cooking techniques, than did the neighboring Mayo. Among the Athabaskan people, some settled down to become sheepherders, blending their culture with that of the Pueblos and taking the name Navajo. Others took only the Spanish horses, and by the 1660s the Apaches, as they were called, had become a menace to both Spanish and Pueblo settlements. Pacification policies encouraged further acculturation through handouts of food and alcohol to make the Apaches dependent on Spanish officials and the distribution of defective firearms to limit the destruction when they did go on raids.[9]

If the spiritual conquest legitimized the colonies, the prospect of making a quick fortune attracted Spanish settlers. After looting the Aztec Empire, the conquistadors set out for the north in search of the fabled Seven Cities of Cíbola, where legend had it that the streets were paved with gold. The expedition of Francisco Vásquez de Coronado reached the Zuni Pueblos in 1540, discovering the reality to be a more prosaic adobe. The silver bonanza at Zacatecas in 1548 attracted the first permanent European settlement in the north and also led to the construction of presidios to protect the treasure on the Royal Road back to Mexico City. Juan de Oñate, a silver miner made wealthy in Zacatecas, established the colony of New Mexico in 1598, although the Pueblo Revolt of 1680 temporarily forced the Spaniards to withdraw to El Paso del Norte. The rest of the Southwest remained unsettled by Europeans until the eighteenth century, when imperial defense requirements promoted a more active Spanish presence. French incursions from Louisiana into Texas led to the foundation of San Antonio in 1718, while Apache raids in Sonora motivated the construction of a presidio at Tucson in 1776. Finally, the appearance of Russian trappers on the northern Pacific coast prompted the crown to transfer troops from Sonora and Sinaloa to new presidios in California.[10]

The new settlers, although generally mestizos from central Mexico, attempted to construct a Spanish society on the northern frontier. The Iberian Peninsula had a medieval tradition of mounted cattle raising—the vaquero culture later appropriated by Anglo cowboys—but the scrawny range cattle were often butchered for their hides alone, leaving the meat behind to rot. The settlers preferred sheep and goats, especially prizing *cabrito asado* (roast kid) as a delicacy throughout the frontier region. Cooking techniques often amounted to methods of preservation such as making cheese or sausage. The colonists also produced large amounts of *carne seca*, a form of jerky made by cutting beef into long strips and drying it in the desert sun inside a cage to keep the flies out. To preserve pork, they made a vinegar marinade called *adovo*, heavily spiced with chiles to distinguish it from similar Spanish preparations. Whenever irrigation permitted, the settlers cultivated the European grain wheat, although the expense of mills and ovens often forced women to grind the grain on metates and cook it in the form of tortillas rather than bread. The pervasive use of chiles in stews and salsas likewise demonstrated the Native American influence on Spanish cuisine. The rich agricultural land of California allowed the production of those Mediterranean staples, wine and olives, unavailable elsewhere in New Spain, but even the wealthiest settlers ate a generally Spartan diet with only an occasional luxury such as imported chocolate. Those sturdy frontier foods later became the foundation for Southwestern cuisine and a bulwark of Mexican American identity.[11]

Deconstructing Chili/e

Chili or chile? Chili con carne or carne con chile? Chile verde or carne verde? Southwestern cuisine often seems as baffling as it is intimidating to newcomers who have not yet developed a tolerance for spicy foods. The confusion derives from both regional and temporal differences; for example, a person who asks, "Red or green?" is now answering the question, "Where are you?" "New Mexico." Prior to refrigeration, the color question was seasonal; had the fresh green chiles ripened and turned red while drying on the *ristra?* But however varied their cooking styles, Hispanics in the Southwest faced a common question that struck to the heart of their identity: were they Mexican or Spanish? For more than a century after the United States annexed the region, former Mexican citizens, accustomed to fluid racial boundaries, struggled to find a place in a society that saw only black and white. They claimed Spanish descent in an attempt to gain equal status as Europeans but, in doing so, often shunned their fellow Mexicans who had migrated north more recently. The permutations of chile reflect the diverse experiences of Hispanics as they encountered Anglo society and established their citizenship in the United States.[12]

New Mexico, the oldest European settlement in North America, also has the most firmly established cuisine in the Southwest. Centered around the capital, Santa Fe, this cooking style extends beyond the geographical confines of the state to include the San Luis Valley in southern Colorado, the mountains around Flagstaff in northern Arizona, and parts of Chihuahua, Mexico (see figure 2). The soul of Mexican cuisine has always been the chile pepper, but while the cooks of Old

Mexico experimented with blending different chiles to make their renowned *mole* sauces, in New Mexico they perfected the cultivation and cooking of a single chile. The state's eponymous pepper forms the basic ingredient for both chile verde and chile colorado, which can be served thick as a sauce or with broth and vegetables as a stew, although in the latter case the green is more common, sometimes with the name carne con chile verde or chile verde *caldo* to distinguish it from the sauce. For those unable to choose between the two sauces, restaurants in New Mexico offer a combination of red and green known as Christmas. Unlike Mexican moles, which gain their taste and texture from freshly ground peppers, chile colorado is often simply a mixture of chile powder and water, perhaps thickened by a roux, with garlic, oregano, and salt to taste. As Santa Fe cooking authority Huntley Dent explains, red chile "savors of mystique, not so much for its own taste, which is earthy and fairly musty, as for its ability to combine with corn tortillas, meat, and cheese."[13]

The traditional cooking of New Mexico comprises a variety of dishes, often made with distinctive local twists. The celebrated blue corn and the little-known *chicos* (roasted green ears) are both hallmarks of the state, which is also the only place cooks serve the hominy dish *posole* as

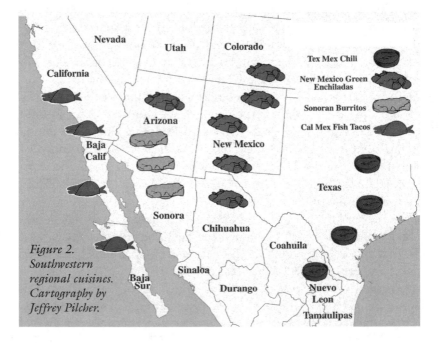

Figure 2. Southwestern regional cuisines. Cartography by Jeffrey Pilcher.

a vegetable side order rather than a meaty stew. Pork rather than beef came to replace kid and mutton as the most common meat, used both for chile stews and the colonial dish *carne adovada,* which remains a favorite in New Mexico. Meals end with such distinctive desserts as the fried-bread *sopaipillas* and *buñuelos* or the enigmatic sprouted-wheat pudding *panocha.* Moreover, different cooking styles appear within New Mexico, particularly in the rivalry between north and south. The residents of Chimayó and Española take pride in the intense flavor their diminutive chiles develop while shivering in the shadows of the Sangre de Cristo Mountains. "Down there in the south," explained farmer Orlando Casados, Sr., "a lot of those chiles are as big as a banana, but they taste like cardboard, no flavor at all. This is the best place for growing chile in the whole world." Nevertheless, people down south in the "Chile Capital" of Hatch, New Mexico, feel equally proud of the *rellenos* (stuffed chiles) served at their annual Chile Festival. Hispanics in Colorado, meanwhile, consider their chile verde superior because of the quality of the local pork.[14]

The regional cooking of Sonora, encompassing both the Mexican state and the southern half of Arizona, gave much less emphasis to the heat of the chile pepper. The classic New Mexico stew carne con chile verde changed so radically when made with mild Anaheim peppers that some Arizona cooks dropped the word "chile" entirely and referred to it simply as "carne verde." The dish also featured beef instead of pork, a tribute to the herds of cattle raised in the valleys of the Sonoran Desert. Even after the advent of refrigeration, one of the most common methods of preparing beef remained the colonial style of jerky, sometimes called *machaca,* for the pounding needed to reconstitute it. Cookbook author Diana Kennedy noted that cooks throughout the state of Sonora kept a large black pebble for this purpose. Flour tortillas, while common throughout the Southwest, also reached the peak of artistry in Sonora, where cooks often roll them out to perfectly round, paper-thin disks a foot and a half in diameter. When wrapped around beef or bean fillings to make burritos, they became "possibly the single heaviest fast-food item in the world," which in turn took the name *chimichanga* (basically meaning "thingamajig") when deep fried.[15]

New Mexico and Arizona shared a common isolation, which kept the territories from reaching full statehood in the nineteenth century and also allowed the Mexican communities to retain their cultural integrity. Of course, Anglos came to dominate politics and most Hispanics remained strictly working class; nevertheless, a substantial Mexican American middle class preserved its economic position and cultural heritage by renaming it Spanish. Eventually, the same rugged mountains and stark desert landscapes that had repelled immigrants in the nineteenth century attracted them when air conditioning and ski lifts arrived following World War II, leading to a real estate boom that drove increasing numbers of Hispanics from their land around Santa Fe, Taos, and Tucson. By contrast, Mexicans in Texas and California did not have a century of isolation to consolidate their social position, for the dispossession of land followed immediately on the Treaty of Guadalupe Hidalgo.[16]

While the origins of Texas's chili con carne remain shrouded in culinary legend, the subsequent development of the dish reveals a process of both racial stereotyping and cultural appropriation. The dish probably began as a stew, made of goat or deer meat as often as beef, and spiced with red chiles, cumin, and oregano, which remain the distinctive flavors of Tex-Mex cooking as cooking expert Marilyn Tausend has observed. Subtleties of taste were lost on Anglo visitors to nineteenth-century San Antonio, who rarely made it past the initial shock of the chile peppers. In 1874, for example, Edward King described "fat, swarthy Mexican mater-familias" offering "various savory compounds, swimming in fiery pepper, which biteth like a serpent." The imagined dangers, both culinary and sexual, of the so-called chili queens on Military Plaza enticed countless tourists, who remembered the city "because of the Chili Stands, the Menger Hotel, and the Alamo." But the Hispanic cooks did not share in the profits from mass-marketing their dish; in 1896, a German immigrant, William Gebhardt, formulated the chili powder known as Tampico Dust, which helped spread the taste for chili across the country. Already tamed down for timid palates, chili underwent other alterations, the side order of beans was unceremoniously dumped into the pot, and it was added to hot dogs and, in Cincinnati, even to spaghetti. Meanwhile, back in San Antonio, after a long struggle with city inspectors, the original chili stands closed down as supposed health hazards in the 1930s.[17]

Chili had been stripped of its ethnicity to become the state dish of Texas, but Mexican Americans retained a repertoire of other foods that affirmed their identity precisely because of the scorn they attracted from the Anglo elite. Although it had lost favor in New Mexico and California, cabrito asado remained as popular in south Texas as in northeastern Mexico, particularly Monterrey, where it attained legendary status. Anglos had little use for goat, but the only beef that poor Mexican Americans could afford was the viscera. One such castoff cut, the diaphragm muscle (*arrachera*), lost its tough texture in a marinade of lime juice and garlic and became quite delicious when grilled on an open fire and served with salsa on hot, fresh tortillas. Perhaps the most beloved dish of working-class Mexican Americans, and the most repulsive one to outsiders, was the pit-barbecued bull head (*barbacoa de cabeza*). The two-day process of preparing the pit, cooking the meat, and serving it up messily as tacos invited communal celebrations, drinking, and dancing among Hispanics.[18]

Legends of Texas chili notwithstanding, the most mysterious branch of Southwestern cuisine is the original art of California ranch cooking. Unlike the thriving Hispanic cultures of New Mexico, Arizona, and south Texas, Californio society now exists only as a memory, distorted by the assimilation of a small elite into Anglo society and by more recent Mexican migrants, who far outnumber the descendants of the original settlers. Nevertheless, a few tastes of that pastoral era can be gleaned from the first Spanish-language cookbook published in the state, *El cocinero español* (1898) by Encarnación Pinedo. An heiress to one of the most prominent Californio families, the Berreyesa clan, she was born in the tragic year of 1848, as a swarm of Anglo fortune hunters descended to swindle away the family estates and to lynch eight of her uncles and cousins. Determined to maintain the dignity of Hispanic culture, Pinedo gave a stinging rebuke to the barbarous Yankee invaders, describing their food as "the most insipid and tasteless that one can imagine." Her own recipes, written in a lively literary style, derived from classical Mexican dishes such as moles, tamales, chiles rellenos, and barbacoa de cabeza, even though she disguised them with Spanish titles. As Victor Valle has observed, "The Mexican roots of [modern] California cuisine can also be detected in her liberal use of fruits and vegetables, fresh edible flowers and herbs, her aggressive spicing, and grilling over native wood fires."[19]

Pinedo's cookbook provided an eloquent example of Hispanics' widespread use of food to affirm their identity against the threat of Anglo encroachment. Jacqueline Higuera McMahan has written a series of nostalgic cookbooks, laden with family history, which describe the culinary encounters of old California. The Yankee newcomers were apparently so astonished to see people eat chiles for breakfast that they attributed to Californios the digestive system of ostriches. The Higueras, meanwhile, repeated the fiction that they had lost their Santa Clara ranch to finance the legendary 1865 wedding festival of Don Valentín's favorite daughter, María. Although declining in society, the family at least took comfort from the belief that they had a more civilized lifestyle than the Anglo land grabbers around them. Twentieth-century migrants brought their own regional dishes with them from Mexico and often used these foods to defend themselves against racial discrimination. Victor Villaseñor, in his best-selling family memoir, *Rain of Gold,* recalled his grandmother's words, "Don't worry about the police. One day we'll feed them tacos with so much old chile that they'll get diarrhea and their assholes will burn for weeks!"[20]

Encounters between ethnic foods and mainstream consumers have remained sites of cultural contention throughout the twentieth century, as Mexicans faced the contradictory impulses to preserve their culture intact or to profit from adapting the foods for a general audience. Enclave restaurants sprang up wherever large numbers of Mexicans settled more or less permanently to work. By the beginning of the century, such small-time establishments existed all along the border as well as in more distant urban areas such as Chicago, St. Louis, and Kansas City. Moreover, many restaurants acquired a Mexican character when Anglo owners discovered the profits they could make by allowing their Hispanic kitchen staff to cook their own foods. One such successful restaurateur, who had started out with just a shack selling hamburgers and barbecue in Tucson and was facing ruin when his Mexican cook quit, begged her to write down the formulas. "Oh, no," Esperanza Montoya Padilla replied, "I'm dumb enough to work for you, but I'm not dumb enough to give you my recipes!"[21]

The combination plate, rarely seen in Mexico but one of the mainstays of Mexican American restaurants, may have originated in Texas early in the twentieth century as an adaptation to Anglo customers. Tacos, enchiladas, tostadas, and burritos, known collectively as *antojitos* (little whimsies), had long provided quick meals to working-class Mexicans, who often ate them standing on a street corner. Mainstream diners required a more formal meal, including a plate and silverware, so Hispanic cooks complied, perhaps spreading quantities of red chili sauce on top because the customers were using forks anyway. Anglo expectations for a quick plate full of food, as opposed to the Mexican preference for separate, smaller courses, encouraged cooks to combine the main dish with rice (usually eaten prior to the main course) and beans (eaten after). Numbering the combination plates relieved non-Spanish speakers of the need to pronounce what they were eating, a strategy also adopted by Chinese cooks seeking a crossover clientele.

About 1940, the combination plate even made its way back to Mexico when flamboyant restaurateur José Inés Loredo created his signature dish, *carne asada a la tampiqueña*. This butterflied and grilled filet, served with poblano chile strips, two green enchiladas, a bowl of frijoles, and a piece of grilled cheese, introduced the regional foods of Loredo's hometown, Tampico, to residents of Mexico City.[22]

Small restaurants have a high mortality rate, and Mexican American establishments are no exception; nevertheless, a few have survived through the years to attain the status of enduring monuments. The names of these restaurants have become local legends: in Los Angeles, El Cholo, founded in 1923 as the Sonora Café; Tucson's El Charro Café, dating back to 1922; La Posta, which opened in Mesilla, New Mexico, in 1939; and Mi Tierra, located on San Antonio's Market Square since 1951. Outstanding kitchens provided the common foundation for these culinary monuments, but their fame spread far beyond their ethnic enclave in part because of celebrity endorsements. El Cholo became a watering hole for Hollywood stars from Clark Gable and Bing Crosby to Jack Nicholson and Madonna. Western movies filmed on location near Tucson in the 1940s gave El Charro an opportunity to bask in Hollywood publicity. More recently, national attention focused on Mi Tierra when a photojournalist caught President Bill Clinton wearing one of their T-shirts while jogging on a beach.[23]

Countless restaurants have sought to lure non-Mexican customers through identification with celebrities, either by decorating their walls with autographed photos or by affixing small plaques to the tables. Such endorsements offered a cheap substitute for advertising in order to build up a brand name as well as a surrogate form of authenticity in a multiethnic marketplace. This familiarity may have been particularly valuable when mainstream eaters lacked sufficient knowledge of an ethnic cuisine to distinguish quality food from bowdlerized imitations. A similar purpose was served by culinary legends, endlessly repeated, about which Southwestern restaurateur named Ignacio invented nachos, or who created the original margarita, or the first green enchiladas with chicken and sour cream. These tales often reveal a desire for acceptance of ethnic foods by the broader society; for example, the owners of El Charro Café recall a visit, in 1946, by Thomas E. Dewey in which the presidential candidate supposedly mistook one of the soft, thin flour tortillas for a napkin and tucked it into his collar. The Dewey napkin exhibited the same characteristics as the legendary origins of Mexican mole, created by colonial nuns out of a mixture of Old World spices and New World chiles—just like the mestizo nation—and served up for the approval of the Spanish viceroy. In the Southwest, these urban legends gently chide Anglos for their unfamiliarity with Mexican food and by extension their society. Perhaps the most famous tells of President Gerald Ford eating a tamale without taking off the husk.[24]

Another route to financial success for Mexican American restaurants in the postwar era came from the development of franchise chains. The largest of these, El Chico, began in 1931 with Adelaida "Mama" Cuellar's tamale stand at the Kaufman County Fair. After losing a number of small-town cafés in the depression, the family moved to Dallas and opened the first El Chico in 1940. When the war ended, the Cuellar brothers began expanding, locally at first and eventually throughout the South and Southwest, before selling the restaurants in the 1990s. Another chain based in the Dallas–Fort Worth area, Pulido's, began in the 1950s with an immigrant family from Zacatecas. The Pulidos weathered economic downturns by self-financing new locations, often taking over defunct restaurants, and by expanding into small towns where they faced little competition. Although the menu catered predominantly to Anglo customers, the tamales retained an authentic Mexican taste because they were made by hand every morning by Mrs. Pulido and her two comadres.[25]

Despite the success of culinary monuments and Southwestern chains, Mexican American food did not attain a national presence until it was taken over by non-Mexican corporations such as Taco Bell. Sociologist George Ritzer has described the spread of fast-food restaurants— "McDonaldization," he calls it—as the continuation of Max Weber's rationalization process whereby technology imposes greater efficiency, predictability, and control on society.[26] This explanation certainly applies to the restaurant chain founded in 1962 by Glen Bell in Downey, California. Rather than compete for the hamburger market with Ray Kroc, in nearby San Bernardino, Bell devised a way to speed up the production of tacos by pre-frying the corn tortillas, thus creating the prototype for the hard taco shell. Mexican-style food was thereby released from the need for fresh tortillas, allowing the chain to expand throughout the country. The corporation went public in 1969, was bought by Pepsi-Cola Co. in 1978, and then spun off in Tricon Global Restaurants with Pizza Hut and KFC in 1997. With more than 4,600 locations worldwide, and with look-alike competitors such as Del Taco, Taco Time, and Taco Tico, Taco Bell defined Mexican food for an entire generation in the United States. The mass-market appropriation of Mexican food, which began with Tampico Dust and racial slurs about chili queens, thus culminated in chants of "Viva Gorditas!" by the Taco Bell dog. Nevertheless, as tourism and migration gave consumers a greater awareness of genuine Mexican cuisine, a culinary renaissance became possible.

THE BLUE CORN BONANZA

Taco Bell had skimmed the surface, or perhaps dredged the bottom, of Mexican American foods, but a wealth of Southwestern dishes await-ed discovery by consumers. Santa Fe finally grabbed the nation's gas-tronomic imagination in the 1980s, after a lengthy search for authentic regional cuisines from the United States that could compete with those of France, Italy, and China. Once the trend began, Southwestern food quickly became so common that, in 1987, M. F. K. Fisher groaned, "If I hear any more about chic Tex-Mex or blue cornmeal, I'll throw up." Nevertheless, her complaints went unheeded, as corporate versions of Mexican food filled supermarkets across the country. That this was not just a temporary fad became clear in 1991, when salsa surpassed catsup as the best-selling condiment in the United States. This rapid success did nothing to diminish but rather heightened the tension between authen-ticity and adaptation that had so long bedeviled Southwestern cooking.27

The birth of a modern, upscale restaurant version of traditional Southwestern cooking had a long gestation period—most notably in the cookbooks, newspaper columns, and ecological awareness of James Beard, Craig Claiborne, and Alice Waters—so that when it final-ly emerged, it soon became ubiquitous. John Rivera Sedlar, a native of New Mexico who pioneered this new style in 1980, recalled, "When I first began serving tortillas, tamales, and chiles in a fine-dining environ-ment, people gasped." Shortly thereafter, Robert Del Grande in Hous-ton and Stephan Pyles in Dallas did for Texas cooking what Sedlar had done for New Mexico. In 1987, Mark Miller, a former anthropolo-gy student with a deep knowledge of the foods and cultures of Latin America, opened the acclaimed Coyote Café in Santa Fe. Where ethnic restaurants had earlier pursued celebrities as advertisements, the chefs suddenly found themselves to be celebrities—for example, television's "Too Hot Tamales," Mary Sue Milliken and Susan Feniger. As the field grew increasingly crowded, Jay McCarthy sought recognition by proclaiming himself the "Cactus King," followed by Lenard Rubin, the "Cilantro King." Of course, much of this nouvelle Southwestern cuisine bore only a superficial resemblance to either Mexican or Mexican American cooking; witness Pyles's signature dish, a seared foie gras corn pudding tamale with pineapple mole and canela dust. Nevertheless, similar concoctions began to appear in some of the most expensive restaurants in Mexico City.[28]

Supermarket sales of tortillas, chips, salsas, and other Mexican foods, meanwhile, grew into a three-billion-dollar market by the mid-1990s, although only a small fraction of this revenue went to Hispanic-owned businesses. Indeed, the industry has been dominated by Anglos since Elmer Doolin purchased the formula for Fritos corn chips from a nameless Mexican American in 1932 and Dave Pace began bottling salsa in 1948. Just three corporations controlled more than half the nation's salsa market: Pace, owned by Campbell Soup Co.; Tostitos, a brand of Frito-Lay; and Old El Paso, a subsidiary of Pillsbury. Boutique producers, meanwhile, contended for a more upscale niche with outlandish claims of authenticity. Fire Roasted Zuni Zalsa attributed its origins to a mythical Mexican past: "The old patron walked down the mountainside overlooking the jalapeño field. He paused, turned to young Josélito [*sic*] and said, 'Make me a salsa, make me a salsa I can't refuse.' " Local Mexican American manufacturers did better with corn tortillas because of their brief shelf life, but the bulk of sales in the United States went for flour tortillas, often stripped of their original ethnic character by cinnamon or pesto flavoring and marketed as "wraps."[29]

Yet the search for authenticity, or at least for product differentiation, led back again and again to Mexico. The quintessential dish of modern Tex-Mex, fajitas, started out as the vaquero's humble arrachera, served up on a fancy grill but eaten in the style of all Mexican tacos, with salsa on hot and, one hopes, fresh tortillas. In the 1980s, the fad drove the price of skirt steak out of the reach of the working-class Hispanics who invented the dish and also led to that oxymoron, "chicken fajitas." One of the hottest items of the 1990s, the fish taco, was discovered by surfers such as Ralph Rubio while vacationing in Baja California and became part of the new Cal-Mex cuisine, especially around San Diego. At the same time, growing numbers of Tex-Mex restaurants in New York City have begun to replace burritos and fajitas with regional Mexican dishes from Oaxaca and Veracruz, dumping the serapes and mariachi music in the process. Even in the Dallas–Fort Worth area, restaurateur Chris Aparicio reported optimistically, "You used to have to have Tex-Mex food to survive. We serve authentic Mexican and our clientele used to be 80 percent Hispanic. Now it's 60 percent Anglo and 40 percent Hispanic. People are catching on to the true flavor of Mexican food."[30]

The real question about the blue corn bonanza remains, who will benefit from it? Mexicans dreamed of finding the legendary Seven Cities of Cíbola for three centuries, only to lose their northern provinces in 1848, a year before gold was finally discovered in California. As Victor Valle has explained, too few of the Anglo owners of Mexican restaurants and food-processing companies are willing to give anything back to the communities that made their fortunes, even by paying decent wages and offering equal employment opportunities. But Valle also strikes a more positive note, pointing to the Mexican immigrants and Mexican Americans who have begun to reclaim their foods in upscale restaurants around the country as well as in factories turning out authentic foodstuffs. Joe Sánchez of the New El Rey Chorizo Company did not feel threatened by large corporate competitors: "So we are not going to disappear. We'll progress. And the big chain stores will have to stock two sections of Mexican food: the tourist food for the Anglos and the real Mexican food for the Mexicans. And then, since many Anglos like real Mexican food, they'll go over to the Mexican section and buy real ingredients, too."[31]

CONCLUSION: WHOSE MEX?

Douglas Monroy titled his study of early California society, "Thrown among Strangers," evoking the similar experiences of Native Americans forced to work on Spanish missions and Hispanic ranchers displaced by Anglo capitalists. For much the same reason, an account of the foods of the Southwest could easily be called, "Fed to Foreigners." Native American women of the pueblos cooked tortillas for the Spanish conquistadors, only to have their Corn Mother deities denounced by Catholic priests in return. Hispanic women in San Antonio served up chili stews to Anglo tourists three hundred years later, losing their businesses to industrial mass producers and city health inspectors in the process. Even their erstwhile compatriots abandoned the Mexican Americans, denouncing chili con carne as a "detestable food with a false Mexican title that is sold in the United States of the North," in the words of linguist Francisco J. Santamaría.[32]

Despite calumny from all sides, Tejanas continue to treasure their "bowls of red" as a hearty, restorative food, made by hand according to old family recipes and served with pride to friends and relatives. Carne con chile verde holds an equally revered status in the kitchens of New Mexico, as do burritos de carne seca in Arizona and tacos de carnitas in California. Even if only once a year at a holiday tamalada, Mexican Americans reaffirm their connections to family and community, the past, and the future through the ritual preparation and consumption of traditional foods. Neither commercialization, mass production, McDonaldization, Yuppification, nor any other menace of modern life has alienated these foods from cooks, both Hispanic and non-Hispanic, who invest the time to prepare them. The "Mex" thus belongs to anyone willing to embrace it. ❖

NOTES

1. For a history of Mexican cuisine, see Jeffrey M. Pilcher, ¡Que vivan los Tamales! Food and the Making of Mexican Identity (Albuquerque: University of New Mexico Press, 1998).

2. The Border Cookbook: Authentic Home Cooking of the American Southwest and Northern Mexico (Boston: The Harvard Common Press, 1995).

3. Victor Valle argues persuasively for the culinary metaphor of the mixed-race mestizo in his scholarly and mouthwatering cookbook, Recipes of Memory: Five Generations of Mexican Cuisine in Los Angeles (New York: The New Press, 1995), 175–77. Another insightful treatment is Amy Bently, "From Culinary Other to Mainstream American: Meanings and Uses of Southwestern Cuisine," Southern Folklore 55, no. 3 (1998): 238–52. On the gendered nature of the frontier, see Fredrick Pike, The United States and Latin America: Myths and Stereotypes of Civilization and Nature (Austin: University of Texas Press, 1992); and more generally Edward W. Said, Orientalism (New York: Random House, 1979).

4. Douglas Monroy, Thrown among Strangers: The Making of Mexican Culture in Frontier California (Berkeley: University of California Press, 1990), 3–18; Edward H. Spicer, Cycles of Conquest: The Impact of Spain, Mexico, and the United States on the Indians of the Southwest, 1533–1960 (Tucson: University of Arizona Press, 1962), 14–15; Martín Salinas, Indians of the Rio Grande Delta: Their Role in the History of Southern Texas and Northeastern Mexico (Austin: University of Texas Press, 1990), 115–20; Carroll L. Riley, The Frontier People: The Greater Southwest in the Protohistoric Period (Albuquerque: University of New Mexico Press, 1987), 298–300.

5. Riley, Frontier People, 184–87, 232–34, 260–63.

6. Ibid., 114–16, 142; Spicer, Cycles of Conquest, 12–14, 541.

7. Ramón A. Gutiérrez, *When Jesus Came, the Corn Mothers Went Away* (Stanford: Stanford University Press, 1991), 14–16; Monroy, *Thrown among Strangers,* 8–9; Spicer, *Cycles of Conquest,* 541.

8. Louise M. Burkhart, *The Slippery Earth: Nahua-Christian Moral Dialogue in Sixteenth-Century Mexico* (Tucson: University of Arizona Press, 1989), 166.

9. David J. Weber, *The Spanish Frontier in North America* (New Haven: Yale University Press, 1992), 92–121, 227–30; Cynthia Radding, *Wandering Peoples: Colonialism, Ethnic Spaces, and Ecological Frontiers in Northwestern Mexico, 1700–1850* (Durham: Duke University Press, 1997), 48–60; Spicer, *Cycles of Conquest,* 542–46, 552; Albert H. Schroeder, "Shifting for Survival in the Spanish Southwest," in *New Spain's Far Northern Frontier: Essays on Spain in the American West, 1540–1821,* ed. David J. Weber (Albuquerque: University of New Mexico Press, 1979), 243–44.

10. Oakah L. Jones, Jr., *Los Paisanos: Spanish Settlers on the Northern Frontier of New Spain* (Norman: University of Oklahoma Press, 1979); Jesús F. de la Teja, *San Antonio de Béxar: A Community on New Spain's Northern Frontier* (Albuquerque: University of New Mexico Press, 1995); John L. Kessell, *Kiva, Cross, and Crown: The Pecos Indians and New Mexico, 1540–1840* (Washington, D.C.: National Park Service, 1979); Max L. Moorhead, *The Presidio: Bastion of the Spanish Borderlands* (Norman: University of Oklahoma Press, 1975).

11. Arthur L. Campa, *Hispanic Culture in the Southwest* (Norman: University of Oklahoma Press, 1979), 277–81; Patricia Preciado Martin, *Songs My Mother Sang to Me: An Oral History of Mexican American Women* (Tucson: University of Arizona Press, 1992), 11, 16, 28; Jones, *Los Paisanos,* 187, 194, 221.

12. Victor Valle, "A Curse of Tea and Potatoes: Reading a 19th-Century Cookbook as a Social Text," *Latino Studies Journal* 8, no. 3 (Fall 1997), 3–18. For a historical discussion that locates Hispanics within U.S. race relations, see Neil Foley, *The White Scourge: Mexicans, Blacks, and Poor Whites in Texas Cotton Culture* (Berkeley: University of California Press, 1997).

13. Dent, *The Feast of Santa Fe: Cooking of the American Southwest* (New York: Simon and Schuster, 1985), 73. See also Cleofas M. Jaramillo, *The Genuine New Mexico Tasty Recipes* (Santa Fe: Ancient City Press, [1942] 1981), 4; Regina Romero, *Flora's Kitchen: Recipes from a New Mexico Family* (Tucson: Treasure Chest Books, 1998), 37–46.

14. Quote from Carmella Padilla, *The Chile Chronicles: Tales of a New Mexico Harvest* (Santa Fe: Museum of New Mexico Press, 1997), 48; Fabiola Cabeza de Baca Gilbert, *The Good Life: New Mexico Traditions and Food* (Santa Fe: Museum of New Mexico Press, [1949] 1982); personal communication from Marco Antonio Abarca, January 25, 2000.

15. Quote from Merrill Shindler, *El Cholo Cookbook: Recipes and Lore from California's Best-Loved Mexican Kitchen* (Santa Monica: Angel City Press, 1998), 85. See also, Diana Kennedy, *The Cuisines of Mexico* (New York: Harper & Row, 1986), 244; Martin, *Songs My Mother Sang to Me,* 17, 59, 155; Jay Ann Cox, "Eating the Other" (Ph.D. diss., University of Arizona, 1993).

16. For just a few examples of this voluminous literature, see Richard Griswold del Castillo, *La Familia: The Mexican American Family in the Urban Southwest* (Notre Dame: University of Notre Dame Press, 1984); idem, *The Treaty of Guadalupe Hidalgo: A Legacy of Conflict* (Norman: University of Oklahoma Press, 1990); Armando C. Alonzo, *Tejano Legacy: Rancheros and Settlers in South Texas, 1734–1900* (Albuquerque: University of New Mexico Press, 1998); Lisbeth Haas, *Conquests and Historical Identities in California, 1769–1936* (Berkeley: University of California Press, 1995); Oscar J. Martínez, *Troublesome Border* (Tucson: University of Arizona Press, 1988); Thomas E. Sheridan, *Los Tucsonenses: The Mexican Community in Tucson, 1854–1941* (Tucson: University of Arizona Press, 1986).

17. The best account of the appropriation of ethnic foods is Donna R. Gabaccia, *We Are What We Eat: Ethnic Foods and the Making of Americans* (Cambridge: Harvard University Press, 1998), quotations are from 108–9. See also Marilyn Tausend, *Cocina de la familia* (New York: Simon & Schuster, 1997), 66; Mary Ann Noonan Guerra, *The History of San Antonio's Market Square* (San Antonio: The Alamo Press, 1988), 14, 48.

18. Mario Montaño, "The History of Mexican Folk Foodways of South Texas: Street Vendors, Offal Foods, and Barbacoa de Cabeza" (Ph.D. diss., University of Pennsylvania, 1992); José E. Limón, *Dancing with the Devil: Society and Cultural Poetics in Mexican-American South Texas* (Madison: University of Wisconsin Press, 1994).

19. Valle, "A Curse of Tea and Potatoes," quotes from 9, 12. The Pinedo volume has been edited and translated by Dan Strehl as *The Spanish Cook: A Selection of Recipes from Encarnación Pinedo's El cocinero español* (Pasadena: The Weather Bird Press, 1992).

20. Villaseñor, *Rain of Gold* (New York: Delta, 1991), 350. See also Jacqueline Higuera McMahan, *The Mexican Breakfast Cookbook* (Lake Hughes, CA: The Olive Press, 1992), 116; *California Rancho Cooking* (Lake Hughes, CA: The Olive Press, 1988), 130–34.

21. Quoted in Martin, *Songs My Mother Sang to Me,* 116.

22. Jamison and Jamison, *The Border Cookbook,* 10–11.

23. Shindler, *El Cholo Cookbook,* 15; Flores, *El Charro Café* (Tucson: Fisher Books, 1998), 3.

24. This discussion was inspired by Tracy Poe, "Food Culture and Entrepreneurship among African Americans, Italians, and Swedes in Chicago" (Ph.D. diss., Harvard University, 1999). See also Flores, *El Charro Café,* 24.

25. Jeffrey Steele, "Mexican Goes Mainstream," *Restaurante Mexicano* 1, no. 1 (January/February 1997): 6–15; interview with Edward Gámez, chairman of the board of Pulido's Restaurants, Fort Worth, Texas, March 26, 1992.

26. George Ritzer, *The McDonaldization of Society* (Thousand Oaks, CA: Pine Forge Press, 1993). See also Warren J. Belasco, "Ethnic Fast Foods: The Corporate Melting Pot," *Food and Foodways* 2 (1987): 1–30.

27. Quote from Sylvia Lovegren, *Fashionable Food: Seven Decades of Food Fads* (New York: Macmillan, 1995), 378.

28. Quote from Barbara Pool Fenzl, *Savor the Southwest* (San Francisco: Bay Books, 1999), 14. See also Mark Miller, *Coyote Cafe* (San Francisco: Ten Speed

Press, 1989); Mark Miller, Stephan Pyles, and John Sedlar, *Tamales* (New York: Macmillan, 1997); Mary Sue Milliken and Susan Feniger, *Mesa Mexicana* (New York: William Morrow, 1994).

29. Gabaccia, *We Are What We Eat,* 165, 219; "Another Round," *Snack World* 53, no. 6 (June 1996): 32; Margaret Littman, "Wrap Up Profits with Tortillas," *Bakery Production and Marketing* 31, no. 16 (November 15, 1996): 40.

30. Mario Montaño, "Appropriation and Counterhegemony in South Texas: Food Slurs, Offal Meats, and Blood," in *Usable Pasts: Traditions and Group Expressions in North America,* ed. Tad Tuleja (Logan: Utah State University Press, 1997), 50–67. Quoted in Julia M. Gallo-Torres, "Salud," *El Restaurante Mexicano* 3, no. 3 (May–June 1999): 14. See also Jane and Michael Stern, "Grill of His Dreams," *Gourmet,* January 2000, p. 40; Eric Asimov, "Beyond Tacos: Mexican Food Gets Real," *New York Times,* January 26, 2000, p. B14.

31. Valle made this point eloquently in a presentation at the Culinary Institute of America's Flavors of Mexico Conference, St. Helena, Calif., November 11, 1999, and in his book, *Recipes of Memory,* quotation on 175.

32. *Diccionario de Mejicanismos,* 5th ed. (Mexico City: Editorial Porrúa, 1992), 385.

U.S. Ports of Entry on the Mexican Border

JOSIAH McC. HEYMAN

U.S. and Mexican ports of entry are the historical bases of most twin border cities, and their importance continues today. San Ysidro, between Tijuana in Lower California and San Diego County in Upper California, is the most heavily traversed land port in the world. Surprisingly little scholarly work has been done on U.S.–Mexican border ports of entry (but see Arreola and Curtis 1993: 192–201). This article aims to rectify that neglect, viewing the U.S. ports in three ways. It first reviews the basic operations of ports, and then turns to the people who operate the port, balancing their work lives and their place in border society. It finishes by examining ports as an arm of the U.S. state. In this regard, the considerable localism of ports on the southern boundary creates tension between the port's mandate to enforce national policies and its adaptation to immediate social, economic, and cultural circumstances. The conclusion offers suggestions for further studies of this vital but neglected institution.

In writing this article, I draw principally on 1992 ethnographic fieldwork (observations and extended interviews) in Arizona and California (Heyman 1995a). Also, in the mid-1980s, I resided in border Mexico for nearly two years, and therefore often participant-observed crossing the port of entry. The 1992 work focused on the Immigration and Naturalization Service (INS), supplemented with some research on the Customs Service. This material has two limitations of which the reader should be cognizant. First, it does not address Mexican-side border ports; and second, some circumstances have changed in U.S. ports. The physical plant of some ports has been improved and expanded through the 1990s, but unlike the Border Patrol, ports of entry have not enjoyed a dramatic expansion in law enforcement staffing.[1] The North American Free Trade Agreement (NAFTA) has reduced some customs duties, but as we shall see, others have taken their place. There is no reason to believe that the basic operations and staffing of ports have significantly changed.

221

The Operations of Ports

In many ways, ports of entry *are* the border (see map). They are as important to the border as the fenced and walled boundary line to which undocumented immigration draws so much attention. There are, for example, vastly more entries and exits through ports than across the rest of the line. More important, the port is where the laws of the nation first take hold for people who ostensibly agree to follow them, so the set of laws, categories, and regulations applied at ports is far richer than are the interdictive functions away from ports. For example, the customs function of the port of entry involves the examination of conveyances, the declaration of merchandise, its inspection concerning that declaration, and the payment of merchandise taxation (tariff duties), as well as the interdiction of contraband. As prosaic as customs (and immigration) processing may seem, its actual port-by-port expression on the border is quite varied and interesting.

Because of the enormous size of the maquiladora industry, all but the most minor border ports have a substantial role in documenting and monitoring the nontaxable parts and finished goods going back and

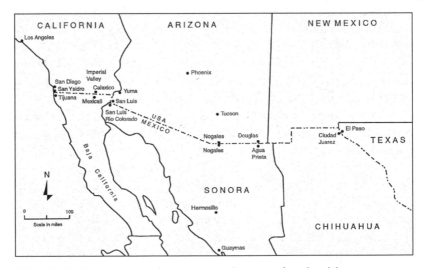

U.S.–Mexico border region, showing ports of entry and major cities. Cartography by Josiah Heyman.

forth. However, other, more distinctly regionalized exports of Mexico shape particular U.S. ports and cities. Nogales, Arizona, for instance, receives from Mexico's west coast up to one hundred fruit and vegetable trucks per day in season, and therefore maintains a customs staff with traditional expertise in commercial agriculture. This, in turn, shapes a town characteristically open to Mexico, historically dominated by a small group of agricultural customs brokers and produce dealers with profound bicultural and binational knowledge, orientation, and webs of confidence. For example, the Customs Service classifies experienced shippers and brokers as trustworthy, thereby speeding entries and reducing their workload by accepting paper declarations of content and value. Customs brokers, in turn, put their finances on the line insuring the legal performance of the entry.

Douglas, Arizona, historically served as a transshipment point for metal ores or concentrates from Mexico. Handled by a few huge, outside corporations, this commerce lacked the binationality of the fruit and vegetable trade through Nogales. Douglas instead functions mainly as a small-town port, with an emphasis on inspectors knowing the repeat daily crossers, their habits, goods, and foibles.[2] Amidst the relaxed inspection of everyday entrants (who might blithely stick a third bottle of liquor in the tire well to circumvent the U.S. legal limit of two), inspectors are on the lookout for contraband narcotics. As a customs officer in charge of regional drug interdiction said, "Douglas and Agua Prieta are a real headache for me." Of course, contraband is crossed at all border ports, and by volume Douglas may be no worse than any other place, but its localism engenders a subtle sophistication of smuggling and shapes a particular cat-and-mouse game with the port inspectors. "At San Ysidro," one customs officer told me, "there is so much traffic they just keep on trying to run it through—you can stop thirty cars, and number thirty-one has a load of drugs in its panels. But in Douglas, they [smugglers] observe you more carefully. If you stop ten cars, then that's it for the day; they know how you are checking." Therefore, Douglas, though closely linked to northeastern Sonora, has not had as binationally oriented a public elite as Nogales, Arizona, partly as a legacy of being a racially segregated company town (Heyman 1993, 1995b) and partly because merchandise brokerage at the port has not been as extensive.

As the brief narrative of these two towns suggests, drug interdiction has become as important as goods inspection and revenue collection for the U.S. Customs Service. In 1992, customs officials in a place as commercially important as Nogales said that drug detection was their first priority and legitimate merchandise their second, though the latter was still accorded attention at a specialized commercial truck port. Alongside laws about legitimate commodities and contraband drugs, the Customs Service also enforces laws against the unlicensed export of guns and ammunition to Mexico and the taking out of the country without declaration of $10,000 or more in cash. This causes the odd phenomenon of port-of-entry inspections on the outbound lane as well as the inbound ones, though in truth such monitoring aims at specific individuals suspected of roles in drug-trafficking organizations. The Customs Service and the INS, as the two principal agencies at ports, enforce law for other agencies, such as the Nuclear Regulatory Commission (restricted movement of radioactive materials), the Department of Agriculture (quarantine functions), and the Fish and Wildlife Service (prohibition of rare animal smuggling).

Ports of entry also enforce immigration and citizenship laws. U.S. citizens can, of course, enter the country without restriction, but on entry all persons have to offer themselves for INS inspection and determination of citizenship because there is no single, definitive document proving U.S. citizenship (that is, no national identification card). Legal permanent residents (immigrants) do carry an identifying green card. Despite this, green carders pose a complication for the INS because the United States allows a small number to live in Mexico and commute to the United States to work. (Otherwise, U.S. law requires that most legal residents not reside outside the nation for more than one year at a time.) Many border commuters lack this permission and reside in Mexico extra-legally while pretending to remain in the United States. As we will see, the near-border labor markets (see Herzog 1990:156–63) and the ports of entry interact on this seemingly obscure issue in fascinating and highly localistic ways. The INS also provides to Mexicans who wish to visit the United States two services: border crossing cards and tourist visas (locally called *permisos*). Border crossing cards give the bearer the right to enter up to twenty-five miles into the United States for seventy-two hours, to shop, visit relatives, and the like—but not to work or reside. The ports give these cards to people from Mexican border cities with proof of established residence and employment, on the assumption that such persons have ties to Mexico that will restrain them from emigrating illegally to the United States. Border card holders and other Mexicans who want to visit the United States for longer times and greater distances require a permiso. Both permits are discretionary, requiring the weighing of commercial tourism against immigration law enforcement, and border ports vary in interesting ways in how they exercise this judgment.

Ports also attempt to detect and halt entries that violate U.S. immigration laws.[3] U.S. law lists categories that may exclude noncitizens from entering the nation, for reasons ranging from violent felonies to controlled substances convictions to possible use of U.S. public welfare services. Certain identified persons appear in a "lookout book" (now on computer), but ports exclude many others. At the Mexican border, the persons most likely to be identified from the lookout book are criminal fugitives. Most immigration-law violators are unknown to the government when they enter, and generally fall into three groups: people who falsely claim to be U.S. citizens; those who use someone else's legitimate documents; and those who use counterfeit or altered documents (e.g., with changed photographs). Occasionally, people crouch in vehicle compartments, hiding from inspection. Although all these acts are prosecutable under criminal law and lead to formal exclusion by an immigration court, the reality is that the INS prosecutes cases tactically. At one busy port, prosecuting officers transmit to the U.S. attorney only those cases involving noncitizens with U.S. criminal pasts making false claims to U.S. citizenship and some of those with commercially purchased fraudulent documents, the latter in an attempt to get them to inform on the seller. However, the INS uses enforcement alternatives, including turning people away at the border, asking them to come back with more documentation, "lifting" papers temporarily on the rationale of needing more "proof," and allowing entry but requiring people to report to the INS for further questioning in their city of destination ("deferred inspection"). This summary offers but the bare bones of immigration law service and enforcement at ports; its enactment, as we will see, is vastly more stressful and challenging.

The reader might notice the phrase "service and enforcement." Unlike the Border Patrol, INS inspectors have many options about how they interact with border crossers. For example, one officer maneuvered the immigration system so that a young deaf-mute woman from Mexico obtained a trainee non-immigrant visa to attend sign language classes on the U.S. side, instead of treating her as "likely to become a public charge," an excludable user of U.S. services. (She has since married in Mexico and her husband has learned to sign.) Ports often seem focused on enforcement, since it draws their energy and attention, but they are best thought of as neither inherently enforcers nor inherently servers, but as the first applier of laws, in many ways, the beginning of the nation-state. For example, although NAFTA has vastly reduced the tariff-oriented controls over commerce between Mexico and the United States, the Customs Service has an important new responsibility in documenting the flow of potentially hazardous materials, often destined for maquiladoras, as they are exported to Mexico and then returned to the United States (by law, anyway). The free-trade era has not so far diminished the border-control functions of ports, because amid open commerce drug and migrant interdiction persists (for reasons explored in Heyman 1999a) and because we live in an era of manifold surveillance, documentation, and regulation, of which boundary ports are central nodes.

WORKING THE PORT

The employees of ports of entry merit attention, not only because of their job functions, but because the Chicanos who work for federal, state, and local police agencies and government organizations generally represent a substantial, but regrettably unstudied group of people in U.S.-side border cities. I interviewed seventeen current immigration inspectors, including managers, and seventeen INS officers who had in the past been inspectors. Of the current inspectors/managers, 71 percent were Chicanos, a remarkably high number even for the INS, an agency with many Hispanic officers (officer ranks in the INS western region were 32 percent Hispanic, mostly Chicano). Notably, much of the current inspections staff comes from the immediate locale: 89 percent of inspectors/managers grew up in border communities and 59 percent were working in their hometown. Finally, inspections has some tendency to be a "pink-collar" job, with a relatively high percentage (33 percent) of women officers in my sample. Therefore, the personal knowledge of people and of border life is high among inspectors, perhaps higher than in any other federal law enforcement agency. As we shall see, this presents inspectors with both ambiguities and refined tools of control.

One Chicana inspector told me that people were "thrilled that she got such a glorified job in Douglas." That she called such a tough duty glorified has stayed with me ever since the interview. It was indeed glorified in her hometown. A federal job looks inward, identifies the bearer with the grandeur of the U.S. nation-state and the practical advantages of citizenship in a town marked by many decades of immigration, ambiguous national identification, and the consequent invidious ranking of U.S. over Mexican, established over newcomer. Also, getting a well-paid civil service job with benefits is an accomplishment in this deindustrialized locale, a scene of grinding poverty and labor markets saturated by layer upon layer of migrants.

To illustrate the path by which Chicana women and men arrive at such "glorified" jobs, let us examine a sketch biography of Ann Calderon (a pseudonym), the INS port director at Nogales, Arizona.[4] Calderon grew up in the near-border city of Yuma, Arizona, the daughter of two parents who immigrated from Mexico. Her father worked as a construction laborer. After high school and trade school, she went to work as a stenographer in local government, and then as a bookkeeper and secretary for a produce company. A girlfriend worked for the Yuma Police Department, so she took an exam and was hired as a dispatcher. Another friend had just moved from the Drug Enforcement Administration (DEA) to be a customs inspector, and she suggested that Ann take her former job as interpreter. Subsequently, Ann worked as an intelligence secretary at the DEA. To move into officer ranks, she put in for work as an immigration inspector at the port of San Luis, Arizona, working there for six years and quickly rising to supervisor. (Interestingly, she recalled some resistance to her being a Chicana and particularly a woman among entrants at the port.) Her next step was to work as a supervisory inspector and then acting officer in charge at Los Angeles International Airport. Having "learned a bit about being in charge," she bid on and obtained the job as INS port director in Honolulu. She then became INS port director in Nogales, which she regards as a promotion to a more demanding and visible port. Of course, hers is an exceptional story, but its elements characterize many border inspectors' lives: working-class origins, social mobility, civil service careers, and love of the border.

However, the inspectors make major sacrifices to hold down these "glorified" jobs. The core of the border port dilemma is the immense workload compared to the staffing. As one former inspector described a Rio Grande crossing, "You'd see miles and miles of traffic stack up from the bridge and feel that you were at the bottom of the mountain. There was never enough manpower to check every person, every vehicle closely, so you could get overwhelmed and depressed, but at the same time there was a frenetic pace, twenty-four hours a day." In early

1992, the port of San Ysidro had just opened a larger pedestrian area to handle the million and a half or so entrants a month. Previously, on weekends the crowd packed into a long, hot hallway so tightly that, reportedly, as people passed out the crowd would simply move them forward. These sorts of work pressures are significant even at medium-sized ports like Nogales: on a weekday I looked out the window of Ann Calderon's office and saw traffic jammed for two blocks into Mexico, and weekends are much worse. Only small border ports are calm and quick, even lonely at night, but they can get just as clogged as large ports on holidays when Mexicanos in the two nations visit their relatives.

One reason for crowding is that land ports are distinctly understaffed compared with the demands put on them. The San Ysidro INS staff in early 1992 had 141 inspectors, including managers, for all shifts of the busiest land port in the world. Customs also faces a heavy workload, with the added burden of commercial processing, but by comparison its staffing shows how overwhelmed the INS is. In Nogales, customs counted 108 inspectors and thirteen import specialists; the INS, twenty inspectors. To compensate for understaffing, the INS demands extensive hours of its workers. One Douglas inspector was "part-time" at forty-two hours a week. At San Ysidro, inspectors were working six-day weeks, and a reform plan was bandied about that would have them work four ten-hour days and an eight-hour Sunday so they could have (in theory, before overtime) a five-day workweek. Some smaller ports are worse in terms of work hours; a former inspector, still in the INS, told me that in the summer of 1988 in San Luis, his first job, "I was most impressed by the amount of work—three to four 16-hour shifts in a seven-day period, a seven-day week was not uncommon, and they called an eight-hour shift 'your day off.' " A district-level INS manager with port-of-entry responsibilities told me that his biggest challenge was getting "adequate staffing down there [at ports] so you can have a family life and a social life as well as a work life." A related problem is standing in the exhaust clouds of vehicular lanes doing primary (initial) inspection. At San Ysidro, an officer on the line remarked that "for the first hour today I felt really dizzy from the smog, but the rain cleared it out so I conducted better interviews." INS management at that port had just agreed with the union to limit time in the fumes to four hours in a twenty-four-hour period; previously, the limit had been four hours of vehicular primary per eight-hour shift, and potentially more during overtime.

Exhaustion and automotive exhaust are the most obviously demanding features of this job, but perhaps psychological stress is worse, stemming from the forced character of interacting with the crossing (and
cross) public. To understand this, it is necessary to digress briefly on the
flow of work at a port. When you or I enter, whether in a car or on foot,
we first go through primary inspection. Customs and INS staff split
primary inspection equally (as best as they can), and inspectors of both
agencies are cross-designated to identify potential violators of the alternate agency's laws (e.g., immigration inspectors can pull aside vehicles
suspected of having narcotics bolted in underbody compartments). Primary demands a snap judgement: admit the people and conveyance to
the United States, or send them for secondary inspection. Officers of
the relevant agency conduct the extended secondary investigation in
pull-aside spaces past the booths of the main entrance. Further questioning of persons, lasting up to four hours, can take place in holding
cells inside the port building, while the front offices team with members of the public of two nations seeking services such as permisos and
border crossing cards.

Many inspectors enjoy serving the public in card interviews and other
helpful functions, and even secondary questioning fulfills their skills as
law enforcement investigators and interrogators. But primary inspection is another thing. The reader has to envision doing the following
in forty-five seconds to one minute (the managerially expected average
time per vehicle in primary at San Ysidro): typing in a license plate number; looking into the window of the car; asking about citizenship for all
passengers, destination, purpose of visit, and whether the people are
bringing anything from Mexico; assessing whether that story makes rea-
sonable sense; examining the demeanor ("nerves") of the people while
also paying attention to what they are saying; looking at their documents for validity, pictures, and dates, looking throughout the interior
and exterior of the vehicle to see any evidence of hidden compartments,
and reading the computer lookout book results on the license plate they
typed in! All of this results in a snap judgment about whether to send
the people over to secondary inspection, and by which agency.

That some effective arrests are made is remarkable. A San Ysidro
immigration inspector recounted this story: "I was pushing traffic real
quick, but one car caught my eye. There was a large green Buick from
Los Angeles, and the driver was not on the computer as the registered
owner. I thought it was drugs, so I sent it to Customs. They found the

body [a live, smuggled person] in the trunk." How do inspectors make such decisions? There are multitudes of factors (including much local knowledge, which we will get to in a moment), but four stand out. Inspectors of both agencies use what they call their "feeling," "reading," or sometimes "sixth sense," which appears to me to be inferences from nonverbal behavior, nervousness, etc. To detect contraband, the Customs Service uses the considerable intelligence loaded on their computer[5] (the basis for 76 percent of port narcotics arrests, according to one customs manager), combined with certain profiles (men between fifteen and twenty-five) and a sprinkling of random pull-asides, just to keep the smugglers on guard. Immigration, in turn, emphasizes the plausibility of the stories of entrants whose documentation or intentions are ambiguous. One interpretative assumption, effective if not always justified, is that Mexican people without significant money come to the United States to work extra-legally, and the converse for those who appear prosperous. I observed an inspector on secondary admit, via deferred inspection, a man who lacked ("had forgotten") a key document issued at the U.S. consulate in the Mexican interior because "he had good-quality glasses, he looked with it." Finally, for immigration, the security points on documents are very important, and inspectors pride themselves on knowing innumerable subtleties in the appearance of various state birth certificates.

The performance of such police skills, especially in primary inspection, is psychologically stressful. As a not-coincidentally former inspector confided, "I really did not enjoy the confrontation even from individuals who do not have something to hide. I feel the inside of the car is their territory, and the II or CI [immigration inspector or customs inspector] has to violate it. So I experienced confrontation after confrontation, especially on a weekend when there are long lines." One Chicana inspector recalled that her trainer subjected her class to a barrage of curses and insults "so we were prepared." Constant and obvious lying, if understandable as part of the failed U.S. immigration system, nonetheless wears on inspectors. An inspector remarked that "the lies get so repetitive—'I found it on the floor'—when there are guys selling bundles of counterfeit border crossing cards just across the line." Finally, most approvals are rapid and unmemorable, limiting the satisfaction derived from serving the public, and "if you spend any time with people, it's confrontational, it's over some negative."

One scene of confrontation is the holding cells inside a port. People can be detained at a port for up to four hours without charges, but as one officer pointed out, in "immigration we work with live people," so they often try to figure out what is going on quickly and either arrest them or admit them in a period of a half hour to an hour. In such a situation, questioning is intense. One officer explained his technique of calm but rapid interrogation: "They have all kinds of memorized stories, but if I ask questions very fast, their memory goes blank. I try not to raise my voice, or they will freeze up." A major problem faced by both entrant and officer is that, apart from official documents, the evidence to reach an adequate resolution is not truly available at the port. A typically ambiguous transnational example is a person bearing no documentation who claims to be a U.S. citizen by virtue of birth north of the border but who was raised in Mexico. Of course, bureaucratic state rule aspires to place complicated social reality into neat legal categories. In this instance, the immigration inspector will grill forcefully the person on the family's jobs and schools, perhaps even threatening him or her with prosecution for making a false claim to a federal officer, all the while looking for psychological cracks or, alternatively, assessing their responses as plausible, in anticipation of admitting them to the United States (Heyman n.d.-a).

The port of entry, then, is a paradoxical institution for U.S. residents of the border: an important institution and appreciated source of "glorified" jobs, it is also—both to its workers and its users—an inherently confrontational location, often tempered but never fully obviated by deep familiarity. For Mexican border residents, too, the port is a source of tension: obviously a place of law enforcement aimed directly at them, it also provides valued services like border-crossing cards and permisos. The U.S. border port is, in either case, a curious branch of the federal government administratively imposed on local life, one in which border communities have a considerable stake. Hence, local communities go to no small effort, conscious and tacit, to bend ports toward the immediate economy, society, and culture.

PORTS AS THE "LOCAL STATE"

Rigorous theories of nationhood tend to be abstract, elitist, and national (Jessop 1982; Block 1987). Studies that are sensitive to local circumstances tend to be about government, a style of analysis often less stringent than state theory. Recently, scholars have connected state theory to observed places and situations (Gupta 1995; Heyman 1998a,

232 ON THE BORDER

1999b; Daniel Nugent 1993; David Nugent 1994; Smart 1989). The useful phrase "local state" implies two converging concerns: that of political elites and functionaries who dominate governance in particular regions; and the operation of arms of the central state that unavoidably interact with, and bend to, local society.

The social web of U.S. and Mexican border towns subtly affects ports. Except for the biggest ports (and even in those to some extent), inspectors come to know frequent local crossers. Border-city residents are relaxed and understanding of the port routine. By contrast, American tourists returning from Mexico often ignore inspectors, not understanding that they too are subject to questioning and review. As a Chicano officer pungently put it, "Can't you see my blond hair, my blue eyes, can't you see I'm not Mexican?" At the same time, locals manipulate the border, sometimes hiding things from inspectors, from the minor prohibited fruits or case of beer, to the girlfriend or boyfriend who has not immigrated from Mexico but is living on the U.S. side. An inspector complained that if you pull regular crossers aside, they say, "Don't you know me? I cross here all the time," while later boasting about how they sneak stuff across the border. But local knowledge cuts both ways. As we know, many inspectors have roots in the modestly prosperous Chicano sector of the U.S. border city. They use community reputation and local gossip ("We more or less know who the dopers are, and the people who are honest, PTA, school friends"). Inspectors were quick to note that one cannot go purely on reputation or appearance; sometimes they are misleading. Furthermore, the most useful local gossip, one inspector explained, circulates among police agencies who are privy to intelligence and details of arrests. This specialization in enforcing the law within and yet against their own communities perhaps engenders ambiguity or estrangement for port personnel.

And that tinge of estrangement may account for tensions sometimes found between port officers of Mexican origin and other Latinos. As we walked about a port, Francisco Encinas (a pseudonym) told me, "You know, they say *lo peor que podemos tener aquí es un Mexicano en la línea*" (the worst thing that we can have here is a Mexican on the line [the border]). Of course, this is an extraordinary generalization, made yet more striking by the notably bilingual, bicultural, binational, and self-confident officer repeating it. He did not mean that it was invariably true; he raised it while discussing troubles some Chicano inspectors might encounter. His explanation (put briefly in my phraseology) was that such officers choose among their culturally supplied models for exerting authority: on the one hand, rigid, gruff, authoritarian; on the other, cool, formal, dominant. I take this argument quite seriously, not least because Francisco was a perceptive and balanced informant. With due respect, then, to his analysis, I suggest other factors also may be at play. First, inspectors working in their own hometowns, surrounded by relatives and friends from both nations, are subjected to open and tacit pressures for special favors they often cannot deliver. Second, Mexican and Chicano crossers who do not know the inspector sometimes appeal to ethnic solidarity, which cannot easily be granted while maintaining integrity of job performance, frustrating Chicano inspectors who feel "put on the spot." Finally, bilingual and bicultural inspectors often penetrate deceptions because of their ability to grasp subtle incongruities of language and behavior and, in their hometowns, because of their mastery of local knowledge. Perhaps Mexican and Chicano crossers perceive this penetration as aggressive and confrontational. (For more on the experiences of Chicano INS officers, see Heyman n.d.-b.)

While some local influences on ports are tacit, other influences are systematically reflected in unofficial port policy. The INS port offices have discretion in some important areas, among them the issuing of permisos to Mexican visitors and, for border crossing cards, the stringency of interpreting established residence and employment. Similarly, port inspectors exercise considerable discretion in how hard they try to make deportation cases against the extra-legal commuting workers described previously. Finally, inspectors must decide how deep to push primary questioning, since deeper inspections mean the slower clearance of traffic. Of course, in almost no cases are these "port policies" explicit. Instead, they vary according to a mix of signals locally and from national INS management. National policy on immigration is almost entirely oriented to enforcement. Non-registered commuters are clearly outside the regulations and law, while facile issuing of border crossing cards and permisos increases the chances of their misuse for undocumented labor and residential migration. But INS port offices weigh national policy against local exigencies. One assumes that comparable statements apply to the Customs Service.

These realities cause port policies to vary in interesting ways. They vary according to the volume of traffic with which they cope, the nature of the Mexican and U.S. economies in the locale and the consequent types of border crossers, and the interests of and degree of attention paid by local and regional elites. Here I sketch differing immigration policies among four ports, taking complete responsibility for these analyses, since ports are not in the position of honestly admitting to significant deviations from official positions. Also, since port procedures may very well have changed since 1992, what follows serves best as illustrations of the "local state" rather than as a definitive cataloging of port policies.

Volume altogether dominated San Ysidro, not surprisingly. The high demand on officer time constrained every activity there, so that interviews for discretionary cards identified only the obvious problem cases and only the highest-priority prosecutions were passed along to U.S. attorneys (e.g., returning deported aliens with criminal records). Even so, San Ysidro generated enormous enforcement activity. Public visibility of traffic flow between the two Californias also shaped San Ysidro's political field, so that managers' greatest fear was criticism of traffic jams and other breakdowns of basic port functions. One response has been a cooperative agreement between Mexican and U.S. authorities to divert vehicles from San Ysidro to the alternate port of Otay Mesa when the former reaches the saturation point. The other three ports—Calexico, Nogales, and Douglas—were less completely dominated by their flows, and thus reflect their locale more actively.

Calexico and Nogales also faced periodic volume problems, which on holidays or weekends limited the ability of inspectors to scrutinize entrants. More distinctively, politically skilled commercial sectors in U.S.-side border cities shaped both ports' policies. Bluntly, U.S. merchants sought shoppers from Mexico, and the way to obtain them was to push ports to issue border crossing cards rapidly and generously. A former INS manager at Calexico described very forceful and direct pressure from the city council and chamber of commerce, even extending to critical attention from regional congressmen. Unlike Nogales, Calexico stood out for its many commuters because it sits astride the agricultural labor artery running from Mexicali to the Imperial Valley. Nogales, in turn, was very generous with permisos, non-immigrant visas for Mexicans going to the U.S. interior. It is the main outlet for Mexico's west-coast highway to the United States and bridges the constant traffic of visitors from Hermosillo and other Sonoran cities to Tucson and Phoenix. As a telling, if a bit backhanded, illustration, the port in 1992 was striving to cut back on the historically large number of multiple-entry permisos issued (a more lax form of visitor control than single-purpose visas). Not being near major agricultural districts or large cities in the United States, however, Nogales admitted fewer commuters than did Calexico.

Douglas represents smaller ports. The Douglas–Agua Prieta crossing in the early 1990s was quiet in many respects (but see note 2 regarding changes in the illegal migration flow). Though there was some awareness of the interests of merchants, there was little overt pressure from the chamber of commerce or the city council. The port was fairly demanding about requiring documentary support before issuing border cards. For example, at San Ysidro, inspectors required only proof of residence for six months, while Douglas inspectors required electrical and water bills and rent receipts or house tax records for twelve months. Douglas, like Nogales, had few commuting workers, but, unlike Nogales, it is not on a main highway to or from anywhere, so inspectors tended to scrutinize strictly permisos for interior Mexicans. However, Douglas manifested one characteristic of a small-town port: that inspectors knew individuals from Agua Prieta and readily granted selected ones permisos to go to Tucson or Phoenix. In addition, the localism of this port sometimes limited the intensity of vehicular inspection: "Calexico is a very thorough port of entry, every vehicle and every person, despite being busy. They open one compartment in each vehicle, and people don't complain because they are used to it. In Douglas, people will complain if you check the compartments. We get to know all the locals, and let them slide through unless we hear something. Inspectors, if they are from the town, pick up the vehicles from out of town." Douglas was a small enough place, with inspectors likely to live in town (rather than driving to work from a larger interior town, as often is the case in Calexico), that if an inspector annoyed locals, even friends of cousins of friends, he or she was likely to hear about it. When I lived in Agua Prieta in the 1980s, long before doing the INS research, I was well informed about the comings and goings and personal affairs of various inspectors.

The port director personifies the port's Janus face. The directorship is a quintessentially political position, the central node in relationships extending upward through the INS and Department of Justice to the policies of Congress and the presidency, and the central state, as well as downward to organized groups and interpersonal networks in the twinned border cities. As a result, the director becomes an important actor in local politics and quasi-politics (e.g., voluntary associations). Ann Calderon, for example, not only fields concerns from Capins and other large stores in downtown Nogales, Arizona, over the processing of border cards, she belongs to a variety of local booster groups:

> I belong to the Arizona-Sonora Commission and the Border Trade Alliance [in 1992], the frontrunners for free trade, so I see a lot of customs brokers. I'm a member to see what's going on, how they feel. I wanted to get involved in this very small community; produce people tend to run it. . . . So I am a member of two groups, the Rotary (one of only two women) and the Business Women's Association. Also, I am on the Nogales Chamber of Commerce "Strategies for the Future" group—it's a wish club.

When asked what she got from these contacts, she told me, "I hear about the need to facilitate traffic through the port of entry. By being in the clubs, I handle issues before they get out of hand, before my boss gets a call—things get settled and handled locally." She also discussed her relationship with the Mexican consul in Nogales, Arizona, and her "very close relationship with the mayor of Nogales, Sonora." Many port-of-entry decisions, whether logistical or in immigration law actions, have ramifications to which the Mexican government pays attention, so perhaps relations outward to Mexico should supplement the model of relations extending upward and downward from the port director, rendering a triangle of pressures. The INS and Customs Service port directors are important and interesting figures in border life and merit attention from historians and social scientists. Identifying such key actors is vital in delineating the "local state" in this region and its role in shaping modern border society.

While U.S. national politics stresses nationalistic responses to cross-border flows like immigration and strains toward subjecting the border to central bureaucratic control (see note 1), the ports of entry maintain within the U.S. state a certain respect for border conditions. On the other hand, their proximate effect is to strengthen local distinctions of power and prosperity. These include mechanisms for dominance by U.S.-side economic elites, whether stores or agricultural employers. A second result is the segmenting effect of well-paid, nationalistic jobs on the Chicano community. Finally, there are different shopping and visiting treatments of wealthy versus poorer Mexicans, an experience of which both parties are aware (Heyman 1997, 172–80). States absorb, select among, and reinforce social inequalities; in this instance, the local state tempers national extremes and exacerbates local ones.

MORE TO BE LEARNED

This article is a preliminary sketch, an outline of what remains to be learned as much as a finished work. My focus on tasks and dilemmas that ports share along a two-state stretch of the border is productive but hardly sufficient. It would be productive to deepen the inquiry into variations in local state and society through a sustained study of a particular border city and its port. In such a study, one might interview and participate with persons who deal with ports, such as importer-exporters, customs brokers, insurers, and truckers (see Alvarez and Collier 1994), as well as the officialdom of the boundary. Parallel work very much needs to be done on Mexican border ports, including the very distinctive roles of Mexican customs and immigration. The local arrangements between U.S. and Mexican ports are particularly intriguing. One topic merits detailed political analysis: the use of boundary blockades by Mexican anti-government protestors for political symbolism and practical effect, and the role of the U.S. government in sheltering such demonstrators.

Wider comparisons also come to mind. One might compare the logistics, legal practices, port policies, and clienteles of southern border ports (facing relatively poor Mexicans) and large metropolitan airports (often facing wealthy and influential international travelers; see Gilboy 1991, 1992). Additional interesting comparisons are to be made with the U.S.–Canadian border and with Europe, especially with the advent of the European Union. As this summary suggests, the U.S.–Mexican ports need further attention and analysis in light of NAFTA, given the ostensibly contradictory functions of the U.S. border regime as barrier to and facilitator of free exchange (see Heyman 1999a). NAFTA heightens the poignant political symbolism of the shared but conflictual U.S.–Mexican boundary where, on any given day, some incident at a port of entry could explode into a public issue in one or the other nation. Then, veils of prosaic routine thrown aside, the ports' importance to the two countries would be rendered visible to all. ❖

ACKNOWLEDGMENTS

This research was generously supported by grants from the Harry Frank Guggenheim Foundation and the Wenner-Gren Foundation for Anthropological Research. I sincerely appreciate the many people inside and outside the INS who have taught me about ports of entry. Drew Wood solicited this article and gave me valuable comments. Still, all responsibility for errors of fact or interpretation remains my own.

NOTES

1. One may speculate about this. The rapid expansion of the Border Patrol, from 4,000-odd officers in the early 1990s to 8,000 officers in the latter part of that decade, was supported by the politics of fear of undocumented immigration among constituencies spread throughout the interior society of the United States, often including groups with little real contact with Mexico (Heyman 1998b:33–43). Given a situation prone to mass-media-based symbolism, Congress clearly favors border patrolling. On the other hand, the constituencies for ports are threefold: local communities that use the ports on a daily basis; the importers and exporters in the two nations; and the similarly fearful politics surrounding drugs that support certain interdiction roles. The local communities of the border are usually far removed from power in Congress or even their home states. Importer-exporters are more influential (as seen in construction of new commercial port facilities), but it is an interesting commentary on the relative weakness of the cooperative relationship between the United States and Mexico that in this epoch of NAFTA, the personnel allocated to closing the border to drugs and immigrants should far exceed those allocated to border facilitation.

2. Recent displacement from California has rendered the Douglas area the focal point of undocumented crossing, drawing unprecedented numbers of entrants. How this affects the port remains to be determined.

3. An important quality of U.S. border ports is that they are the maximal legal expression of U.S. state sovereignty. There are very few restrictions on search and seizure; there is little privacy. On entry, contraband and documentary searches on persons or vehicles are altogether unrestricted, and holding a person for questioning or further documentary investigation requires only an "articulable reason" from the government officer (warrants or searches and questioning after observed violation stops in the interior of the nation demand the higher standard of probable cause).

4. Every port has two directors, one from customs and the other from INS.

5. Heyman (n.d.-c) delineates INS and customs computer databases and their increasing role in surveillance of the borderlands.

REFERENCES

Alvarez, Robert R., and George Collier. 1994. The Long Haul in Mexican Trucking: Traversing the Borderlands of the North and South. *American Ethnologist* 21:607–27.

Arreola, Daniel D., and James R. Curtis. 1993. *The Mexican Border Cities: Landscape Anatomy and Place Personality.* Tucson: University of Arizona Press.

Block, Fred. 1987. *Revising State Theory: Essays in Politics and Postindustrialism.* Philadelphia: Temple University Press.

Gilboy, Janet. 1991. Deciding Who Gets In: Decisionmaking by Immigration Inspectors. *Law and Society Review* 25:571–99.

———. 1992. Penetrability of Administrative Systems: Political "Casework" and Immigration Inspectors. *Law and Society Review* 26:273–314.

Gupta, Akhil. 1995. Blurred Boundaries: The Discourse of Corruption, the Culture of Politics, and the Imagined State. *American Ethnologist* 22:375–402.

Herzog, Lawrence A. 1990. *Where North Meets South: Cities, Space, and Politics on the U.S.–Mexico Border.* Austin: Center for Mexican American Studies, University of Texas.

Heyman, Josiah McC. 1993. The Oral History of the Mexican American Community of Douglas, Arizona, 1901–1942. *Journal of the Southwest* 35:186–206.

———. 1995a. Putting Power in the Anthropology of Bureaucracy: The Immigration and Naturalization Service at the Mexico–United States Border. *Current Anthropology* 36:261–87.

———. 1995b. In the Shadow of the Smokestacks: Labor and Environmental Conflict in a Company-Dominated Town. In *Articulating Hidden Histories: Exploring the Influence of Eric R. Wolf.* Jane Schneider and Rayna Rapp, eds., 156–74. Berkeley and Los Angeles: University of California Press.

———. 1997. Imports and Standards of Justice on the Mexico–United States Border. In *The Allure of the Foreign: Post-Colonial Goods in Latin America.* Benjamin S. Orlove, ed., 151–84. Ann Arbor: University of Michigan Press.

———. 1998a. State Effects on Labor Exploitation: The INS and Undocumented Immigrants at the Mexico–United States Border. *Critique of Anthropology* 18:155–79.

———. 1998b. Finding a Moral Heart for U.S. Immigration Policy: An Anthropological Perspective. Monograph No. 7. Washington, D.C.: American Ethnological Society.

———. 1999a. Why Interdiction? Immigration Control at the United States–Mexico Border. *Regional Studies* 33:619–30.

————. 1999b. *States and Illegal Practices.* Josiah McC. Heyman, ed. Oxford: Berg.

————. n.d.-a. Class and Classification at the U.S.–Mexico Border. *Human Organization,* forthcoming.

————. n.d.-bINS. Officers of Mexican Ancestry as Chicanos, Citizens, and Immigration Police. Manuscript in files of author.

————. n.d.-c. United States Surveillance over Mexican Lives at the Border: Snapshots of an Emerging Regime. *Human Organization,* forthcoming.

Jessop, Bob. 1982. *The Capitalist State.* New York: New York University Press.

Nugent, Daniel. 1993. *Spent Cartridges of Revolution: An Anthropological History of Namiquipa, Chihuahua.* Chicago: University of Chicago Press.

Nugent, David. 1994. Building the State, Making the Nation: The Bases and Limits of State Centralization in "Modern" Peru. *American Anthropologist* 96:333–69.

Smart, Alan. 1989. Forgotten Obstacles, Neglected Forces: Explaining the Origins of Hong Kong Public Housing. *Environment and Planning D: Society and Space* 7:179–96.

Slab City: Squatters' Paradise?

Travis Du Bry

Photographs by Dominique Rissolo

> Every American is a squatter at heart.
> —W. W. Robinson, *Land in California*

On the southeastern edge of the Salton Sea in Imperial County of Southern California lies a place called Slab City (see figure 1). It is a popular wintering destination for northern-based RV owners seeking the hot and arid climate found in the Colorado Desert. It is also an area where some individuals and their families have chosen to settle permanently, thus pursuing their own version of the American dream. These modern-day squatters and their unauthorized settlement on California desert land are the subject of this article.

Figure 1. The entrance to Slab City.

CALIFORNIA AND SQUATTERS

The Homestead Act of 1862 held out the promise of settlement for those venturing west past the Alleghenies and into the frontier zone. Yet this promise was adamantly denied to the would-be farmers and landowners that flooded into California in search of arable lands. Chief among the barriers to settlement were railroad and agricultural interests, maneuvering within and outside the law to monopolize the control of land. Instead of finding open lands ready to be developed and farmed, settlers met notices of previous ownership. In instances where they attempted to settle, they were met with threatened and actual eviction. Any land that was available for settlement was often marginal.

The unwelcome climate in California toward settlers led social critic Carey McWilliams to comment, "One of the most striking respects in which California differs from the other western states consists in the manner by which it skipped or omitted the frontier phase of land settlement." The well-known Mussel Slough incident of 1880, in which five farmers were killed during the eviction of squatters from Southern Pacific Railroad land, is testimony to the level of violence that occurred all too frequently.[1]

Historian Donald Pisani documents that for the most part, squatters in California history have been viewed as lawless settlers, ostensibly working under the cover of mob rule. However, in a period of land monopolization, legal and judicial abuses, and the entrenchment of elite interests, the squatters were but another symbol of "a society out of balance" in the latter half of the nineteenth century. In such a situation, the actions of squatters ranged from sabotage tactics to patient maneuvering through the legal system. Past and present experiences with authorities and their agencies continue today to contribute to a conflicted image of California squatters.[2]

PATTERNS OF LAND OCCUPATION

The area in Imperial County now known as Slab City has accommodated diverse forms of occupation. Native American Cahuilla would camp along the banks of the intermittent lake that would form from the flooding of the Colorado River. In 1848 the area where Slab City is located was designated as Section 36 land: property set aside for the benefit of publicly endowed schools. Revenue generated from Section 36 lands in the state has gone not to local schools, but rather into the state teachers' retirement fund. The U.S. military constructed a long-range gunnery range and Marine training camp there during World War II. Since then, the area has become a regular destination for snowbirds in their seasonal migration from the north.[3]

Probably the period when heavy activity first came to the area was in the mid-1940s, when it was a military facility named Camp Dunlap. It was chosen for development as a Marine training ground because of its close resemblance to terrain the troops would face in North Africa. It was at this time that basic infrastructure was first constructed in the area: water, electricity, telephones, sewage treatment, and roads were developed for the camp by the military. Camp Dunlap operated for a total of three years and five months, from 1942 to 1946. The property then reverted back to the state and was allowed to deteriorate.[4] All that was left behind by the military were concrete guard boxes, several bunkers, and the concrete foundation slabs for their buildings, the latter forming the basis for the moniker Slab City (see figure 2). Adjacent to Slab City proper, the military still operates the Chocolate Mountain Gunnery Range, an active range where artillery is dropped almost daily from fighter planes. Some Slab City residents, called "scrappers," make a living from clandestine forays into the range to collect scrap metal.

Figure 2. A bunker dating from the Camp Dunlap era.

It was not long after World War II when the slabs began being put to use. The postwar rise in the popularity of recreational vehicles led many individuals to use the level, concrete slabs as parking pads for their vehicles. The warm winter weather and the free use of the site attracted them. The area is administered by the Bureau of Land Management (BLM), so individuals have rights as squatters to settle on the land.

SLAB CITY RESIDENTS

While snowbirds are probably the most visible residents of Slab City, they are seasonal dwellers from only about October to April. Less visible is a large contingent of permanent settlers on the land, year-round squatters numbering in the hundreds. The appeal of living temporarily or permanently in Slab City has to do with more than just the warm weather. The apparent absence of rules regulating behavior and the freedom to create a community based on individuality play a large role in the popularity of living at Slab City.[5]

There is some evidence of community formation throughout Slab City. A bulletin board stands on the main boulevard of slabs, allowing people to post information or publicize events (see figure 3). A church is located in a small trailer to attend to residents' religious needs (see figure 4). The local school bus makes a stop in the Slabs to pick up resident children.

An academic study on Slab City by Dorothy Ann Phelps divides the year-round residents into two groups. There is a group termed "bush bunnies" by the locals, individuals who are barely managing to sustain their existence. They live in and amongst the creosote and palo verde

Figure 3. The community bulletin board.

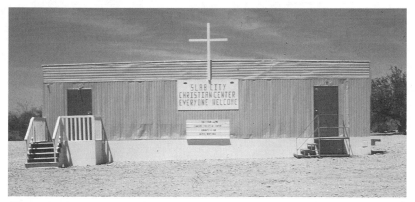

Figure 4. The community church, located in a trailer.

trees, south of the concrete slabs. The other group is made up of families that have made the slabs their homes, living in carefully built compounds peppered with signs to keep out (see figure 5). A third segment of seasonal dwellers identified by Phelps is migrant farm laborers, who have been using the slabs for more than twenty-five years when they are harvesting crops in northern Imperial County.[6]

The persons living in Slab City all have found their way to the area in different ways, all with unique stories. Dominique Rissolo and I spent several days in September 1999 observing the daily life and activities in Slab City. Residents were interviewed at their compounds while they

Figure 5. A typical living compound.

went about their routines. The pattern of questioning was open-ended and designed to capture the interviewees' sentiments about and motivation for settling in Slab City. In a place where residents cherish their privacy, we expected some resistance to revealing information, but instead found that residents were forthright in discussing their past and present circumstances. The following vignettes of three individuals are representative of the general circumstances in which permanent residents find themselves.

Tommy

Tommy, in his late fifties, deals in wrecked cars, bringing them to his claimed lot in Slab City and tearing them down for scrap. He has lived in Slab City for five years. Originally from Florida, Tommy worked with several wrecking yards in the San Bernardino area, in towns like Rialto and Colton. He had heard about Slab City over the years and had come to see it for himself. Eventually he tired of working for others and decided to move to Slab City and become his own boss. He has been running a wrecking business, tearing down cars found out in the desert or brought to him by locals. Tommy uses car batteries for lights or just goes without. He obtains his water in town and stores it in tanks.

Recently, he ran into some trouble with the California Highway Patrol (CHP). The CHP cited Tommy's lot as a nuisance and danger to the community (see figure 6). Officers also suspected Tommy of accepting stolen cars. Several weeks previously, CHP officers had come out to Tommy's place while he was gone on business and, armed with spray paint cans, began marking all of the wrecks that were to be confiscated. Tommy returned to find a portable car crusher processing all of his cars and a competitor buying his cars for scrap. Unable to produce titles of ownership for all of the vehicles, Tommy was left with fewer than ten cars.

Tommy said this happened to him because he is a squatter. He has rights over his domicile and his personal belongings but because he is squatting on the land, he has no property rights over the land or anything contained on it. However, even the status of his domicile seemed rather tenuous, as evidenced by the words "Have Permit" spray-painted on it to dissuade the authorities from confiscating the trailer as well. Tommy said his situation is common among those living year-round in Slab City.[7]

Figure 6. Economic resources—or junk?

Floyd

Unlike most others at Slab City, Floyd, in his mid-fifties, claims to own a total of 640 acres on a ninety-nine-year lease. The land was purchased privately through an acquaintance. Floyd has been living year-round at his compound in Slab City for five years now. Also living at the compound are extended family members, but during the hotter months of the summer they live in nearby Niland to escape the intense heat. Originally from Oklahoma, Floyd makes his living selling junk and used items to passersby and especially to the snowbirds. Floyd told us that September was a busy time for him as he was trying to get all of his items out in time for the annual arrival of the snowbirds in October.

Floyd is acquainted with all of his neighbors and other residents of Slab City, viewing them as community members. All of Floyd's possessions and items for sale are constantly out in the open and unprotected, yet Floyd feels no cause to worry about them (see figure 7). Everyone knows what everyone else has, so if neighboring children decided to pilfer something, everyone would know exactly where it came from (see figure 8). This contributes to a feeling of safety Floyd described to us: there exists an unwritten code of behavior for residents in which they are free to do as they wish as long as it does not interfere with others' freedom. Floyd described how much he enjoyed living in Slab City. He is an independent businessman, selling items to bring in some income.

He told us that he did not receive any welfare or Social Security checks. He described himself as self-sufficient, dependent upon no one, and living in freedom on land he owns.[8]

Lacking a working infrastructure to provide basic utility needs, Floyd relies on solar power for electricity, a renewable resource of which, thankfully, the desert has an endless supply. Water for drinking, cooking, and bathing is stored in large tanks and purchased in Niland. Also in Niland is a post-office box for mail.

Leonard Knight

Leonard Knight is an internationally known environmental folk artist. His major work, Salvation Mountain, is a monument made of adobe and paint and built into the side of a bluff at the entrance to Slab City (see figure 9). Living as a modern ascetic, Leonard spends most of his time painting and augmenting the mountain (see figure 10). He enjoys the support of the local community and visitors, many of whom donate paint and various sundries to him. Recently a major piece of his was

Figure 7. A denizen of Slab City with his wares for sale.

Figure 8. Claimed property.

included in a traveling folk art exhibit. Originally from Vermont, Leonard has been living at Slab City since 1986.

Even though Leonard's work has been discussed and documented by museums, art critics, documentary filmmakers, and journalists and is visited by a constant stream of private individuals, it has come under fire from county and federal officials. Charges of environmental degradation were leveled in 1994 against Leonard and Salvation Mountain, with officials saying that paint runoff from the mountain has harmed the local environment and has been implicated as one factor in the damage to the nearby Salton Sea. Various agencies threatened to destroy and remove Salvation Mountain, viewing it as a hazardous waste site to be cleaned up.

Officials were somewhat surprised by the degree of support that materialized on Leonard's behalf. Petitions, media coverage, and a grass-roots campaign to save Salvation Mountain resulted in the reversal of the decision to demolish the work. Today, Leonard and Salvation Mountain are as popular as ever. Many of those who find themselves at the entrance to Slab City are there because they came to see Leonard and his art.[9]

Figure 9. Salvation Mountain.

Figure 10. Leonard Knight at work.

COMMON THEMES

There are some unifying themes in the preceding vignettes. Many of those with whom we spoke indicate that they can live more freely in Slab City than elsewhere. They talk about individualism, self-sufficiency, and self-government. They police themselves and follow implicit rules of behavior. In Slab City, people are free to do as they wish as long as it does not interfere with the liberty of others. These, of course, are basic themes of democracy with which most Americans would agree. However, the residents of Slab City suggest that their practice of democracy is a reality, not just an ideal.

A recurring theme is the conflict between various authorities and the squatters. Individuals have the right to occupy the land within Slab City under BLM policies, yet they still come into conflict with authorities over their particular actions and use of the land. This is most obviously seen in Leonard's case with his art and also on a lesser scale and more frequently in cases such as that of Tommy and his vehicles.

Conflict arises over the scrappers and their activities on the adjacent gunnery range. In their search for scrap metal for cash, scrappers tres-pass onto government land and potentially put their lives at risk. Unexploded artillery litters the range. The military has responded with patrols designed to discourage the scrappers, yet the threat of apprehension and prosecution has done little to dissuade scrappers from making a living from scrap-metal collection. Their nocturnal forays onto the range continue unabated.

The conflicts between authorities and squatters are unique in content but not in context. Although different from the experiences of the nineteenth century, there is the common thread of confrontation. Residents in Slab City do not live in fear of harassment by the authorities but view such events as necessary evils in the course of their residency there. According to those who spoke with us, the price of capricious official action against them is worth paying in exchange for the experience of freedom that is potentially more enriching than can be found outside of the slabs. As Floyd told us, "I couldn't dream of living anywhere else. Here I'm my own boss, with no one telling me what to do."[10]

WHY SLAB CITY?

Charles Erasmus's book, *In Search of the Common Good,* documents the establishment, growth, and failure of utopian communities throughout the world. Central to the book is an investigation of why such communities appear and disappear in recorded human history. Erasmus had four requirements for considering a community a "true democracy": (1) small in size, (2) simple and unsophisticated, (3) social and economic equality, and (4) life without luxury.[11] While a "true democracy" is obviously an intellectual ideal, in most ways Slab City appears to meet the criteria. The residents of Slab City did not plan to create a community based on utopian idealism. Their pursuit of personal liberty led to the organic growth of a community based on the tenets of democracy.

Settlement in Slab City can be seen as an adaptive strategy for some to deal with poverty. Some of those currently located in Slab City have opted or felt inclined to reside there out of economic necessity. It is simply less expensive to live in Slab City without housing rents than it would be in urban or suburban areas with their associated costs. The migration of poor families and individuals into the countryside is becoming a common strategy for adapting to low-income situations.[12] But some Slab City residents described their residency there as a choice, a choice they made in conjunction with specific ideals they hold to be important.

Have Slab City residents found a squatter's paradise in decidedly anti-squatter California? Without a doubt, there are some pressing social problems in the area, including inadequate sanitation and various health risks. Most of these problems are directly related to the complete lack of an infrastructure to serve the residents. Because of its remote location, Slab City has occasionally been witness to some criminal activity. However, the residents of Slab City ultimately would prefer to see themselves, and have others see them as well, as individualists in pursuit of liberty. Despite the inherent tentativeness of the situation, squatting on BLM land in a remote region of the state can afford them the opportunity to follow their ideals of self-sufficiency. As an apparent effect of establishing themselves upon the land, they have also created a fledgling community of like-minded individuals. The degree to which they actually function as a community is uncertain. Their policing of themselves and Slab City in their own way conflicts with the stereotype of lawless squatters that we are left with from California history. Perhaps they have found their version of paradise after all. ❖

NOTES

1. Carey McWilliams, *California: The Great Exception* (Berkeley: University of California Press, [1949] 1999), quotation on 100, for the Mussel Slough incident, see 93–94; W. W. Robinson, *Land in California* (Berkeley: University of California Press, 1948), 159–60.

2. Donald J. Pisani, *Water, Land, and Law in the West: The Limits of Public Policy, 1850–1920* (Lawrence: University Press of Kansas, 1996), 62–63. Refer to the sensationalized treatment of Slab City denizens in Mark Schone, "I Was a Teenage Coyote," *Spin* (October 1999) and the more evenhanded account by Dorothy Ann Phelps, "A Singular Land Use in the California Desert" (master's thesis, Department of Geography, University of California, Riverside, 1989).

3. Phelps, "Singular Land Use," 36, 6–7.

4. Ibid., 43, 52

5. Ibid., 57.

6. Ibid., 59.

7. Travis Du Bry, interview with Tommy, Slab City field notes, 11 September 1999.

8. Du Bry, interview with Floyd, Slab City field notes, 11 September 1999.

9. Du Bry, interview with Leonard Knight, Slab City field notes, 12 September 1999.

10. Du Bry, interview with Floyd.

11. Charles J. Erasmus, *In Search of the Common Good: Utopian Experiments Past and Present* (New York: The Free Press, 1977), 115.

12. Janet M. Fitchen, *Endangered Spaces, Enduring Places: Change, Identity, and Survival in Rural America* (Boulder: Westview Press, 1991).

Juan Soldado: Field Notes and Reflections

PAUL J. VANDERWOOD

In February 1938, an eight-year-old girl was raped and murdered in Tijuana, Mexico. The next day a twenty-four-year-old Mexican soldier named Juan Castillo Morales was arrested as a suspect. The following day, according to newspaper accounts, Morales confessed to the crime. The ensuing day—now the third day in these events—the military executed Morales in the local cemetery. Soon thereafter, people visiting his gravesite reported strange happenings. Blood bubbled up out of the soldier's grave, and Juan's *ánima*, his soul, was said to be drifting about the site crying out for revenge. Spectators perceived a divine presence and began to venerate Morales as Juan Soldado, John the Soldier. Miracles occurred at the scene: the blind saw, and the lame walked. The faithful declared Juan a saint, or at least a blessed ánima worthy of their prayers and petitions. Today a chapel covers the gravesite and devotees regularly visit to pray to or just pass some time with Juan Soldado. I am researching this extraordinary story. My field notes and thoughts on a recent visit to the shrine follow.

June 24, 2000. Today is San Juan Day at the cemetery. The day is set aside on the Catholic calendar to honor John the Baptist, but a steady stream of people coming here are celebrating the birthday of their *santo*, Juan Soldado. No one is sure of Juan's birth date, but some years ago his followers proclaimed this date his special day, and they sing *Las Mañanitas* to him. With their music—*mariachis* smartly dressed in their typical bolero jackets and tight-legged pants, *conjuntos*, *bandas*, strolling guitarists in common street clothes, and a boom box—and picnic fare including *pollo*, *tamales*, Cokes, and Tecates, they make a colorful assembly, visiting the shrine to pay their respects or ask for a favor and sitting with family members on gravestones in shaded areas on this hot (it must be in the mid-eighties), beautifully sunny day. Mexicans have a knack for settling themselves in the slightest sliver of shade on such days. It makes picture taking hard, especially for amateur photographers like me who can barely handle a point-and-shoot camera. The automatic light meter likes to play games with me. The faces inevitably print out too dark, the backgrounds too light. Still, the whole *ambiente* is luscious and divine.

This is an especially important research day for me. In an attempt to give the project more shape (mainly to calm colleagues who demand "discipline and rigor"), I have designed a questionnaire for the faithful, tested it on two recent occasions, and assembled an *equipo* to help administer it. Those who helped to try out and revise it were Flor Salazar and her husband, Sergio Canedo Gamboa, both history graduates of the Universidad Autónoma de San Luis Potosí doing doctoral work at the University of California, San Diego. Right off, we learned two important things: (1) the *inquesta* had to be administered to respondents; we could not just hand it to them and say, "Please fill it out"; and (2) the questioners had to be native speakers. My accented Spanish, especially coming from a gringo here on the border, made people leery. It closed them down rather than opening them up.

Those assisting me this San Juan Day were my ex-student, good friend, and colleague, Raúl Rodríguez, who teaches history at the Centro de Enseñanzas Técnicas y Científicas (CETYS) in Tijuana as well as at several community colleges in San Diego; José Armando Estrada, a historian now employed with the local branch of the Consejo de Cultura y Arte, who also teaches history at CETYS; Ariel Mojica, a senior student of Armando's who specializes in religious history; and Daniel Vega, a graduate student in Latin American Studies at San Diego State University, who phoned me one day saying, "I'd like to help you with your project." All of these cheerful, intelligent people not only lent me heaps of their youthful energy in administering questionnaires but provided cultural insights that greatly informed my study in progress.

8:30 A.M. The cemetery usually opens at 9 A.M., but today the heavy, rusting iron gates swing back a half hour early to accommodate expected crowds. The gatekeeper, a middle-aged woman, gripes about having to open early and receiving no extra hourly wage. This is a municipal cemetery, and the municipality pays her to be there from 9 A.M. to 4 P.M. No overtime pay is forthcoming.

Two entrepreneurs who sell Juan Soldado remembrances are setting up their carts just off the curb on the street outside the gate. They sell scapulas and cheap metallic frames that carry *the* picture of Juan Soldado. I put *the* in italics because it seems to be the only picture of Juan in circulation—Juan standing there, posed, in neat army uniform, with necktie and cap, one hand resting on a half pillar beside him like some great Greek solon. He resembles a baby-faced boy of about fourteen or fifteen years, but this fellow has status, or likes to think that he does. There are also numerous candles with a wraparound paper that carries the image and a special prayer to Juan Soldado, plus a few plaster of Paris, hand-painted statues of the soldier. Some of these statuettes are modeled after the photo and portray Juan standing up (see figure 1). Others are busts of the soldier. The clean-shaven faces of these figures are a creamy white; this soldado is no mestizo. I have seen casts of Juan where the soldier has *bigotes* (a mustache), which make him look a little older, but no such statues are here today.

The same merchants seem to be here every time I visit the cemetery. They have a kind of concession on the business outside the gates. They say that they cast and paint the busts themselves. There are big companies that manufacture and sell the bottled candles (votives), which are wrapped with the prayers of major (best-selling) saints, such as San Martín de Porres or El Niño de Atocha. But the vendors said that Juan Soldado commands no such business, so they buy the candles in a grocery store, tear off the labels honoring other saints, and put on their own Juan Soldado wraps, which they have had made in the local print shop. Very enterprising people, these vendors. Still, I do not understand how they can maintain their concession, apparently unchallenged by others, outside the cemetery. I shall have to ask them about this on my next visit.

Here comes a mariachi band dressed in typical *charro* outfits. They have been paid—at the rate of $200 per hour—by a man who lives outside Los Angeles, California, and is thanking Juan Soldado for the miracle of stopping his heavy drinking. He promised Juan that he would hire mariachis to serenade the santo every year on his birthday if the drinking stopped. It did, and this was the fourth consecutive year that the middle-aged man had made a pilgrimage with his family to Tijuana to honor the saint.

One of the hallmarks of this pilgrimage site is the way the faithful come as families—extended families—with many children in tow (see figure 2). Fathers often carry their children on their shoulders; mothers cradle them in their arms. The youngest baby I have seen at the site was only two weeks old. Parents explain the story of Juan Soldado to their children. Inside the shrine itself, parents help their youngsters to light

Figure 1. Ceramic statue of Juan Soldado. (Photo by the author)

candles and hold them so that they can touch and rub the busts of Juan. They point out the many offerings to the soldado—crutches, locks of hair, dolls, wedding veils, and the marble plaques on the walls, all of them testimonials to favors received. They also note the hundreds and hundreds of *peticiones* asking favors, some scrawled on the wall, many accompanied by pictures of the solicitors. The families tend to congregate for long periods of time around the shrine, eating, drinking, laughing, singing, but mostly chatting. Not all of the relatives actually enter the shrine; some say they do not believe in the miracle-working powers of Juan Soldado. One man said he was an Adventist and did not "at all" appreciate this sort of worship, but he wanted to be with his family. Another claimed he was there because his father had relatives working in Tijuana who were devoted to Juan Soldado. "While they go inside the shrine," he said, "I make small talk with their daughters." This practice of family observance is very important, for it demonstrates how the Juan Soldado story is passed from generation to generation and also how the faithful perceive Juan Soldado: he is "family" to them. Not all say they come by the cemetery to ask a favor of Juan. Some say they visit "just to say hello" or "to see how he's doing." When one incorporates a santo into his or her family, it represents a new level of belief, one that goes beyond church attendance, regular or not.

The young girl who was raped and murdered in 1938 was named Olga Camacho. Her family plot, well kept and with an impressive crypt of its own, is located within easy sight of the Juan Soldado shrine. However, the little girl is not buried in the family plot. She lies in another cemetery, Number Two, just up the street from the site of Juan's grave. Some say that she was moved there to put some distance between her and the soldier executed for her death. A watchman at the Juan Soldado cemetery said that when the Camacho relatives visit their family plot, they shout invectives at those calling on Juan, saying his veneration is the work of the devil. Of course, those who pray to Juan in the main find him innocent of any wrongdoing in the matter.

Blame for little Olga's death, however tragic, lies elsewhere. A woman explains, "Following the execution, a military buddy of Juan's drew up and circulated fliers proclaiming the innocence of his friend. That is how the cult began."

There is a second *capilla* honoring Juan Soldado at the back of the cemetery on a hill where the execution allegedly took place. Later the body was buried down below at the main chapel site. In the upper chapel

Figure 2. Family waiting to enter shrine on San Juan Day. (Photo by the author)

a large number of little stones have been placed on a low altar in front of a framed embroidery of Juan Soldado. The stones are said to have come from the soil of the cemetery surrounding the site. When a person asks Juan for help, he or she takes a stone and keeps it in a pocket or pocketbook, or on a home altar, until the requested miracle has been granted. Then the stone is returned to the shrine and the recycling continues. One woman said she had been carrying such a stone for ten years waiting for her miracle to occur. She was not at all disappointed by the delay. "It will come, when Juanito is ready," she assured me.

A new mariachi band has arrived at the main site. It has been hired by a swarthy young man, perhaps twenty years old, dressed in blue jeans, T-shirt, and baseball cap turned backwards, which is *de rigueur* among many youngsters today. He is accompanied by two other youthful males. Friends? Acquaintances? Bodyguards? Who knows? The young man struts and swaggers around, resembling a bullfighting matador who has just completed a beautiful and daring pass with a cape or achieved a good kill of the beast. This fellow is obviously full of himself and has money. Twice he returned to the shrine with large bundles of candles to be lighted in honor of Juan Soldado. He seemed to be buying candles by the dozen. His buddies did not enter the shrine. When asked by Daniel for an interview, the youth said, "más tarde," but in a disdainful voice, as if he did not have time for such frivolities. Later on, Ariel approached him and received a similar response. Of course, anyone has the perfect right to refuse to answer a questionnaire, but in general those asked to participate in the inquesta responded with warm enthusiasm. They *wanted* to talk about Juan Soldado and what the santo means to them. So the youth who declined raised some suspicions—quite possibly completely unfounded—that he could have been involved in the drug business so prevalent in Tijuana. It has been said by others that the *narcotraficantes* pray to Juan Soldado for protection, although I have found no evidence of this in the hundreds of petitions that I have read at the shrine. Juan has been asked to perform a kaleidoscopic panoply of miracles, and his devotees claim that he grants them for a variety of concerns, but Juan Soldado is no Jesús Malverde, the acknowledged santo of the traficantes around Culiacán in the state of Sinaloa.

One of those administering the inquesta, Raúl Rodríguez, remarked that virtually all of those he interviewed seemed to be working-class people. Then he began to query an elderly lady and her daughter. It turned out that the son of the younger woman (the grandson of the older lady) was currently one of his students at CETYS, a private, quite costly institute that specializes in business training for the better off. The session confirmed what had become obvious to me on other occasions at the cemetery—that the devotion to Juan Soldado cuts a broad swath across class and gender lines, encompassing people at all age, income, occupational, and educational levels. In this case, the son was not a devotee of Juan, but the mother confirmed that her son respected the santo and those who worshiped him. At any rate, a greater number of the faithful carried cell phones at the shrine this year.

Practically nothing is known about the life of Juan Castillo Morales before his encounter with military justice and subsequent veneration as a santo. Newspaper reporters covering these events in 1938 evidently did not render the kind of background reportage common to journalism today, especially for these sorts of macabre stories—at least to date I have been unable to uncover any such reports. My research in this regard reminds me of the search for the historical Jesus: lots of speculation, theorizing, and possibilities, mostly based on the Gospels, which themselves are in many respects considered suspect, or at least subject to an evangelistic spin. The followers of Juan Soldado have not bothered to create much of an earlier life for the santo, which is an important cultural factor in itself. But tidbits creep in here and there. During this visit, one woman told me that as a child of six or seven she had been given a *paleta* (ice cream) by Juan Castillo Morales, whom she claimed frequently gave sweets to children around the military *cuartel* (army barracks) where he was posted. Another visitor related that at age four, she had been a schoolmate of a sister of Olga Camacho, the victim of the crime, and that Private Morales was well known in various *colonias* (neighborhoods) where he taught youngsters how to play sports—to hit a ball with a stick as in *beisbol*, and to kick a *futbol*—activities through which the soldier aimed to steer them from becoming *vagos* and ne'er-do-wells. Such images establish Morales as a kind, good, likable young fellow doing good works in the community. He was like—how anyone would want their son to be.

I was very grateful to the devoted for their willingness to share their knowledge of and feelings for Juan Soldado with me. When I had finished an especially enlightening and entertaining interview with an older woman, I turned to her adult daughter to say how much I appreciated her mother's time and openness. As the daughter was quite round of stomach, I politely asked her when she was expecting her baby. And she replied, "I am not pregnant. What you see is all me." I slumped down; I could have died. I apologized; I felt like lighting a candle to Juan Soldado, asking forgiveness. But the daughter and her mom passed off the faux pas with a hearty laugh and the offer of a Tecate, which I accepted. Devotees at the shrine are curious about why a gringo wants to know so much about Juan Soldado, but they are appreciative that an outsider is trying to understand their santo and their culture.

Three people have approached the shrine to pay a *manda*—a debt for a favor received. They have crawled on their knees on a very rough cobblestone pathway from the entrance of the cemetery to the shrine— some fifty yards in all—to reach the chapel. Family is with them. As they progressed toward their goal, a family member spread a long carpet in front of them to somewhat protect their knees, but it remained a rugged, painful crawl. On other occasions I have seen the faithful do the same but without the carpet. Their knees become bruised and bloody. They need to stop quite frequently to ease the pain, but they never leave their knees. Onlookers pay them little attention. It is as if the pilgrims are doing what is expected of them, or that their style of devotion is no one's business but their own. Family members may chat about miracles received by those in their own group, but they do not nose into the devotional needs and findings of others.

The Juan Soldado shrine reminds one of those many smallish, humble homes that dot the hillsides of Tijuana. It is located in the central part of the cemetery, surrounded by other gravesites with their variety of mostly white marble monuments. The chapel stands out partially because of its design but mainly because of the line of people waiting to enter it. The basic structure, constructed of cinder blocks, is some fifteen feet wide, twenty feet long, and eight feet high. A covered walkway with arches painted bright red to resemble large bricks or blocks extends out from the front doorway some ten yards into the cemetery. This is the only entrance into the chapel, which has two small windows that provide a half light to the interior. The curious visitor might well find the inside cramped, stuffy, messy, and unclean. The devoted describe it as inviting, even cozy like home, and sacred. The entire structure, with its additions and improvements, has been donated by individuals in fulfillment of promises made in exchange for wishes granted. The gray outside walls of the main building are covered with plaques attesting to miracles received. A random pile of personal paraphernalia, such as crutches, an arm splint, or a leg brace, left inside but later removed to make space for other offerings, are piled on the roof. The caretakers, municipal employees who periodically clean up the shrine, claim that nothing is destroyed or discarded from the site. This seems improbable, as over time pilgrims must have deposited tons of materials at the shrine.

Today the shrine is filled to overflowing with flowers and floral wreaths. One icon of Juan Soldado is so covered with flowers that only the eyes, nose, and mouth of the santo are visible. Peticiones, often with photographs, cover all the walls. There are three statues of Juan at the front. The middle one is encased in a glass box, and an image of the head of the Virgin of Guadalupe hangs on a wall to the left. A long wrought iron table, serving as a kind of altar, fills the center of the room. Here is where the faithful light and leave their candles. Today these candles also fill the space under the table and spread into other parts of the interior. There must be four hundred or more candles at the site. At the end of the table that faces the door sits a money box. Today it is overflowing with nearly as many U.S. dollars as Mexican pesos. The caretakers say that municipal officials come by periodically to empty the money box. One of my interviewers reports that money seen earlier in the day on top of the box is now (at mid-afternoon) missing.

There are two kneeling benches at the front of the chapel. Before lighting their votive candle, the faithful kneel there and usually recite the special prayer to Juan Soldado printed on the paper wrapped around the candle. Some just kneel and meditate, but almost all—virtually all—make the sign of the cross in the traditional Catholic manner while kneeling. Many do the same on exiting the chapel. Without a doubt, there is a good deal of what one might call "official Catholicism" embedded in the practices of the faithful, although the Church has strongly discouraged any devotion to Juan Soldado. A woman said, "I pray to Juan Soldado even if the Church does not approve. I do not think that God minds." And so for her *that* issue is a closed one.

Most of the pilgrims have left the cemetery by 4 P.M., the usual closing time. Now the watchman comes to shoo out the remaining few, including my colleagues and myself. A guitarist from one of the conjuntos wanders by for a final word. He says that the day was not as profitable for his group (he charges five dollars a song) as in the previous four years that he has been coming to the cemetery on San Juan's Day. He says he believes in Juan Soldado but attends the celebration mainly to make a living. He asks me if I intend to write about Juan Soldado.

"Well, maybe," I reply. "I really don't know."

"You'd better write a *good* book about him," he says.

"I don't know enough about Juan yet. I can't promise anything."

"Whatever you do, you'd better do it *right*."

"If I do anything," I replied, "you can be sure that it will be done with *mucho cariño*." ❖

The Oaxacan Enclaves in Los Angeles: A Photo Essay

DEVRA WEBER

Immigrants from the state of Oaxaca have gravitated to California in large numbers since the 1980s. They are largely indigenous Mixtecs, Zapotecs, Mixes, Triques, and Chontales. In Los Angeles, the majority are Zapotecs, from the Isthmus of Tehuantepec, the Sierra Juárez, or the Valley of Oaxaca, who have formed enclaves around the city. People from Tlacolula have settled in Santa Monica; a group from Macuiltianguis lives in Burbank. In Oaxaca many had been teachers, nurses, merchants, or craftspeople, but in the United States, most find work in the service sector, as busboys, domestic workers, food vendors, gardeners, and janitors. There are now established restaurants, small businesses, and a biweekly newspaper, *El Oaxaqueño*.

Indigenous communalism remains part of their lives, despite pulls of an individualistic consumer culture. There is evidence of mutuality and communalism in a group of men fixing a *país años* roof. They perform *tequios*, or community service, in their hometowns; they send money from California to support hometown projects. In fact, Oaxacans are famous for the plethora of organizations they support. They form hometown organizations, from the two dozen who support their small town of Yaganiza, to the large and sometimes divided groups from Yatzachi el Alto or Malcuiltianguis. They have formed a regional organization, ORO (Organización Regional de Oaxaca) out of these local associations and are part of the large, binational FIOB (Frente Indígena Oaxaqueño Binacional), active in California, San Quintín, Baja California, and the state of Oaxaca. Some are active in Mexican political parties and elections.

Immigrants have brought dances, music, celebration, and foods of Oaxaca to their new city. The *guelagetza*, which brings together dancers and the ubiquitous bands from different Oaxacan communities, was originally established by the PRI as a tourist draw in the city of Oaxaca. The high price made it prohibitive for Oaxacans, but once in Los Angeles, they have made it their own. Each summer several guelagetzas are held in Los Angeles, where immigrants and children who have learned the dances perform.

269

Immigrants talk of returning to Oaxaca, either "soon" or when they retire. Few are able to do so. They become part of the Los Angeles economy, and over the years they marry, and have children and grandchildren who strengthen their ties to this city. Their children are of the culture here, and while many celebrate customs and visit Oaxaca, most will remain in Los Angeles and maintain long-distance relationships with the towns of their parents. ❖

A woman of Yalalag selling tamales at the guelagetza held at East Los Angeles College. Note the Spago apron. (All photos courtesy of Devra Weber)

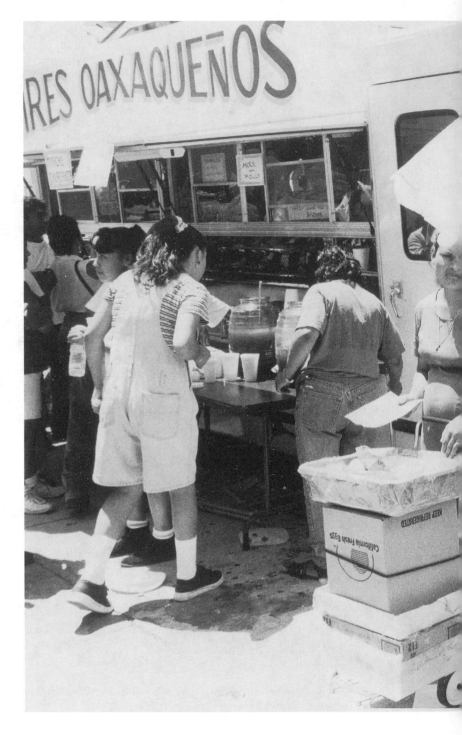

Amalia López and her daughter, Erika, selling at the guelagetza., July 1995, Normandy Park. Amalia, who has been active in ORO, travels to Oaxaca to buy foods to resell to homesick immigrants.

*July 1995, woman selling
horchata at the guelagetza.*

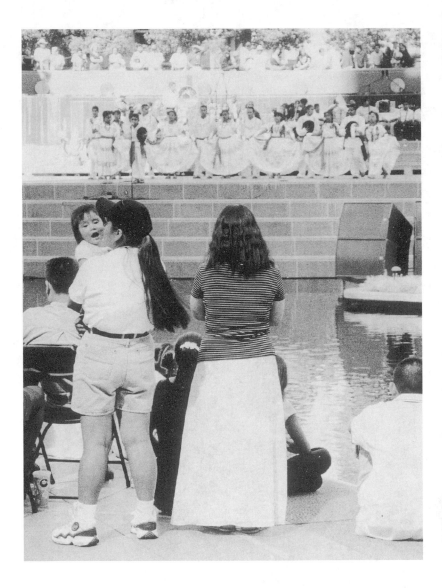

July 1998, the FIOB-sponsored guelagetza at the downtown California Plaza that introduced the celebration to the broader LA community. The event brought together a cross-section of Los Angeles: Latinos, African Americans, Anglos, and Asian Americans as well as Oaxaqueños.

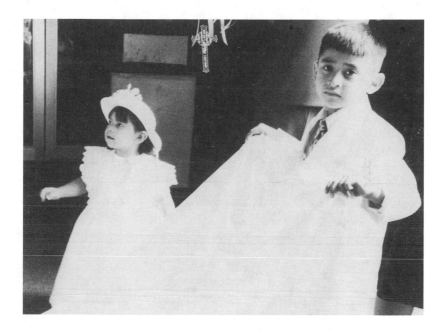

Johnny López and his sister, Ana Patricia Martínez, in 1997 outside Santo Tomás church where their grandparents were repeating their wedding vows after twenty-five years of marriage. Friends from Tlacochahwaya joined the celebration, videotaping the event so those unable to come could vicariously participate.

In the spring of 1999, FIOB hosted a guelagetza in Highland Park.

Mauricio Chávez Bell, March 1994. Mauricio sells elotes, *corn smothered in crema and dusted with chili powder and dry cheese. A knowledgeable opera aficionado, he has since moved to New York and plans to go to Paris.*

Binational feet at a jaripeo, *December 1993, in Yatzachi el Alto in Sierra Juárez. On the town's saint day, the diasporic population returns from Oaxaca, Mexico City, and Los Angeles to celebrate with the dwindling number of people who still live there. A highlight of the celebration is the bull-riding contest— the jaripeo—held in a makeshift ring and watched by, among others, these boys perched on the fence.*

Yatzachi el Alto, December 1993. Men from Los Angeles and Oaxaca play basketball, a game with ancient antecedents in Oaxaca.

Ismaela Erasto de Bautista rolls out a clayuda on a metate, and María Bautista lays it out on a wood-fire-heated metal pan in preparation for a Christmas celebration. Yaganiza, Sierra Juárez, December 1993. Both women are trilingual and have worked as domestics in Los Angeles for a number of years.

María Bautista and her first grandson, Victor Bautista, 1993. Victor is now living in Los Angeles with his uncle, Maurilio Bautista, and has joined the workforce.

Damiana Hernández at the entrance to her kitchen, December 1993, in Yatzachi el Alto. Damiana returned to Yatzachi after working in Los Angeles for more than thirty years. Strong-minded, she was active in ORO and the early days of the FIOB. The local school is in the background.

How Would You Like an El Camino? U.S. Perceptions of Mexico in Two Recent Hollywood Films

ANDREW GRANT WOOD

For nearly two hundred years now, Mexico and the United States have viewed each other with suspicion. Following the Mexican War, *gringos* were generally thought to be aggressive, land-hungry agents of imperialism. On the other side, many in the United States acted on the belief that Mexicans were mustachioed *machos* if not *banditos*—a people, in other words, not to be trusted. Accordingly, media forces on both sides—initially, newspapers, and in the twentieth century, radio, cinema, and television—have generally only added to the bad blood between the two countries through continued stereotypical portrayals.

From the Mexican perspective, films depicting life for immigrants to the United States, beginning with the 1922 silent film *El hombre sin patria,* have tended to offer audiences the message that if you go to the United States, you will experience certain racism and oppression. On the other side, Hollywood films dealing with Mexicans and Mexican immigration have usually pitted a heroic actor (from Tom Mix to Charles Bronson and Jack Nicholson) against a vaguely defined "gang" of undocumented workers seeking entry to the United States. Saying little about the diverse cultures of either country or the causes, experiences, and, ultimately, contributions of Mexican immigrants, these often low-budget "B" movies have reflected past assumptions, fears, and misunderstandings on both sides.[1] Yet, with increased trade and a significant rise in the Mexican population in the United States over the past decade, the film industry in both countries has again begun to produce cinematic responses to changing social, cultural, and historical realities.

Taking into account the ever-changing relationship between the United States and Mexico, recent Hollywood films offer interesting commentary. *The Mexican,* starring Julia Roberts, Brad Pitt, James Gandolfini, and Gene Hackman, is a romantic comedy that plays on binational stereotypes of "Old Mexico" and the "bumbling gringo." In contrast, the Steven Soderbergh-directed blockbuster *Traffic,* starring

Michael Douglas, Catherine Zeta-Jones, and Academy Award-winner Benicio del Toro, examines the current international drug trade through portrayals on both sides of the border. While very different films, each offers a curious mix of old stereotypes and new perspectives regarding U.S.-Mexican relations.

In *The Mexican*, "the Mexican" is a valuable pistol that Jerry (Brad Pitt) is sent to Mexico to find. At the beginning of the film, we learn that Jerry and his girlfriend (Julia Roberts) are a typical crazy gringo couple—she wants stability and marriage and he, mixed up with the mob, is trying to do right but can't seem to get it together. Somehow the forces of fate conspire to put Jerry on a plane to Mexico City where he soon collects his baggage and begins his odyssey. A stranger in a strange land, our protagonist first tries in vain to call his girlfriend by inserting his American Express credit card in a Telex public phone. Frustrated but not discouraged, Jerry then walks up to a rental car agency desk.

In a parody of middle-class American tourists, Jerry and a savvy Mexican car agent go about making a deal. "Do you speak English?" Jerry asks. "Yes," the agent responds, "how can I help you?" After filling out the paperwork and giving the agent his American Express card, Jerry tells the agent he does not want to rent a Chrysler because he can get "one of those" in the States. "Is this your first time to Mexico?" the agent asks. "Yes," Jerry acknowledges. "Well, then, would you like something a little more . . . ?" the agent inquires. "Um, something," Jerry shrugs, "a little more . . . Mexican!" Having sized up his customer, the agent then tells Jerry with a kind of Cheech-and-Chong Hollywood Chicano accent, "Oh, I have just the thing. . . . How would you like an El Camino?" With this, Jerry's Mexican car rental expectations are more than met, and soon he is on his way in his souped-up, blue El Camino—complete with windshield decoration and a Virgin of Guadalupe statue on the dash.

Not surprisingly, scenes in *The Mexican* offer many of the usual stereotypes of Old Mexico, complete with peasant women offering directions along the roadside, *campesinos* and mule carts, colonial villages, fiestas and fireworks, and, of course, seedy cantinas filled with tough guys drinking tequila. In search of the famed antique pistol, Jerry drives into a colonial town and walks right into a cantina where an unshaven, glass-eyed bartender calls him "America" and asks if he is a "bandito." Characteristically, Jerry shrugs and pays for his tequila with a U.S. twenty-dollar bill. Coming out of the bar, he finds that his car has been stolen, and in its place he is offered a burro.

The next scene finds Jerry the following morning, not very far from where he was the night before. Frustrated with the slow-going burro, he flags down a pick-up truck with three Mexican guys in the cab. Acting out another cross-cultural comedy of errors, Jerry this time confidently says, "Buenas noches," to which the Mexicans jokingly reply, "Buenas nachos." Jerry then tells them, "I need a ride . . . but I have no money, *no dinero*," emptying his pockets to show them. Having fun with their gringo hitchhiker, the Mexicans laugh, "Sí, Robert Dinero." Undeterred, Jerry improvises and tells them, "I need a lift in your truck-o to the next town-o, village-o . . . *pueblo*." With the word "pueblo," the three Mexicans motion for Jerry to hop in the back of the truck, and away they go.

Other adventures ensue in the quest for "the Mexican." Along the way, Jerry gets his car back by chasing down the robbers, finding them in a small town, and forcing them at gunpoint to obey him. A little later, Jerry is questioned by a Mexican sheriff outside a store where he is enjoying a green-colored Jarritos soda. "I'm an American," Jerry tells the lawman. "No shit," he replies in English, "and I'm a Mexican." "Cool," Jerry replies, smiling, and with this the sheriff asks him for his passport. Jerry's response to the sheriff is appropriate for these times. Mexico, in the eyes of many North Americans today, is "cool"—especially if that means thinking that Mexicans drive exotic, tricked-out El Caminos and old Ford pick-up trucks, take siestas, and live in dusty old rural towns.

In *The Mexican* we eventually learn that the quest for the antique pistol is ultimately all about honor. And, as Julia Roberts—while captivated by a *telenovela* on television—tells her boyfriend Jerry when he asks her why she is even watching the show, "emotion transcends language." Following the lead of our two most youthful and glamorous actors, American audiences realize that some kind of dialogue with Mexicans—however embarrassing at times—must begin.[2] In the case of *The Mexican*, "playing" with old stereotypes in a new way might be one way to start a more meaningful cross-cultural dialogue.

Quite different from the ironic and often humorous situations portrayed in *The Mexican*, *Traffic* dramatizes different aspects of the drug trade between Mexico and the United States. Making a powerful statement about the widespread demand for narcotics north of the border, director Steven Soderbergh suggests that huge profits accompanied by even greater social costs will continue as long as Americans have a seemingly insatiable desire for a fix. Taking little comfort in the efforts of lawmakers on either side of the border, *Traffic*'s assessment of the current drug situation paints a bleak picture.

The story is divided into three parts. The first is set along the U.S.-Mexico border and follows the work of two Mexican policemen—Javier and Manolo, played by Benicio del Toro and Jacob Vargas—as they apparently battle against powerful drug lords headquartered in Tijuana and Ciudad Juárez. Next we are introduced to federal judge Robert Wakefield (Michael Douglas), who has just been appointed the nation's drug czar by the president. On fact-finding missions to the border and to Mexico City or at home in suburban Cincinnati, Wakefield is naïve but nonetheless earnest in fulfilling his role as America's leading crusader in the war on drugs. The third segment is set in San Diego, where Catherine Zeta-Jones plays the wife of a wealthy drug dealer who has recently been busted and awaits trial.

In a powerful, socially conscious film, Soderbergh shows us the seductive power of drugs and money. As the drama unfolds, all the players on the American side gradually lose whatever innocence they may have had and become embroiled in a drug-driven fiasco with no easy answers or happy Hollywood endings. Yet while *Traffic* has generally been praised for its complexity and social realism, it portrays Mexico largely as an ill-fated land. With the Tijuana scenes photographed with a gritty yellow frontier look, viewers are taken across the border into a cinemascape filled with stock characters: drug lords, paramilitary men, corrupt police, whores, and madonnas. In nearly all of the south-of-the-border scenes, the only person apparently wearing a white hat in the dusty Old Mexico town of Tijuana is policeman Javier Rodríguez, who cleverly plays both sides. Certain character ambiguities notwithstanding, Javier is pictured as the last decent Mexican standing in a drug war that has largely been lost.

From the highest echelons of power to the street dealers and sidemen, Soderbergh's portrayal of life across the border establishes Mexico (and by extension, all of Latin America) as wholly corrupt. From the very first scene, when the two policemen sit idly in their vehicle waiting for suspected smugglers, Javier tells his partner Manolo of a dream in which his mother was tied up in a chair with a plastic bag taped over her head. "There was nothing I could do to help her . . . *chingao!*" he exclaims. Introduced to Javier through a surreal story of cruelty and frustration, the audience is given a hint of what he will be up against as he wages his own fight along the drug superhighway between Mexico and the United States. Yet in portraying Javier as a noble soldier while nearly all his compatriots fall prey to kidnapping, assassination, torture, and betrayal, *Traffic* offers a skewed portrait of Mexican society in getting its antidrug message across to American audiences. While taking great care to factor in the complicated U.S. side of the drug equation, Soderbergh's version of Mexico is another in a long history of film oversimplifications.

As we see the day-to-day scenes of crowded northern Mexican city streets through Soderbergh's tobacco-stained lens, other, more insidious, underworld transactions between various drug runners, police, and politicians add up to one big Mexican competition for control of the U.S. drug trade. Watching as lawmen Javier and Manolo cautiously make their way through a Byzantine maze of criminal plots and counterplots, some viewers might argue that this portrayal of Mexico is "real."

While not wanting to ignore the fact that in real life Mexican drug cartels do inflict considerable terror and command significant aspects of the transnational political economy, a critical screening of *Traffic* nonetheless reveals Soderbergh's focus on the dark side of Mexican culture, community, and commerce. Shots of ramshackle houses in Tijuana tend to reinforce U.S. impressions of Mexican society as largely poor and uneducated.[3] Images of broken-down fences further send a message that suggests that law-abiding citizens have totally lost a moral and political struggle against influential criminal forces.

Nearly all of the Mexican scenes give us the idea that imprisonment, torture, and death await any person who dares to take a stand against the monopolizing control of the Tijuana and Juárez cartels. At one point, General Salazar, talking in his overly drawn-out *mexicano* accent, notes the bruises on one of his enemies and asks the henchman who carried out the torture, "Are you responsible for this? *We are not savages.*" Here, obviously, the viewer—having seen the violence—catches the heavy-handed irony of this remark.

When Judge Wakefield travels to Mexico City to meet with General Salazar (who has just been appointed Mexico's chief of antinarcotics operations), we are presented with a series of heavy-handed cinematic treatments. Off-center camera angles for the arrival of Wakefield's helicopter in the Plaza Zócalo suggest that the bureaucrat has entered the belly of the drug-trafficking beast. Ensuing scenes in the National

Palace quickly lead us to the realization that in Mexico corruption exists at the highest levels as we watch General Salazar politely greet Judge Wakefield. Adding to the intended contrast between "American" and "Mexican" government responses to the crisis (and by extension each culture's alleged respect for life itself), Salazar cynically informs his guest that Mexico has no programs for the treatment of drug addiction. Instead, he calmly says to Wakefield (whose daughter is not coincidentally caught up in a dramatic struggle with her own cocaine demons) that "addicts eventually overdose and die . . . and then there is one less to worry about." As viewers watch this and other scenes in which drug-related violence shapes the fate of criminals and innocent victims alike, we are encouraged to think of Mexico as basically a wasteland inhabited by a lost people. The message set forth in the Mexican scenes in *Traffic* is that drugs and anarchy have already taken over; and, if we are not careful, *the same thing will happen in the United States.*

In some ways, *Traffic* is an old story with a postmodern twist. Previous treatments of illicit trade along the border have similarly cast Mexicans as a people with dubious motives while law-abiding border patrolmen have stood by to uphold the higher principles of "Anglo civilization." Maybe the only difference with *Traffic* as compared to earlier films is that this time we have a Mexican rather than a gringo as our hero. Yet, to be fair, Soderbergh and his team have given us an intelligent, well-crafted film that deals primarily not with the history and culture of Mexico but with a serious drug problem currently corrupting individuals, families, and communities throughout the Americas. Unfortunately, the film too often drives home its message in a way that exoticizes and oversimplifies Mexico rather than painting a more informed social portrait. Like the *narco-ficheras* produced for borderlands immigrants, Soderbergh's *Traffic* is marketed to U.S. audiences. Too bad that in getting the message across, Mexico too easily becomes identified as the exotic source point for drugs and corruption.[4] As Soderbergh and his cast surely know, the real story is a bit more complicated.

Despite many misunderstandings, U.S. perceptions of Mexico and Mexicans are changing in positive ways. Compared to past representations that portrayed Mexicans as the stereotypical exoticized "other," increased contact and communication, closer ties, and even the sharing of a few laughs between the people of two countries are leading to greater levels of tolerance and trust. A recent survey by the California-based Tomás Rivera Policy Center in conjunction with the University of Tamaulipas indicated that out of more than 2,000 residents sampled along the border, a majority favored officially opening *la frontera* to greater work and study exchanges on both sides. According to Jorge Santibañez, director of El Colegio de la Frontera Norte in Tijuana, "Integration has happened . . . [and is happening] despite Mexico City and Washington."[5]

In the coming years it will be interesting to observe not only the continued trajectory of migration and trade negotiations taking place at diplomatic levels but also how the film industry both in the United States and in Mexico portray the current demographic and cultural transformations taking place along the U.S.–Mexico border as well as throughout all of North America. Given the changing political climate that came in the wake of the September 2001 terrorist attacks in New York and Washington, one can only hope that growing cross-cultural familiarity will prevent the occurrence of any kind of renewed anti-immigrant backlash that would set back the real progress made in recent years between people in the United States and Mexico. ❖

NOTES

1. For a discussion of immigration films, see David R. Maciel and María Rosa García-Acevedo, "The Celluloid Immigrant: The Narrative Films of Mexican Immigration," in *Culture across Borders: Mexican Immigration and Popular Culture*, ed. David R. Maciel and María Herrera-Sobek (Tucson: University of Arizona Press, 1998), 149–202.

2. Adding to the "western comedic" tone, the film features a soundtrack somewhat derivative of Ennio Morricone's "The Good, the Bad, and the Ugly."

3. The same can also be said of the scenes in downtown Cincinnati.

4. Similarly, the recent film *Blow* starring Johnny Depp and Penelope Cruz includes scenes from various "south of the border" sites in Mexico and Colombia as source points for drug traffic.

5. *Tulsa World*, September 9, 2001, p. A2.

Index

About the Contributors

ANDREW GRANT WOOD was born in Montreal, Canada, and is the author of *Revolution in the Street: Women, Workers, and Urban Protest in Veracruz, 1870–1927* (2001), which won the 1999 Michael C. Meyer Prize for best first manuscript in Latin American history as well as the 2002 Thomas F. McGann Prize for best book published by a member of the Rocky Mountain Council for Latin American Studies. Presently, Wood is writing a biography of Mexican songwriter Agustín Lara, coediting a volume on tourism in Mexico, and producing a DVD/documentary on the history of Carnival in Veracruz. He received his Ph.D. from the University of California, Davis, and worked as a postdoctoral historian at the University of California Institute for Mexico and the United States (UC MEXUS). He teaches at the University of Tulsa.

LAWRENCE D. TAYLOR is a researcher with the Departamento de Estudios Culturales at the Colegio de la Frontera Norte, Tijuana, Mexico. His books include: *El nuevo norteamericano: La integración continental y su impacto sobre la cultura y la identidad nacional en la época del TLCAN* (2001), *Guía general de las fuentes de la región Ciudad Juárez-El Paso para la investigación de la historia de Chihuahua* (1996), *La gran aventura en México: El papel de los voluntarios extranjeros en los ejércitos revolucionarios mexicanos, 1910 a 1915* (1993), *La campaña magonista de 1911 en Baja California* (1992), and *Revolución Mexicana: Guía de archivos y bibliotecas, México-Estados Unidos* (1987). Taylor completed his Ph.D. at the Colegio de México, Mexico City.

DANIEL D. ARREOLA has published extensively on topics relating to the cultural geography of the Mexican-American borderlands. He is the author of *Hispanic Spaces, Latino Places: Community and Cultural Diversity in America* (2004), *Tejano South Texas: A Mexican American Cultural Province* (2002), and *The Mexican Border Cities: Landscape Anatomy and Place Personality* (with James R. Curtis, 1993). Arreola serves on the editorial boards of several leading geography journals and of an international cross-cultural architecture journal and is a contributing editor to the Hispanic Division of the Library of Congress. He is a past president of the Association of Pacific Coast Geographers. Presently, Arreola is professor of geography and an affiliate faculty member with the Center for Latin American Studies at Arizona State University. Born in Los Angeles, he holds a Ph.D. from the University of California at Los Angeles.

Víctor Manuel Macías-González teaches history and is the director of the Institute for Latino/a and Latin American Studies at the University of Wisconsin, La Crosse. With Anne Rubenstein, he has coedited an anthology on Mexican masculinity (forthcoming). He has written widely on the history of the art, gender, class, consumer culture, and etiquette of nineteenth-century Greater Mexico. Macías-González is finalizing a study on the aristocracy during the Porfiriato. He received his Ph.D. from Texas Christian University in 1999.

Eric Michael Schantz completed his Ph.D. at the University of California at Los Angeles in 2003. He has taught at California State University, Los Angeles, and is currently researching Chinese immigration to Mexico during the nineteenth century.

Vincent Cabeza de Baca teaches history and Chicano Studies at Metropolitan State College in Denver. The Colorado Historical Society awarded him the 1999 Leroy Hafen Prize for contributions to Colorado history for his editorship of the anthology, *La Gente: Hispano History and Life in Colorado* (1998). He earned his Ph.D. at the University of California, San Diego.

Juan Cabeza de Baca attended St. John's College in Santa Fe, New Mexico.

María S. Arbeláez was born in Bogotá, Colombia, and received her Ph.D. from the University of Miami in Coral Gables, Florida. She currently teaches history at the University of Nebraska at Omaha. Arbeláez has contributed articles to *Journal of the South West*, *Great Plains Research*, *Journal of the West*, and *Historias*. She has authored and coauthored several other publications for the Instituto Nacional de Antropología e Historia in Mexico. Arbeláez is also the editor of the *Journal of Latino-Latin American Studies* of the Office of Latin-Latino American Studies of the Great Plains in Omaha.

Jeffrey M. Pilcher has published *Cantinflas and the Chaos of Mexican Modernity* (2001) and *¡Que vivan los tamales! Food and the Making of Mexican Identity* (1998), his first book, which won the Thomas F. McGann Prize of the Rocky Mountain Council for Latin American Studies. He is also the editor of *The Human Tradition in Mexico* (2003). His current research is on Mexican American cuisine. Pilcher completed his Ph.D. at Texas Christian University and teaches at The Citadel in Charleston, South Carolina.

Josiah McC. Heyman teaches sociology and anthropology at the University of Texas at El Paso. He is the author of *Finding a Moral Heart for U.S. Immigration Policy: An Anthropological Approach* (1998) and *Life and Labor on the Border: Working People of Northeastern Sonora, Mexico, 1886–1986* (1991) as well as the editor of *States and Illegal Practices* (1999). He has written articles and essays on border culture, work, consumption, migration, border law enforcement, and state power, including "The Inverse of Power" in *Anthropological Theory* 3 (2003). In his current research, Heyman is revisiting ports of entry in the era of homeland security and free trade.

TRAVIS DU BRY does ethnographic research that focuses on settlement, socioeconomic mobility, and community-building efforts by farm laborers in the Coachella Valley of Southern California. He was a researcher in residence at the University of California, San Diego, for U.S.-Mexican Studies in 2001–2. Du Bry completed his Ph.D. at the University of California, Riverside.

DOMINIQUE RISSOLO earned his Ph.D. at the University of California, Riverside. Primarily a Mesoamerican archaeologist, Rissolo has also participated in applied anthropological research projects along the U.S.-Mexico border. He is an avid photographer with extensive experience in desert landscapes, caves, and environmental folk art. Rissolo's publications include a book on ancient Maya ritual cave use as well as articles on Maya pottery and rock art. He currently teaches in the Department of Anthropology at San Diego State University.

PAUL J. VANDERWOOD is Professor Emeritus of Mexican History, San Diego State University. He is the author of several books and articles on Mexican history, including *The Power of God against the Guns of Government: Religious Upheaval in Mexico at the Turn of the Nineteenth Century* (1998), *Border Fury: A Picture Postcard Record of Mexico's Revolution and U.S. War Preparedness* (with Frank Samponaro, 1988), and *Disorder and Progress: Bandits, Police, and Development* (1981). His latest book is *Juan Soldado: Rapist, Murderer, Martyr, Saint* (2003). After working as a reporter, Vanderwood earned his Ph.D. at the University of Texas.

DEVRA WEBER is the author of *Dark Sweat, White Gold: California Farm Workers, Cotton, and the New Deal* (1994). Her research interests include immigration and Latino communities in the United States. She earned her Ph.D. at the University of California at Los Angeles and teaches at the University of California, Riverside.

Latin American Silhouettes

*William H. Beezley and
Judith Ewell*
Editors